TOO GOOD TO
BE TRUE

TOO GOOD TO BE TRUE

TORONTO IN THE 1920S

RANDALL WHITE

Dundurn Press
Toronto & Oxford
1993

Editor: Judith Turnbull
Design: Andy Tong
Cover photographs: John Boyd, Globe and Mail Collection, City of Toronto Archives,
    SC 266-7579 (front), SC 266-45 (back)
Front cover hand-tint: Ted M. Smith
Printed and bound in Canada by Gagné Printing Ltd., Louiseville, Quebec, Canada

The writing of this manuscript and the publication of this book were made possible by support from several sources. The publisher wishes to acknowledge the generous assistance and ongoing support of **The Canada Council**, **The Book Publishing Industry Development Program** of the **Department of Communications**, **The Ontario Arts Council**, **The Ontario Publishing Centre** of the **Ministry of Culture, Tourism and Recreation**, and **The Ontario Heritage Foundation**.
    Care has been taken to trace the ownership of copyright material used in the text (including the illustrations). The author and publisher welcome any information enabling them to rectify any reference or credit in subsequent editions.

J. Kirk Howard, Publisher

Canadian Cataloguing in Publication Data

White, Randall
    Too good to be true : Toronto in the 1920s

Includes bibliographical references and index.
ISBN 1-55002-197-4

1. Toronto (Ont.) – History. 2. Toronto (Ont.) –
Biography. I. Title.

FC3097.4.W45 1993   971.3'541   C93-094435-6
F1059.5.T6857W45 1993

Dundurn Press Limited
2181 Queen Street East
Suite 301
Toronto, Canada
M4E 1E5

Dundurn Distribution
73 Lime Walk
Headington, Oxford
England
0X3 7AD

Dundurn Press Limited
1823 Maryland Avenue
P.O. Box 1000
Niagara Falls, N.Y.
U.S.A. 14302-1000

CONTENTS

ACKNOWLEDGMENTS

My first debt is to Kirk Howard, president of Dundurn Press, for his interest and faith in this project, from start to finish. I am also grateful beyond words for the steadfast assistance and support of Jeanne MacDonald.

I owe several other debts to the staff at Dundurn Press. Judith Turnbull has edited my original manuscript with skill and sensitivity. She has left the reader with a finer text than I could offer on my own, and somehow managed to make the editorial process an enjoyable and creative experience. Andy Tong has taken much-appreciated pains to fashion a book design that similarly complements and extends the original concept. In more diffuse ways I am indebted as well to Eileen Craig, Karen Heese, Ian Low, Nadine Stoikoff, Shawn Syms, and Michèle Wilkie.

I have spent several years intermittently collecting material for this book in the newspapers department of the Metropolitan Toronto Reference Library. I have always been impressed by the unfailing courtesy and good cheer of the rather peripatetic staff. I am also indebted in a broader way to the staff and resources of the Metro Reference Library at large.

I am beholden to Ted Smith for exertions above and beyond the call of duty in hand-tinting the photograph that appears on the cover, and to Sue Berkley for discovering the photograph in the first place. I would like as well to take this opportunity to thank Rex Williams for his efforts on my behalf in this and other projects. And I am grateful to the Ontario Arts Council for a Writers' Reserve grant.

Steve MacKinnon at the Archives of the City of Toronto has provided valued advice and assistance with the John Boyd photographs that do so much to illustrate the text and bring it alive. I would also like to thank the city archives for permission to use the Globe and Mail Collection from which these photographs have been taken. Again I owe broader debts to the archives' staff and resources, and to those of the John P. Robarts Library at the University of Toronto.

I am indebted to Alfred White for access to his private archives, including a photograph of the Band of the Governor-General's Body Guard militia regiment, and to Alfred White and Albert Linington for advice on the Toronto advertising industry of the 1920s. I am also indebted to Louise Reynolds for access to her private collection of inter-war memorabilia, and to Christopher White for recurrent help in my struggles with the mysteries of late twentieth-century computer technology.

My Linsmore Institute colleagues, Peter Carruthers and David Montgomery, kindly read strategic excerpts from the original manuscript, and provided valued written comments. John Hughes offered information on real estate conditions in Los Angeles during the 1920s that prompted me to rethink my views on the scene in Toronto. Charlie Bigenwald and John Purdon provided opportunities that inadvertently helped subsidize costs incurred in researching and writing the book. Gene Lees graciously responded to a specific query about the jazz age. Recurrent explorations of Toronto geography today with Michael Seward have helped sharpen my feeling for the urban geography of the 1920s.

All too many years of conversation (in one sense, and in another, all too few) with family members and family friends, who actually lived in the Toronto of the 1920s, are reflected in the pages that follow – in a way that defies specific enumeration. With a related eye on the future, I am grateful to Joseph MacDonald White and William MacDonald White for various forms of assistance and forbearance during the course of this project.

My original assumption about the newspaper ads that complement and extend John Boyd's photographs in illustrating the text was that if they ever were subject to copyright, they are no longer. This drew initially on information in Philip Marchand's 1989 biography of Marshall McLuhan. After consulting several authorities, Kirk Howard advised that the point seemed not altogether certain: for my own protection and peace of mind, I ought to go through the process of soliciting formal permissions to use the ads, wherever at all possible.

Diligent efforts have been made to contact potential holders of rights for every ad used in the text. In a few cases it has seemed clear that there are no such individuals or organizations extant today. In the great majority of cases I have been pleasantly surprised by the warmth and enthusiasm I encountered – a sign, I would like to think, that many local economic institutions are aware of the various advantages in taking an interest in their collective past.

I am grateful in particular to J.B. Agnew, Hudson's Bay Company; Lori A. Ball, Carling O'Keefe Breweries of Canada Limited; Robert Brockhouse, the Royal Alexandra Theatre; Bill Burak, Lake Simcoe Enterprises Ltd.; Brian A. Butters, *The Province* (Vancouver); Susan Cade, Toronto Transit Commission; Christine Coleman, Moir's Chocolates; Ted Cowan, Toronto Star Syndicate; Bill Croke, the King Edward Hotel; Paul Edmonds, Cadbury Beverages; Danielle M. Frizzi, the Gillette Company; Mark Gryfe, United Jewish Appeal of Toronto; Martha Heighington, Nesbitt Thomson; Charles Heintzman, Heintzman Pianos Limited; Jon Hodgins, CCM sport Maska inc.; Dale Hodson, The Toronto-Dominion Bank; Alan Hurst, Toronto Hydro; Rose Marie Ip, Canadian Pacific Hotels Corporation; M.L. Issac, Canadian Imperial Bank of Commerce; John Jursa, The Toronto Harbour Commissioners; Charles A. King, Liberal Party of Canada; Sylvie Lafleur, Canada Steamship Lines; Amanda J. Lang, Globe Information Services; D.S. Low, General Motors of Canada Ltd.; Doris M. Lunney, Kodak Canada Inc.; Michael E. Matthews, CN North America; Peter J. Moore, Exhibition Place; Lyndsay Morrison, National Trust; N.A. Morrison, Camco Inc.; Judith Lynn Nefsky, Canadian Pacific Archives; Maureen O'Brien, Northern Telecom Canada Ltd.; John N. O'Shea, Warner-Lambert Company; Randall Pierce, Progressive Conservative Party of Canada; John Rajanayagam, Lanka-Ceylon Tea Company; J.-Jacques Samson, *Le Soleil* (Quebec City); P.K. Sheard, Canada Life; Roger Smith, Eddy Matches; Melanie A. Warr, Westinghouse Canada Inc.; Craig Wilson, GE Canada; and P.J. Wilson, Eaton's.

I am grateful as well for some observations on the story of the Casa Loma Hotel from Mr. Rand Sparling.

R.W.
Fernwood Park
Toronto
July 1, 1993

Children looking at toys in window. (December 1922)

THE INTRIGUE OF THE 1920S

North of the North American Great Lakes, the 1920s started as the age of the farmers' revolt. But in cities like Toronto a new kind of urban life was putting down roots. Radio was in the air. Ice boxes had at least begun to give way to electric refrigerators. Though there were still horses on the streets, there was also the McLaughlin-Buick – "Canada's Standard Car."

In March 1922 the Toronto St. Patricks defeated the Vancouver Millionaires in the Stanley Cup finals at the Arena on Mutual Street. Five years later the St. Pats had become Conn Smythe's Maple Leafs, in a new ten-team National Hockey League with a Canadian and an American division. The year before, the Toronto Maple Leafs baseball club had defeated the Louisville Colonels in the "Little World Series."

By 1925 Canada had embarked on a brief but resounding economic boom. In August 1926 the Diwan of Bahadur from the Indian subcontinent officially opened the Canadian National Exhibition. Ontario's version of prohibition ended in 1927. Early in 1928 the Casa Loma Orchestra was pioneering the swing era in big-band jazz. Ernest Hemingway had already passed through town. He inspired the local writer Morley

Callaghan to publish his first Toronto novel – aptly entitled *Strange Fugitive*.

There was a downtown building boom at the end of the decade. The economic bustle in the country at large was boosting Toronto's challenge to Montreal's traditional status as Canada's business capital. The Royal York Hotel opened in June 1929. By the time the stock market crashed in October, work had begun on the new headquarters of the Canadian Bank of Commerce – "the tallest building in the British Empire."

THE ALMOST MYSTERIOUS PAST

Objectively, one might say, the decade of the 1920s was a fascinating and important time in almost every part of the globe. Toronto in the 1920s intrigues me for more subjective reasons.

I am now approaching the age of fifty – a distressing thought. Except for a few brief periods, I have lived in Toronto all my life. The place has changed enormously since I was born. The older I've become, however, the more I've felt that the evolution of Toronto I've seen with my own eyes is incomplete. I took my seat, as it were, in the middle of the movie. Lately, I've had a sense that this particular movie has ended. And I've grown more and more interested in seeing the earlier part I missed. I think Toronto today has finally evolved into something that it started to become in the 1920s. That's why I've tried to learn about an era in the city that, though I never saw it myself, still seems a part of my own Toronto life.

There are some obvious respects in which Toronto started to become what it is today long before the 1920s. Its modern history began with Iroquois villages on the northwestern shore of Lake Ontario, in the second half of the seventeenth century. They were followed by Mississauga villages and French fur trade and military outposts in the first half of the eighteenth century. Then there was the founding of the British North American town of York, in August 1793. Even the corporate entity still known as the city of Toronto was established as long ago as 1834.

By 1850 there were some 30,000 people in the city. There are a number of Toronto buildings from this period that still stand today. The *Globe* had already begun the story of what is now known as the *Globe and Mail*. By 1900 Toronto had about

200,000 people, some electric lights, and regular streetcar service. The old city hall and the present provincial parliament buildings at Queen's Park were in place. So were a number of structures on the downtown university campus. The *Toronto Daily Star* had begun the story of what is now more simply called the *Toronto Star*.

By the 1920s we are suddenly much closer to our own time. The growth of the modern suburbs that would eventually bring more than four million people to the Greater Toronto Area of today had just started. But the original city of Toronto, in its still current official sense, had something quite similar to its boundaries in the 1990s – and to its present population of around 600,000 people. Though the multiculturalism that would blossom in the metropolis after the 1960s was still muted, it too had begun in earnest. Already there were recognized Jewish, Italian, and Chinese communities. Vestiges of the city's small but ancient black population, with roots that stretched back to the origins of the town of York, had ever so gently begun to revive.

In 1921 the local art critic Barker Fairley, reviewing some paintings of old Toronto houses by Lawren Harris, wrote of "a vast gulf between the city's present and its immediate but somehow almost mysterious past." Here is where the young and still too callow metropolis we inhabit in the late twentieth century really starts to rise.

A NOTE ON SOURCES

In 1923 a youthful Ernest Hemingway reported that "Canadians ... don't believe in literature" and "think Art has been exaggerated." According to the historian Frank Underhill, in the 1920s Canadians read newspapers, not books. With this kind of testimony in mind, newspapers have been my primary sources for learning about Toronto in the 1920s. The key to my sense of the decade has been cut by several years of intermittently pondering endless rolls of microfilm, in the newspapers department at the Metropolitan Toronto Reference Library.

I have examined other sources as well. Both sets of my grandparents came to Toronto in the early twentieth century. One set were immigrants to Canada, or North America. Both my parents and an assortment of uncles, aunts, and in-laws lived in the city during the 1920s – as did the ancestors of some friends and acquaintances. So I have had contact with live travellers from the past I am writing about.

I have also explored the historical collection of *Might's City Directories* and related items at the Metro Reference Library. I have consulted records at the Archives of the City of Toronto, at the new city hall. On several occasions I have turned to the closely watched wisdom at the John P. Robarts Library, on the University of Toronto campus.

Again and again, however, I have come back to the newspapers. For certain kinds of research, in both the past and the present, they have all-too-obvious limitations, but for my purposes here they have proved more alive and revealing than any other material. Newspapers are also the major source of the illustrations that accompany the text to the book. Some work I did a few years ago inadvertently suggested that the newspaper advertising of the 1920s has a unique capacity to evoke the spirit of the age.

At first I thought that the ads in the papers should be the book's sole source of illustrations. Then my favourite adviser on such matters convinced me that a number of local photographs of the 1920s, in the Globe and Mail Collection at the city archives, were too good to pass up. These pictures are the work of the late John H. Boyd, staff photographer at the *Globe* (and later the *Globe and Mail*) from December 1922 to February 1963.

I have examined a diverse enough collection of sources to appreciate the naivety of pretending to capture the full richness of an entire decade in one slender volume. Though I have tried to present a well-rounded series of snapshots of what happened in Toronto during the 1920s, I am all too aware of how much I have had to leave out. I have nonetheless made some effort to keep in mind the obscure lives of ordinary people – alongside the larger events that dominated the news of the day. In one sense, I think that what is most impressive and most interesting about Toronto, even in the late twentieth century, is the setting it offers for ordinary life.

TOO GOOD TO BE TRUE

This book is not meant to be a serious discourse on urban problems – in Toronto or anywhere else. But in the 1990s it is impossible to write about Toronto in the 1920s without saying a few words on what many rightly regard as serious issues.

C.S. Clark first published his book *Of Toronto the Good* in 1898, coining a phrase that would live on long after his death. It summarized a side of the city's consciousness that endures in some degree even today. The outside world may have been rampant with evil, but Toronto the Good – "the city of churches" – was not as bad as other places (especially those south of the undefended border). It was a refuge for some higher morality.

In fact, when the 1920s began, the sale of alcoholic beverages had been illegal for almost four years, but the city of churches had a drug problem. Though the multicultural society of our own era had started to show its face, the Canadian federal government's Chinese Immigration Act of 1923 stiffened an earlier Anglo-Protestant tribalism. Municipal politics in Toronto may not have been as corrupt as in other locations, but the Orange Order ran its own powerful and exclusive local political machine. Though the city still preserved what the American literary critic Edmund Wilson would later call "a British tradition of good order and capable handling," Toronto's colonial obsession with the British Empire blunted its early discovery of the northern wilderness romance of Canada, from coast to coast to coast.

Many among us in the late twentieth century would add still more to the indictment. The city in Morley Callaghan's *Strange Fugitive* was, according to the back cover of a much more recent edition of the book, lamentably "narrow" and "provincial." White males ruled the roost, and everyone else languished under their domination. A big economic boom was under way by the middle of the 1920s, but there had been hard times earlier in the decade. There was virtually no social safety net of the sort we argue about in the 1990s. Victims of economic dislocation had to fend for themselves – including those who had only recently risked their lives, or lost family and friends, in the terrible Great War in Europe.

I count myself among those who would stress that this was not at all the whole picture. It is juvenile to judge the past by the standards of the present (especially when these standards are themselves the subject of so much controversy and uncertainty). My thesis, however, is that the era of the city's history that began in the 1920s has now come to an end. When an era is over we can recognize its beginnings for what they were. In Toronto the Good today, I think it's worth remembering that, in several important senses, Toronto in the 1920s was too good to be true.

A BEND IN THE RIVER

Some friends whose opinions I value have urged that this is the wrong theme for the book. They argue that it conceals more than it reveals – and that the legend of Toronto the Good, for all its smug hypocrisy, has brought tangible benefits to many different kinds of people. A place that claims a superior morality is at least occasionally forced to live up to its ideals. "Deconstructing" the positive myths of the past can just as easily lead to nihilism and violence as to fresh breezes of candour and creative equality.

I do have some deep sympathy for this point of view. The problem isn't just that it is juvenile to judge the past by the standards of the present. The world is also a complicated place, and real social change is a highly complicated and protracted process.

During the era that followed the First World War, Toronto did not accept its embryonic multiculturalism as it does in the 1990s, but it did not decisively repress it either: new cultural currents had some room to grow. Though a few white males dominated the city's public life, this did little for the status of the great majority of the species. There were "working girls" in the 1920s, and the decade saw the emergence of Toronto's first women politicians. The city *was* narrow and provincial, but it was also somewhat broad-minded. It was a more lively and interesting (and even dangerous) place than its current reputation implies.

At the same time, I think that Toronto today, like other parts of "northern North America," has reached a stage where it ought to start re-examining its past. In some often neglected respects we have still not progressed as far from the 1920s as we sometimes imagine. In his late 1970s novel, *A Bend in the River*, V.S. Naipaul, a writer whom I admire a great deal, recounts the adventures in a Canadian city of an Asian character whose "family have been traders and merchants in the Indian Ocean for centuries."

The city would seem to be Toronto, but it could equally be Vancouver, or even Montreal, or several other places. Naipaul's character is not impressed by the people he comes across in this neighbourhood of the global village: "They thought they were part of the West, but really they had become like the rest of us who had run to them for safety. They were like people far away, living on other people's land and off other people's brains, and that was all they thought they should do."

This harsh evaluation is bound to strike someone with my background as uncharitable, and – as the mere act of writing this book itself implies – I do not think it is altogether correct. Yet it does seem to me that Naipaul's character makes an important point. I think that Toronto in some collective sense is starting to appreciate this point. It has begun to ponder what should be done.

This is part of what I mean when I suggest that the particular stage in the evolution of Toronto that began in the 1920s has lately come to an end. Like others, I have recently had a sense of some vast curtain falling on the city's past. If this sense is even half right, the 1990s, or perhaps the first decade of the new century, will also be, like the 1920s, a time when a new stage in the evolution of the city that was too good to be true starts to take shape.

I hope these final slightly sombre introductory thoughts do not mislead anyone into expecting a more serious book than the one I have written. My main purpose in putting together the words and pictures that follow has been to entertain myself. Nonetheless, though I do not believe that history offers any lessons in any simple sense, if we let it, history can do a little more than entertain us. In the story of Toronto in the 1920s there are premonitions about the story of Toronto that lies ahead.

Snow shovellers on Queen Street. (December 1922)

CHAPTER ONE

A KIND OF REVOLUTION

It would be wrong to start the story too dramatically. At the time, the place had several dull edges. Economically Toronto was becalmed. In this part of the world, the decade would be almost half over before it really roared.

Nevertheless, the 1920s in Toronto did begin in the middle of what passed locally for radical events. The *Globe*, the city's oldest newspaper, had just announced a "political revolution." This revolution came as a great surprise. Its origins went back to October 1919, but it would not be confirmed until the middle of February 1920.

Strictly speaking, what was happening was only an unusual change of government in the Canadian province of Ontario, of which Toronto was, then as now, the capital city. A Conservative regime, headed by William Howard Hearst, had called a provincial election for Monday, October 20, 1919. The Hearst Conservatives had put on a smooth and even progressive show. They had expected to win. On October 18 the newspapers were still predicting what had seemed inevitable: "HEARST IS LIKELY TO HAVE MAJORITY OVER ALL GROUPS."

Some odd breezes, however, were in the air. Women voted for the first time in the 1919 Ontario election. The First World

The 1919 Ontario election took place in the wake of the First World War.
Exactly how many Canadians "commenced to eat Moir's Chocolates while in
service overseas" is not known, but more than 626,000 participated in the
conflict (from a total population of less than 9 million), and more than
68,000 were killed. (June 1920)

War, in which the Canadian forces of the British Empire had made great sacrifices, had ended less than a year before. There was postwar turmoil in many parts of the globe.

In the countryside outside Toronto, a still youthful association known as the United Farmers of Ontario (the UFO, inspired by the earlier United Farmers of Alberta) had decided to run protest candidates. In the province's rising cities, a loosely knit organization called the Independent Labour Party, or just the Labour Party, had resolved on a parallel gesture of concern.

When the votes were counted, the Conservatives took only 25 of the 111 seats in the Ontario Legislative Assembly. Their traditional Liberal opponents won 28. The United Farmers won 45 seats, and Labour 11.

After much debate, the United Farmer and Labour members decided to form a coalition government, commanding the barest of legislative majorities. They resolved to ask Ernest Charles Drury, an austere and scholarly family farmer from Simcoe County, north of Toronto, to be their leader. He formed a government on November 14, 1919.

The forty-two-year-old Drury, though a leading member of the UFO, had not bothered to run in the election. He could not be the premier of Ontario without a seat of his own in the assembly. On January 20, 1920, John Ford, the United Farmer member for Halton, west of Toronto, resigned, making way for Drury in a by-election. This was held during a driving snowstorm, on Monday, February 16. Drury won handily enough.

Drury was not fond of city life, believing the family farm had created "the finest yeomanry that civilization had yet produced." He would occupy the premier's office at Queen's Park for the next three and a half years, at the head of Ontario's first third-party government. This new regime was dominated by untried politicians who advocated "moral uplift." After his by-election victory, Drury proclaimed that people were "tired of the old game of politics. They want to see the creation in some way of a new order of things."

SERGEANT-MAJOR MACNAMARA

The 1919 Ontario election was only a mild local variation on more dramatic events in the world at large. At the top of the list, the Bolshevik Revolution had burst upon Russia in 1917. In various senses, it was still in progress in 1919. Two days before the Farmer-Labour victory in Ontario, the *Toronto Daily Star* had reported: "KRONSTADT FALLS, PETROGRAD NEAR SURRENDER."

In Ontario the 1919 election result was in part a protest against the decline of the old agrarian democracy, which was based on the North American family farm. In 1871 some 78 percent of all Ontario residents had lived in rural areas. By 1911 this had shrunk to 47 percent – less than a majority for the first time in the province's history.

Another local ingredient was the protest against the role assigned to the new industrial work force in Ontario's rising cities. The strongest Labour support came from such smaller industrial centres as Hamilton, Kitchener, Peterborough, and St. Catharines.

Toronto, in its narrowest official sense, had ten seats in the provincial parliament. In October 1919 five of these went to the traditional Liberals, and four to Hearst's Conservatives. Only one seat – Riverdale, in the recently developed area east of the Don River – opted for a candidate who would ultimately support the new Farmer-Labour coalition.

The victorious candidate in Riverdale, Sergeant-Major Joseph MacNamara, was variously described in the press as "Independent" or "Soldier-Labor." He defeated the official flag-bearer of the Independent Labour Party, John Vick, as well as the Conservative candidate, W.D. Robbins, and George Lockhart, a Socialist fringe candidate.

During the campaign MacNamara had urged that if "men were willing to go overseas to fight for the country at the call of the Government," then "the Government ought to be willing to conscript the wealth of the profiteers for the benefit of the widows, orphans and the broken wrecks of the war." Putting his finger on an issue that would finally do much to defeat the Drury government in 1923, he had also boldly declared: "I want my beer."

A NEW TYPE OF ARTIST

While the farmers of Halton County were confirming E.C. Drury as Ontario's new premier, some citizens of the province's capital city pondered another milestone. In the *Globe*, on Saturday, February 14, 1920, the Art Gallery of Toronto (known as the Art Gallery of Ontario today) ran a small advertisement announcing an exhibition of "Paintings by Tom Thomson and Japanese color prints," from "13th to 29th February, inclusive."

This was only a prelude to a more elaborate display some three months later. In May 1920 the art gallery would hold an exhibition of "Paintings by a Group of Seven Canadian Artists." This marked the first collective public showing of some innovative local art.

Many more Torontonians would go to see such things as Genaro and Gold in a "Musical Melange" at Loew's, on the east side of Yonge Street just north of Queen. The exhibit at the Art Gallery of Toronto nonetheless demonstrated that, after a long study of models in other places, Toronto had begun to discover its own geography. The geography involved was not inside the city itself. Then as now, this was less than overwhelming, but the geography that shapes a city is not just within the city boundaries. In the first formative era of the late seventeenth-century Iroquois villages, Toronto's strategic significance had turned around a canoe portage and water route, running north to Georgian Bay.

This "Toronto Passage" was also behind the Mississauga villages and French outposts established in the area in the first half of the eighteenth century. The same trail would have recurrent echoes – from Yonge Street, started by John Graves Simcoe in the 1790s and then improved by the Montreal fur-trade enterprise known as the North West Company, all the way to the multilane Highway 400 after the Second World War.

If you move further on along this northward pathway, up the eastern shoreline of Georgian Bay, you come to the dramatic rocky wilderness of the Canadian Shield, in the districts of Muskoka and Parry Sound. This is the truest romantic heartland of the Toronto region, in its widest sense. It starts about 130 kilometres north of the city limits. And it has everything that the landscape inside the city boundaries lacks.

The Group of Seven helped Toronto appreciate this wider regional geography. Its unofficial leader was Lawren Harris, a legatee of the Massey-Harris agricultural machinery fortune. The other six original members – Franklin Carmichael, A.Y. Jackson, Franz Johnston, Arthur Lismer, J.E.H. Macdonald, and F.H. Varley – were all Toronto commercial artists. They went on canoe trips up north and painted in their spare time.

According to the journalist F.B. Housser, they invented a "new type of artist" who "paddles, portages and makes camp" and "sleeps in the out-of-doors under the stars."

Though the 1920 exhibition inaugurated their collective career, they had formed personal friendships before the First World War. They had various inspirations. Harris and Macdonald, for example, had been impressed by an exhibition of Scandinavian art at the Albright Gallery in Buffalo in 1913.

Even before the Group of Seven went public, Tom Thomson had become its symbiotic martyr. He was born in 1877 on a farm in Grey County, near the southwestern shore of Georgian Bay. By 1904 he was working as an engraver in Toronto. In 1912 he started sketching the wilderness in Algonquin Park, a public forest reserve east of Parry Sound.

Not long after this ad ran, the old Grand Trunk system would become part of the new Canadian National Railways. (May 1920)

Courtesy of CN.

Over the next five years Tom Thomson caught the magic of the Canadian Shield as no one had done before. He died on July 8, 1917, in a still-mysterious canoe accident on Canoe Lake in the southwestern corner of Algonquin Park.

NATIONAL GEOGRAPHIC

By 1920 the stark and rocky wilderness north of the old Toronto Passage had begun its history as the preferred recreational retreat for jaded urbanites from the regional metropolis. Already it was Toronto's most coveted summer cottage country.

Soon enough it would be clear that this stretch of wilderness was only the city's closest point of access to the rugged northern geography that marked all Canada, from the Atlantic to the Arctic to the Pacific oceans. By 1924 four of the Group of Seven would be sketching the Rocky Mountains. Lawren Harris would go on to paint his own stark impressions of the Canadian Arctic. He would spend the last thirty years of his life in Vancouver, British Columbia. Harris had studied painting in Berlin before the First World War. According to the critic Dennis Reid, the "firm training in the business of commercial art" enjoyed by the rest of the group "led them to strive for qualities of eye-catching design and immediacy of impact." They could have drawn cartoons for Walt Disney but they had chosen something quite different.

During my youth I became acquainted with a University of Toronto character called H.N. "Bud" Milnes. I still remember a winter night at his house in the late 1960s. A group of young people who knew much more about art than I did were enthusiastically discussing the limitations of the Group of Seven. At one point someone asked Bud what he thought.

He agreed that Tom Thomson, Lawren Harris, A.Y. Jackson, and the others were not like Picasso, but he urged that some of them had some distinction. They had "said something" with real conviction, for the first time. They had said "look at this: it isn't Europe, but it's interesting."

IN THE BRITISH EMPIRE

It has been a regret for some that Toronto is not a part of Europe. Even worse, beyond its primary allegiance to the rugged northern physique of Canada, geographically (and in other ways as well) it is part of the North American Midwest. Toronto is on the Great Lakes, not the eastern seaboard or the Atlantic Ocean.

The North American Midwest has been a widely despised part of the planet. As if to counteract the stigma, *Might's Directory* implied in the 1920s that Ontario's biggest city actually was located somewhere else. It had "the largest university," the "largest exclusive furriers," and the "largest Board of Trade" – not in Ontario, or Canada, or North America, but "in the British Empire."

The newspapers of the day resound with endless variations on this theme. When the Group of Seven had its first public exhibition, there were countless signs of an already "global-ized" British imperial civilization in the city. In 1867 Canada had become the first self-governing dominion in the British Empire, but it was not until the late 1920s that the principle of full political autonomy for British dominions would even start to acquire legal recognition. The official act that enshrined this principle – the Statute of Westminster – would not be passed until 1931. In the 1920s there were Union Jacks flying all over Toronto. (As people of my generation can testify, they would keep on flying until the late 1960s, or even the early 1970s.) Today there are strong pressures to forget all this. Some flow from high-minded impulses. One of them involves Canada's still-earlier French imperial history. Toronto had its own highly muted French Canadian community in the 1920s. But that is a story for later on.

THE KING OF CASA LOMA

Though colonialism breeds mimicry, ardent colonialists see the metropolis not for what it is, but for what they think it ought to be. Toronto's version of British imperial civilization had several ambiguous aspects in the 1920s.

Sir Henry Mill Pellatt – knight bachelor, commander of the Royal Victorian Order, doctor of civil law, knight of grace in the Venerable Order of St. John of Jerusalem, and colonel of the Queen's Own Rifles militia regiment – personified a once-bubbling current that was starting to dry up.

Pellatt was born in Kingston, Ontario, in 1859. As a very young child, he moved with his parents to Toronto. His father would establish one of the first successful stock brokerages in

British Grown
for British Taste

This new tea called Lanka is British through and through, the perfected blend of finest varieties the hill gardens of Ceylon can produce. It comes straight to us from the Island of Ceylon through the Keystone Port of Vancouver—a direct route which saves freight charges and import duty. Thus, although super-quality, Lanka is sold at the popular price of 75 cents a pound.

Once you have tasted it, once you have enjoyed its incomparable flavor, Lanka will be your final choice of tea. . No other varieties satisfy after you have once enjoyed the wonderful flavor of Lanka.

Lanka Tea is further distinguished by its beautiful bright sparkling color, by its captivating aroma, as irresistible as the bouquet of rare wine.

You will see the handsome Lanka package illustrated in this advertisement on your grocer's shelves. Leading dealers everywhere have welcomed the chance to offer their customers the supreme quality of Lanka.

Imported and packed by

WM. BRAID & COMPANY
Vancouver, Canada

LANKA TEA

Tea from the Empire in South Asia for the people of Toronto, imported via Vancouver on the Pacific northwest coast. (January 1920) the city. Pellatt's parents were somewhat struggling immigrants from the United Kingdom, and most of his formal education took place at the Toronto Model School, not the more locally prestigious Upper Canada College. Young Henry, however, would make a grand tour of Europe before joining his father's firm.

No matter how or where he had grown up, Henry Pellatt would likely have left some mark on the world. Despite the immense girth of his later years, as a young man he excelled as an amateur runner. In 1879 he ran the mile in a near-record four minutes and forty-two and four-fifths seconds, at a race in New York City. And once he settled down in his father's office, Pellatt developed a reputation as a daring investor. He was dubbed "Pellatt the Plunger" by his peers.

Then the early twentieth century brought a great boom to Canada. The modern Canadian economy went into its "take-off" between 1896 and 1914. In some ways the phenomenon has never been equalled. During the four years preceding the First World War, Canada achieved immigration levels that have yet to be matched.

The boom made Henry Pellatt's fortune, built around early hydroelectric power development in Ontario and real estate in western Canada. For Pellatt, however, money was only a means to an end. His guiding passion was the romance of the British Empire. He devoted his fortune to cultivating a self-invented persona as a local hero of the global Raj. By 1905 he had managed to procure a knighthood. His imperial patriotism had a public-spirited, almost populist side. He was a patron of the Queen's Own Rifles militia regiment in Toronto, and in 1910 he financed an extended regimental excursion to England from his own pocket.

In the same year, work began on the foundations of Pellatt's grandest project and most enduring legacy to Toronto. It was "a castle" on the bluffs of the primeval Lake Iroquois shoreline (what Lake Ontario used to be, before the end of the last ice age), due northeast of Walmer and Davenport roads.

The place was called Casa Loma, which means "house on the hill" in Spanish. Why the name should be Spanish is unclear. But "no where in America," a later guidebook would explain, can "be found a more accurate or exact reproduction of the medieval architecture of the British Isles or Europe."

Pellatt moved into the building when it was still not quite finished, in 1914. It would never be quite finished, but even unfinished it was impressive enough.

It had 98 rooms, 30 bathrooms, 3 bowling alleys, 25 fireplaces, 52 telephones, 5,000 electric lights, a built-in vacuum system, an indoor swimming pool, a shooting gallery, an electric elevator system, and the largest wine cellar on the North American continent.

URBAN DEMOGRAPHY AFTER THE FIRST WORLD WAR

Willing and Williamson, Booksellers and Stationers, published a map of Toronto in 1878, when Henry Pellatt was nineteen years old (and E.C. Drury had just been born). At that point the city took in a modest rectangle of territory, stretching from Lake Ontario north to Bloor Street, and from Dufferin Street on the west to just east of the Don River. According to the 1881 Census of Canada, it was home to only some 86,000 people.

By 1920 more than half a million people lived in Toronto. Through a series of annexations, culminating during the half-dozen years between 1906 and 1912, the official territory had expanded to something not far short of its configuration today. The modest rectangle that had defined the city in Henry Pellatt's youth now reached from Bloor Street north to St. Clair, from Dufferin west almost to the Humber River, and from the Don River east to Victoria Park Avenue.

Mimicking the old Toronto Passage, a new, much narrower rectangle, along the Yonge Street corridor from St. Clair north to Hog's Hollow, had been placed atop the earlier figure. Already there was growth outside these boundaries. "Toronto" had started to imply a range of geography beyond the city of Toronto itself. And the earlier age of annexation was close to some kind of limit.

Inside and outside the city's official boundaries, the geography involved was not at all as compelling as the nearby Canadian Shield country, but it could boast some small attractions. Toronto's Lake Ontario vista had impressed the visting Walt Whitman in the late nineteenth century. Anyone who has ridden a bicycle around the place knows the steep hill that marks the shoreline of the primeval Lake Iroquois.

Lake Simcoe ice houses, in thirty-two different locations, were one way in which "the country came right into the city" in the 1920s. (June 1923)

Neither the Don nor Humber River amounts to much. Yet they are part of a minor but extensive watershed that has made Toronto a city of ravines, even today. The nostalgic local journalist Robert Thomas Allen has stressed that in the 1920s the place "was criss-crossed with ravines that a boy could reach in fifteen minutes, from the time the schoolbell rang, and lose himself in until suppertime ... The city didn't sprawl into the country then; the country came right into the city."

According to the decennial Census of Canada, the official city was home to just under 522,000 people in 1921. Using the same data, urban analysts have subsequently estimated that the 1921 population of the larger Toronto metropolitan region was approximately 686,000. *Might's Directory* estimated that in the same year there were 671,661 people in what it called "Greater Toronto."

By either set of figures, Toronto in the 1920s was still playing second fiddle to its bigger, older brother, Montreal – the traditional economic capital of Canada, in the old province of Quebec. According to census data, the larger Montreal region was home to some 796,000 people in 1921.

Canada itself was still a small colonial pond. At this point neither Toronto nor Montreal (to say nothing of Winnipeg, Canada's third-largest city in 1921) had real big-city muscle, as such things were reckoned in the neighbouring colossus of the United States of America. As early as 1900 New York City had taken in some 3,470,000 people. Chicago had been able to boast 1,699,000, and Philadelphia 1,294,000.

As best we can tell, however, the world's population was much larger in the early twentieth century than it had ever been before. Many more places had passed some creative threshold of city size than would have been conceivable in earlier eras. By the end or even the middle of the 1920s, the greater Toronto region would have as many people as the ancient city of Rome, at the height of the Roman Empire.

THE IMMIGRANT CITY

For Henry Pellatt, and many other people, what most distinguished Toronto from its U.S. neighbours in the early 1920s was the city's continuing allegiance to the British Empire. Demography reveals some visceral underpinnings to this allegiance. To an even greater extent than other parts of Ontario,

Toronto had a well-established history as a magnet for migrants from Great Britain. In the 1850s and 1860s, just before the Canadian Confederation of 1867, the majority of people living in the city had actually been born in the United Kingdom.

The British Dominion of Canada's first generation was thwarted by economic hard times. This dampened immigration profoundly. The share of Toronto's population "born in Canada" peaked at 73 percent in 1901. With a new burst of prosperity on the horizon, it would never reach so high a level again.

The Canadian boom of the early twentieth century that brought Henry Pellatt the money to build Casa Loma also brought a fresh wave of British immigrants to Toronto. In 1921 only 62 percent of all city residents had been born in Canada. Almost three out of every ten had been born in the United Kingdom.

There was as well a much newer trend bubbling among the latest population statistics. By the 1920s cultural demography in Toronto had started to become a complicated subject.

In the first two decades of the twentieth century, for the first time in the official city's still youthful history, significant numbers of non-British migrants were coming to Toronto. They had backgrounds in Europe beyond the United Kingdom, even beyond such European places as Germany and France, and even (to a much smaller but still noticeable degree) in parts of the world beyond Europe altogether. By 1920 the broader multiculturalism that would blossom so boldly after the Second World War had put down its first deep roots.

Throughout the nineteenth century, the share of the Toronto population with what documents of the day called "British racial origins" – whether born inside or outside Canada – had remained well over 90 percent. By 1921 three out of every twenty city of Toronto residents were reporting one form or another of non-British origins. By the end of the 1920s the proportion would rise to two out of every ten.

Though "the British" remained the dominant majority throughout the decade, more than a few classed in this group by government statisticians had begun to see themselves as more Canadian than British.

AN AMBIGUOUS AND IRONIC PLACE

Sir Henry Pellatt was on the elite side of the city's British colonial culture. Among members of the oldest branches of the local establishment, he was a parvenu with a populist touch. He was not above dealing from the bottom of the deck, but no one doubted that he was a man of the classes, and not of the masses.

For Ernest Charles Drury and his supporters, this was one of the problems with the British Empire. It elevated certain classes and repressed the masses. They spoke with an English-speaking Canadian variation on the voice of the North American frontier. This voice had been discovered on the independent family farm, an ocean away from the aristocratic European past. Locally it had been trained by George Brown of the *Globe*, who had lionized "the rural population, the reading population," in the pre-Confederation "Canada West."

The most extreme cadences of the voice had been raised by "the Firebrand," William Lyon Mackenzie. He was the first mayor of the city that had been erected on the foundations of the old British North American town of York, in 1834. He was also the leader of the failed Upper Canadian Rebellion of 1837.

In Toronto during the 1920s all this was still living history, in a way that has not quite survived into the present. Some of the most fertile personalities in the early twentieth-century city had grown up on Canadian versions of North American family farms.

By this point, however, Toronto had become entangled in the ironies and subtleties that help explain its still-prevalent reputation for irksome ambiguity. Already it was almost impossible to say anything straightforward about the place without inviting pedantic contradictions. George Brown had been both a warm admirer of Abraham Lincoln in the United States and a staunch supporter of "British institutions" in Canada. Towards the end of his life, even the fiery Mackenzie, back home after a period of enforced exile in upstate New York, had confessed: "Republican rule is far less pure than I thought until I lived in the republic."

In still other ways, allegiance to the Empire in Toronto during the early 1920s was as strong as it was because it was not just an affair of the classes. It had its own mass base, with its own collective memories, populist pedigrees, and popular voices.

*Bloor Street, east of Dundas and west of Lansdowne, when the romance of
the nineteenth-century railway age that had begun in George Brown's day
was still more alive than it is today. (February 1923)*

TOMMY CHURCH

The strongest of these voices belonged to T.L. "Tommy"
Church, who served his last term as mayor of the city in 1921.
When I was growing up after the Second World War, his name
was still in the air. Eventually it struck me that this was partly
because he stood for so much that was bad in the old Toronto
the Good.

When my most progressive aunt talked about Mayor
Church, it was in a voice of warning. He personified a world we
had grown out of, and we were lucky. It was a world where the

Orange Parade on the 12th of July was still a big annual event. Swaggering British Protestant young men marched around the downtown streets, banging ominous drums to reaffirm the message that the real Toronto belonged to them, and no one else.

Tommy Church's city was a place that still revelled in a late nineteenth-century notoriety as "the Belfast of North America." Tommy Church himself was a big man in the Orange Order, and a particular kind of Conservative.

Charles Dickens had visited Toronto on his first North American tour in the middle of the nineteenth century. He had written to his friend, John Forster, that the "wild and rabid Toryism" of the place was, "I speak seriously, *appalling*." Out of one side of his mouth, Tommy Church was still speaking for this wild and rabid Toryism in the early 1920s. He raised at least one tribal voice of the old WASP majority in the city. It was not always a sweet voice to hear.

A photograph of "his worship Mayor Church ... at his desk this morning" glares out from a page of his staunchest journalistic supporter, the *Evening Telegram*, for Tuesday, December 21, 1920, at the start of his last victorious municipal campaign. He has a hard scowl that says, "Don't mess with me." He looks cold, opinionated, suspicious, and unpleasant.

Yet, in Toronto, a place already entangled in ironic ambiguities, this harsh caricature demands some qualification. Orangeism in old Toronto, in fact, did not have all that many real teeth. And it was far from ubiquitous. For every friend Tommy Church had at the *Telegram*, he had an enemy at the *Daily Star*.

Even when it was bad, then as now, Toronto the Good had good manners. The voice raised by the likes of Tommy Church had its circumspections. You can hear them in the excuses offered by Church's friends at the *Telegram* for his unusually slender margin of victory in the municipal election of 1920. Apparently, there had been some "Knights of Columbus activity against T.L. Church" during the campaign, and the "Roman Catholic Church in Montreal is one of the great money powers in Canada." Such explanations cleverly blend anti-Catholic with both anti-French and anti-Montreal bigotry. But they achieve their sordid purposes politely, and in a moderate way.

There were still more subtleties. Not all Orangemen were Tories. Not all were ethnophobic. Orangeism had some positive sides. Not everyone who voted for Tommy Church was an Orangeman. Mayor Church himself was more than this. He was also a populist and even a progressive of sorts. In January 1921 he described his last electoral triumph in the Toronto mayoralty as "the people's victory for public ownership ... and public rights."

During the 1920 campaign Mayor Church linked himself with Sir Adam Beck – "the Hydro Knight." Beck had briefly been considered a possible leader of the new Farmer-Labour coalition in Ontario, until the mantle finally settled on Drury. From this other side of his mouth, Mayor Church spoke with the voice of what later generations would call a "progressive conservative" or even "a Red Tory."

Tommy Church was first elected mayor of Toronto in 1915, in the middle of the First World War. He would be elected again in 1916, 1917, 1918, 1919, 1920, and 1921. But 1921 would be the last year he served as mayor. By the 1920s the world he personified, like the world of Sir Henry Pellatt, king of Casa Loma, had begun to disappear.

PUBLIC TRANSIT

Until after the Second World War, municipal elections in Toronto were held annually, on New Year's Day. In the elections of 1920, along with electing politicians, voters were asked to declare the will of the people on six local policy issues, in what a *Daily Star* editorial called "The Referendums."

In one of these referendums the people of Toronto endorsed the establishment of a publicly owned and operated mass transit system. This led to the creation of the Toronto Transportation (later Transit) Commission (TTC), which finally opened for business on Thursday, September 1, 1921.

In the early 1920s mass transit in Toronto already had a respectable history. The city's two major earlier systems, however, had been privately owned and operated monopolies, granted by city council for thirty-year periods.

The Toronto Street Railway Company, established in 1861, had run a system of horse-drawn streetcars. When the TSR franchise expired, a new enterprise, called the Toronto Railway Company, was commissioned to operate a system of electric streetcars. Popularly, the "TRC" was still often referred to as the "TSR." In 1921 the expiration of its franchise made way for the

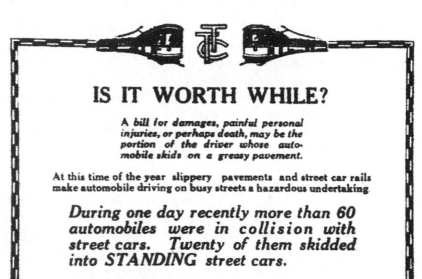

IS IT WORTH WHILE?

A bill for damages, painful personal injuries, or perhaps death, may be the portion of the driver whose automobile skids on a greasy pavement.

At this time of the year slippery pavements and street car rails make automobile driving on busy streets a hazardous undertaking.

During one day recently more than 60 automobiles were in collision with street cars. Twenty of them skidded into STANDING street cars.

MOTORISTS! Remember that a street car cannot dodge. Automobiles which stay off the street car tracks are in no danger of colliding with a heavy street car.

PRACTISE SAFETY FIRST, LAST AND ALL THE TIME

The surest way to avoid accidents is to

RIDE IN THE STREET CAR

The cost of one accident will pay your street car fare for a long, long time.

THE INSIDE OF A STREET CAR IS THE SAFEST PLACE ON TORONTO'S BUSY STREETS

Toronto Transportation Commission.

The TTC was less than two and a half years old when this ad on the perils of the new automobile age ran in the papers. (December 1923)

TTC. In effect, the TTC bought out the private corporation and operated it as a public enterprise.

At the time, enthusiasm for public enterprise was not confined to supporters of the revolutionary Drury regime at Queen's Park. In 1906 the Whitney Conservatives had established the Hydro-Electric Power Commission of Ontario (known today as Ontario Hydro). Masterminded by the Hydro Knight, Sir Adam Beck, it was North America's first publicly owned hydroelectric power enterprise.

There was also a more strictly expeditious aspect to the birth of the TTC. This flowed from the unhappy fate of the take-off in the Canadian economy that had occurred between 1896 and 1914. Nothing lasts forever. By the early 1920s, according to a youthful Ernest Hemingway, Canada was in the middle of "a kind of busted boom."

The leading figure in the privately owned Toronto Railway Company was Sir William Mackenzie (no relation to William Lyon Mackenzie, or to several other unrelated Mackenzies who have played prominent roles in Canada's past). The TRC was only one of many enterprises in a commercial empire that Sir William had built up during the late nineteenth and early twentieth centuries. The empire's crown jewel was the Canadian Northern Railway – Canada's third major transcontinental rail line.

By the end of the First World War, Sir William Mackenzie's empire was in tatters. It had become clear that Canada probably did not need more than one transcontinental railway. It certainly did not need three. The two privately owned rivals of the original Canadian Pacific Railway found themselves in profound financial trouble. To avert disaster, the Canadian federal government bought them out, to form the publicly owned Canadian National Railways. And the city of Toronto bought out William Mackenzie's Toronto Railway Company, to form the TTC.

THE ONTARIO TEMPERANCE ACT

Beyond the bonds of the British Empire, Toronto in the 1920s, like the rest of Canada, was inescapably a part of North America. Both the Hydro-Electric Power Commission and the TTC were variations on a wider progressive impulse in both Canada and the United States.

Another sign of continental trends was a piece of provincial legislation known as the Ontario Temperance Act (OTA). Passed by the Hearst Conservatives in 1916, it prohibited the sale of alcohol in the province, except for "medicinal, mechanical, scientific and sacramental purposes."

Hearst's legislation had left some doubt about whether "the OTA" would remain in force after the First World War, but a

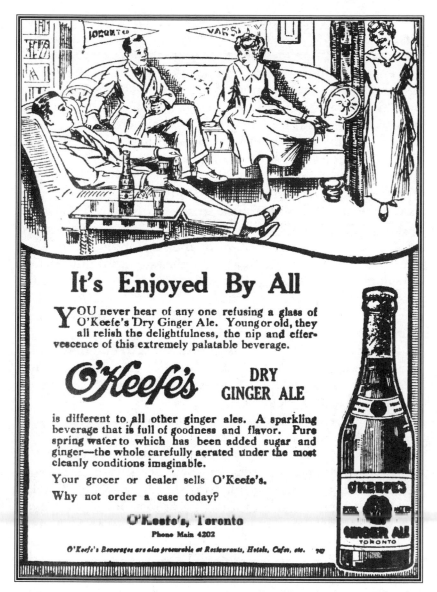

When selling alcoholic beverages was illegal in Ontario, companies that would sell beer to a later generation sold ginger ale. (February 1920)

referendum accompanying the 1919 provincial election made clear that a decisive majority of Ontario voters continued to support prohibiting the sale of the demon rum.

These feelings were passionately endorsed by the United Farmers. The endorsement was taken to heart by E.C. Drury and his attorney general, the eccentric Toronto lawyer W.E. Raney. To the distress of Sergeant-Major MacNamara and others among the government's Labour supporters, a still stronger Ontario Temperance Act became a key element in the surprising political revolution.

There was a temperance movement in the United Kingdom as well as in the United States, but it was only in the United States and English-speaking Canada that enthusiasm for temperance led to the prohibition of the sale of alcoholic beverages by law. In the 1920s what both places had that the United Kingdom did not was a still-strong memory of the wild habits on the Anglo-American frontier.

At the same time, there were a few significant differences between prohibition in the United States and Canada. At midnight on January 16, 1920, the Eighteenth Amendment to the U.S. Constitution took effect. It prohibited the sale of alcohol, under federal law, throughout the United States. It would not be repealed until December 5, 1933.

Except for a brief so-called emergency period towards the end of the First World War, there would be no federal prohibition in Canada, but by 1916 every Canadian province except Quebec had passed provincial laws against the sale of alcoholic beverages. Before the end of the 1920s, however, all English-speaking provinces except Prince Edward Island would convert their prohibition laws into government-controlled systems of legal liquor marketing.

Government-controlled liquor marketing would not arrive in Ontario until 1927. Meanwhile, in the early 1920s, the 1919 lifting of the short-lived Canadian federal prohibition posed a problem for the Drury regime and the OTA. While the OTA prohibited selling alcoholic beverages, it did not prohibit buying them. Once the brief period of Canada-wide prohibition ended, thirsty customers in Toronto could legally order cases of whatever they liked from solicitous merchants in Montreal. This problem led to another provincial temperance referendum, on Monday, April 18, 1921.

The 1921 Ontario referendum posed the question: "Shall the importation and the bringing of intoxicating liquors into the province be forbidden?" In Ontario at large a majority voted "Yes." Though everyone in the province had to abide by this decision, the majority in Toronto and other larger urban centres voted "No."

There had been another notable loophole in the original OTA. Apart from their availability through the inevitable bootlegging and illegal speakeasies, alcoholic beverages could still be legally purchased "for medicinal purposes" – under a doctor's prescription. In these circumstances many confirmed drinkers found themselves subject to recurrent illnesses that only alcohol could cure. Some doctors were sympathetic.

In 1920 it was reported that 90 percent of the prescriptions issued by doctors for quart bottles of liquor were medically unnecessary. One doctor had prescribed for more than 2,000 patients in one month. Another had treated 487 in a single day. In its continuing campaign to strengthen the OTA, the Drury regime took steps to restrain such sympathies. In 1921 doctors were legally limited to 40 liquor prescriptions a month.

COCAINE AND MORPHINE

Drinking the demon rum for non-medical reasons was not the only illegal form of local drug use during the early 1920s. In February 1920 the *Globe* ran an ad touting the current issue of *Maclean's* – "Canada's National Magazine," published in Toronto – in which the lead article was on "The Growth of the Deadly Drug Habit."

According to the ad, in 1912 "only 35 ounces of Cocaine" had been "imported into Canada. Last year the imports had jumped to 12,333 ounces"; in 1907 "Canadians imported 1,523 ounces of Morphine. Last year we imported 30,000 ounces." The result was that the "drug habit is growing in Canada – growing so fast that it has become a national menace."

The article was written by Emily Murphy – a prominent early twentieth-century Canadian journalist and political activist. She was "police magistrate of Edmonton" and said to be popularly known as "Janey Canuck."

In Toronto the Good recurrent items in the press suggest some grounds for Emily Murphy's concern. On February 20,

Some two years after she wrote about the "Deadly Drug Habit," Emily Murphy (top right) appeared in this fountain-pen ad. (March 1922)

Courtesy of Waterman Pen Company.

1920, the *Globe* ran an article headlined "CHARGES DRUG TRAFFIC AMONG THE CHILDREN."

Several months later, in June, an item appeared in the *Daily Mail and Empire* under the headline "SCATTERED DOPE ON CITY STREET." On Mutual Street police had arrested a Benny Herscourbitz of Montreal. He had in his possession "nearly $1,000 worth of cocaine and morphine, both pills and powder."

In December 1920 another *Globe* article, headlined "GATHERING IN OF 'DOPESTERS,'" reported that the "Morality Department has spread a net over the Chinese colony, which, it claims, is the centre of the drug trafficking which has been going on in an extensive way."

In July 1922 the *Daily Star* reported on the case of a local "drug dealer" called Edwin Mcguire. He had been apprehended some time before. On July 3 he was given the choice of paying a $1,000 fine or serving one year "at the Industrial Farm" (otherwise known as the Don Jail).

In February 1923 Dr. Charles Hastings, Toronto's medical officer of health, released a special report titled "The National Curse of the Drug Traffic." A key cause of drug abuse, he argued, was simply "modern living, with its combination of monotony and stress."

As Heather MacDougall, the late twentieth-century historian of the city health department has explained, Dr. Hastings was especially concerned about pushers who sold "pleasure powder" or "snow" (a combination of cocaine and boracic acid) to young men at Toronto dance halls. Young men, apparently, were more attracted to the deadly habit than were young women, but according to an article in the *Star* for Tuesday, March 16, 1923: "WOMEN FORM THIRD OF DRUG ADDICTS." As viewed in some quarters, this was only one aspect of a new liberation.

On the boardwalk at Sunnyside. (April 1923)

CHAPTER TWO

POPULIST ADVENTURES

About a month after the 1921 prohibition referendum, Howard Ferguson, the new leader of the Ontario Conservative Party, gave a speech in Ottawa. In Toronto it was prominently reported by the *Mail and Empire,* companion morning voice for those who read the *Evening Telegram* at night.

According to Ferguson, there had recently been "a most marked change in the attitude of the public toward the Drury Government." He maintained that when "a general election was next held," the unusual Farmer-Labour coalition "would be decisively driven from office."

The prophecy probably pleased many readers of the *Mail and Empire;* yet for some Torontonians it was beside the point. They might think it a good thing that Toronto was the capital city of Ontario, but provincial politics was only the minor league. The big action was in Ottawa, capital city for all the Dominion of Canada.

Three and a half months later, just as the TTC was starting to operate the city's first publicly owned streetcars, citizens of Toronto had their own chance to play in the political major league. On September 1, 1921, Arthur Meighen, prime minister of Canada, called a federal election for Tuesday, December 6.

In Canada at large the 1921 federal election is memorable for several reasons. To start with, it was the first time since Confederation in 1867 that no political party had won a governing majority. The simple reason was the new Progressive Party, which took 64 of the 235 seats in the Canadian House of Commons of the day.

The Progressives in Canada were the federal big brothers of such provincial organizations as the United Farmers of Alberta and the United Farmers of Ontario. In 1921, except for one seat in New Brunswick, they won nothing east of the Ottawa River, but they took 2 seats in British Columbia, 10 in Alberta, 12 in Manitoba, 15 in Saskatchewan, and 24 in Ontario.

Arthur Meighen's Conservatives fared badly, much like the Hearst Conservatives in the 1919 Ontario election. They took only 50 seats: 37 in Ontario and 7 in British Columbia.

The federal Liberals, under their new leader, William Lyon Mackenzie King, did better. They took 116 seats – just two short of a bare majority. They won 25 seats in Atlantic Canada and 21 in Ontario. Mackenzie King had carefully posed as the loyal Liberal disciple of Canada's first French Canadian prime minister, Wilfrid Laurier. He had the staunch support of several Quebec native sons, including his close political friend and colleague Ernest Lapointe. On December 6, 1921, the Liberals took all 65 of Quebec's 65 federal seats.

On December 29 Mackenzie King formed his first cabinet in Ottawa. Technically it presided over a minority government that leaned on the support of at least two independent members from western Canada. Mackenzie King nonetheless began his career as the country's longest-serving prime minister. The Liberals began an even longer history as Canada's natural "governing party" at the federal level. They would not lose this status until 1984.

THE LONG SUNSET OF TORY TORONTO

William Lyon Mackenzie King was born in 1874 in Berlin, Ontario (or "Kitchener," as it was renamed after the First World War broke out). He liked to remember that he was the grandson of William Lyon Mackenzie, first mayor of the city of Toronto and leader of the failed Upper Canadian Rebellion of 1837.

Conservative Party advertising in the Toronto papers, four days before the December 1921 federal election.

King's own seat in the federal Parliament in 1921 was York North. It was in the farming district due north of Toronto, which had been a bastion of support for his grandfather some eighty years before. Both the *Globe* and the *Daily Star* supported Mackenzie King in the 1921 federal election.

The five Toronto seats won by the Ontario Liberals in the 1919 provincial election had seemed to undercut an earlier local Conservative dominance. "Tory Toronto" had a history that went back even further than the rabid enthusiasms that had so appalled Charles Dickens in the middle of the nineteenth century. Yet by 1920 a new kind of rising young metropolis was already showing a kaleidoscopic face. It embraced a wide variety of people and points of view – culturally, economically, politically, socially, and in almost every other way imaginable.

In local politics, however, the 1921 federal election signalled that the 1919 provincial election had only started a long process. It would take decades to complete. Reports of the death of the old Tory Toronto were premature. After the unusually strong showing of Sergeant-Major MacNamara and the provincial Liberals in 1919, Conservative candidates would return to sweep the city in the three federal and three provincial elections of the 1920s.

In December 1921 Meighen's federal Conservatives advocated a "Canada for the Canadians." Their Canada, though, was still a robustly loyal part of the British Empire. The Conservatives stood for a protective tariff, especially against manufactured goods from the United States. They spoke to the rising cities.

Mackenzie King's Liberals leaned towards a more autonomous Canadianism, less entangled with the Empire and the Old World. They had more enthusiasm for free trade or "reciprocity" with the United States. They still had roots in the values of the North American family farm. In the age of Laurier (and Oliver Mowat at Queen's Park), the Liberals had discovered the traditional rural virtues of the ostensibly pious Catholic *habitant* in Quebec.

Just after the election was called, a somewhat convoluted headline in the *Star* inadvertently summed it all up: "FARMERS HIS CHIEF FOES IN GENERAL ELECTION / AND THE ISSUE IS FREE TRADE OR PROTECTION / SAYS MEIGHEN IN ANNOUNCING APPEAL TO THE

PEOPLE BEFORE YEAR-END." On December 6 all nine federal ridings in "Toronto and District" returned Conservative members. Sensing that his municipal career was approaching its limits, Tommy Church ran in North Toronto. Like every other Conservative candidate, he won.

AGNES MACPHAIL

Tommy Church was definitely a Tory, but he was also a populist of sorts. In 1921 it was still too early for the local Tory revival to bring about the sudden death of radical postwar populism, even in Toronto. The federal Progressives had grabbed the limelight in the political major league at Ottawa. Mackenzie King's Liberals had formed the new federal government. Out in the rural hinterland of Toronto there had been a still more radical event.

As they had provincially in Ontario in 1919, in 1921 women cast their first votes in a Canadian federal election. Some men found the prospect amusing, and the editors of the *Daily Star* felt called upon to condemn those who worried aloud that women would simply vote for the most handsome male candidates. But by the early 1920s women could do more than just vote. They could run for office. On December 6, 1921, both men and women in one federal riding cast so many votes for a female candidate that she actually won a seat in the Canadian House of Commons.

On the testimony of her friends, Agnes Macphail was a warm and attractive lady. She liked to wear capes "because they swing when you walk." Though she would remain single all her life, she apparently turned down numerous proposals of marriage.

She was born in 1890 on a family farm in Grey County, Ontario – the same part of the province Tom Thomson was from. She started as a country schoolteacher. Then she became active in the United Farmers of Ontario and made her first trip to the organization's head office in Toronto. In the 1921 federal election she ran with the Progressives in her home county and won.

Agnes Macphail has traditionally been viewed as the first woman elected to the Canadian federal Parliament, although some ambiguous recent evidence on a nineteenth-century man

Like the lady here, Agnes Macphail began her working life as a schoolteacher, but it's hard to imagine her taking heart and nerve pills. (January 1921)

who may have really been a woman has clouded the issue somewhat. Macphail's public career sharpened her awareness of women's issues. She once declared that "she would not like to see any other woman go through what she had to go through when she first came into the House of Commons." Yet her political vision transcended the narrowest concerns of her own sex. Her maiden speech in Ottawa, reported in the Toronto *Globe* on March 28, 1922, dealt with the problems of "small-salaried workers." Several months later a "Spotlight" article on "AGNES MACPHAIL, M.P." in the *Daily Star* stressed how she had just refused a salary increase voted by the previous Parliament.

Actions of this sort would not have endeared Agnes Macphail to the powers that were, even if she had been a man. The popular historian Valerie Knowles has called her a "hard-working, sharp-tongued pioneer." To make things worse, she had a sense of humour as well. She once asked a male heckler, who had been urging her to get a husband: "What guarantee have I that anybody I married now wouldn't turn out like you in ten years?"

Her career in Canadian federal politics would last until 1940. In 1943 she reappeared in the Ontario legislature as an independent-minded supporter of the Co-operative Commonwealth Federation (ancestor of today's New Democrats). But hard-working, sharp-tongued pioneers of either sex are often not rewarded for their struggles. Agnes Macphail would die in Toronto in 1954, short of money and after a long period of poor health.

LADIES MAY SOON TRIM MERE MEN

Even before Agnes Macphail's triumph in the federal election of 1921, Toronto's "first woman alderman," Mrs. Constance Hamilton, had won a place on city council in the municipal election of 1920. Mrs. Sidney Small joined her in 1921.

Readers of the local press could see that this was part of an international trend. An article in the *Star* in June 1922 reported that "a councillorship on the Madras Corporation has been offered to Mrs. Devados, wife of a local judge. The offer is the first made to a woman in India."

As in other parts of North America, Toronto women were also identified with the righteous cause of prohibition. Agnes Macphail's friend Nellie McClung was prominent in the Women's Christian Temperance Union (WCTU) out west. The Toronto branch of the WCTU was prominent in the local struggle against the demon rum.

Early in April 1921 Stephen Leacock from Montreal gave a popular lecture in Toronto, arguing for the wet side in Drury's second prohibition referendum. He claimed that beer was no more harmful than cucumber. A few days later Mrs. Gordon Wright, dominion president of the WCTU, demanded that Leacock apologize to the cucumber. On April 18 a front-page headline in the *Daily Star* proclaimed: "ONTARIO WOMEN ARE PILING UP 'DRY' MAJORITY."

Women's early political strides in the 1920s had an economic base in a new and increasingly urban labour force. Agnes Macphail was born on a farm, but she would die in a Toronto duplex. Women were in demand as nurses, salespeople, schoolteachers, secretaries, and telephone operators.

During the First World War women had filled jobs in factories, vacated by men who had gone overseas. When the war was over, male employers, politicians, and clergymen urged women to return to the home and give the jobs back to discharged veterans. The boom that had busted in Toronto during the early 1920s strengthened these pressures. The majority of women in the city still aspired to be housewives.

Even so, by the 1920s there was a strategic minority of "business girls," "office girls," and "working girls." It included some married women. It included women who would never marry and would work all their lives. They did not have anything like the best jobs. They were not well paid. But a movement that would gradually broaden into the mainstream of working women in Toronto today had started. "A Shaw School graduate," explained a classified ad under "Help Wanted – Female" in the *Mail and Empire*, for Saturday, March 25, 1922, "is seldom without lucrative employment."

Already there were some countervailing pressures against the male employers, politicians, and clergymen who urged that a woman's only permanent place was in the home. According to Agnes Macphail, a woman's place was "any place she wants to be."

In April 1921, in the middle of the second prohibition referendum campaign, the American Women's Club of Toronto invited the iconoclastic American author Sinclair Lewis to town, to lecture on the role of women in business. The crux of his message was "that women, with a little training, could be better business successes than men." Or, as the front-page headline in the *Star* for Tuesday, April 12, put it: "EVEN IN BUSINESS LADIES MAY SOON TRIM MERE MEN."

BANTING, BEST, COLLIP, AND MACLEOD

The drug scene in Toronto during the early 1920s involved more than the illicit use of cocaine and morphine. In the history of today's global pharmaceutical industry, the city rates an honourable mention as the birthplace of insulin – still the major drug used in the treatment of diabetes.

On the old orthodox version of the story, the hero was Dr. Frederick G. Banting. He discovered insulin in 1921, perfected it in 1922, and won the Nobel Prize for medicine in 1923.

Banting was born in 1891 on a family farm near Alliston, Ontario, in the hinterland north of Toronto that had once harboured such staunch support for Mackenzie King's grandfather. Banting was the kind of hero that Toronto in the early 1920s liked. He was a simple farm boy who hit on a bright idea

City of Toronto Archives SC 266-1261

Like Agnes Macphail and other influential figures in Toronto during the 1920s, Frederick Banting started his life on a family farm. The combined binder/thrasher here is at work in the Agincourt area, just east of the city. (August 1923)

and made good in the big city. In March 1922 an article in the
Star captured the image: the discoverer of insulin was "strangely slow in speech and unassuming," but "also strangely he soon
won the reputation of coming across with the punch at the critical moment."

The *Star,* with its particular political bent, was strongly pre-
disposed to heroes of this sort. A year later even the *Mail and
Empire* lionized Banting – "YOUNG SCIENTIST MODEST IN CLAIMS
REGARDING NEW TREATMENT." In March 1923, before a prestigious crowd of local notables at the King Edward Hotel,
Banting was awarded a life membership in the Canadian Club.
When he received his award, an "outburst of cheers ... showed
the high esteem in which Dr. Banting is held." When he
addressed the audience, "in simple language," the great men of
the city "listened with the utmost attention."

Research by the late twentieth-century historian Michael Bliss
has taken much of the homespun gloss off the local insulin legend. Banting graduated in medicine at the University of
Toronto in 1916. He then served as a medical officer in France,
where he was wounded and decorated for valour. After the war
he qualified as an orthopaedic surgeon. He went into private
practice in London, Ontario.

His academic record was not brilliant, and he was not a
well-trained medical research specialist, but late in 1920 he
came up with the idea of isolating the internal secretion of the
pancreas. His idea would ultimately lead to the creation of
insulin. Banting developed a research proposal, which won support from the University of Toronto. In May 1921 he began his
work under the supervision of J.J.R. MacLeod, professor of
physiology. MacLeod was a Scotsman some fifteen years older
than Banting, with an extensive medical education in the
United Kingdom and Germany. Banting was assisted by C.H.
Best, a twenty-two-year-old postgraduate student.

Banting and Best's initial research was crude. It was promising, but not successful. In the winter of 1921–22 the biochemist
J.B. Collip joined the team. Collip, born in Belleville, Ontario,
was only a year younger than Banting. A skilled technician, he
had received a Ph.D. from the U. of T. in 1916. Collip – not
Banting – actually produced the first insulin suitable for use on
human beings, early in 1922.

When he received his life membership in the Canadian Club in March 1923, Banting did acknowledge the assistance of Best, MacLeod's supervisory work, and the invaluable help of other individuals and institutions. The international medical community understood the extent to which the discovery of insulin in Toronto was the achievement of a research team, and not of one individual alone. In 1923 Banting and MacLeod were jointly awarded the Nobel Prize for medicine.

Banting, however, did not get along with MacLeod, or, initially, Collip. Banting and Best maintained that MacLeod's supervisory work was mostly tiresome interference. Banting and Collip would become friends in the 1930s, but they quarrelled bitterly in the early 1920s. Banting resented sharing the Nobel Prize with MacLeod, and to show his feelings he gave half his prize money to Best. MacLeod, with his own resentments, gave half his prize money to Collip.

Despite the number of players, it was Banting, or at most Banting and Best, who attracted the local media of the day. MacLeod was a Scotsman who had only come to Toronto, and Canada, in 1918. He would only stay until 1928. He was one in a long line of British professionals who had long dominated Toronto academia and taken scarce jobs away from local boys. Banting was the local boy who made good. The press liked his story best.

U.S. BRANCH PLANTS IN CANADA

For the world of today, the most significant point about the story of Banting, Best, Collip, and MacLeod is probably what happened to insulin after its discovery in Toronto.

If the local notables who cheered Banting at the King Edward Hotel in March 1923 had been different kinds of people, it might have occurred to them that they had just been presented with a unique economic opportunity. But they were not, and it did not. Insulin would first be marketed commercially by the U.S.-based drug manufacturer Eli Lilly.

A local newspaper reader who wanted an explanation might have consulted an editorial in the *Mail and Empire* in the later part of March 1922. Entitled "THE AMERICAN INFLUX," it began by noting with satisfaction that the "steady influx of United States business firms into the Canadian field, mainly by the establishment of branches in Ontario, is having considerable

This U.S. branch plant in Toronto's closest big-city neighbour was "the most modern Lamp Factory in the British Empire." (November 1921)

effect on commercial real estate." It went on to stress that "Canadians have always welcomed the establishment of United States branch plants or warehouses here."

According to the Dominion Bureau of Statistics, the editorial continued, "in 1918 34 per cent of the securities of our manufacturing companies were owned in the United States." What's more, along with "about 600 recognized branches of United States manufacturing companies, there are several hundred so-called Canadian plants that are, in reality, controlled from New York, Chicago, or other large financial centres."

With the "incoming of so much constructive enterprise," the *Mail and Empire* of Toronto concluded, the "outlook is bright for solid progress all round."

THE EARLY NHL

All this raises a question once put to me by a friend in Toronto today, who was born in a distant place: "What, really, is Canada all about – besides hockey?"

It is a good question, and there is still no short and simple answer. It is certain, though, that by the early 1920s Canada – and Toronto, too – was at least about hockey, played on ice, and known locally as "the fastest sport in the world."

In the late nineteenth century the Ontario Hockey Association played a seminal role in the early amateur organization of Canada's national sport. By the First World War professional hockey had arrived. In 1917 the National Hockey League was born.

The NHL went through two main evolutionary phases in the 1920s. The second didn't get under way until later in the decade. The initial phase had two principal features, the first being simply that all teams in the league were from Canadian cities. The second is more complicated.

In the early 1920s, NHL teams only represented cities in Ontario and Quebec. But competition for the Stanley Cup – symbol of "world supremacy" in professional hockey – included teams from western Canadian cities. The Stanley Cup was not yet the unique trophy of the National Hockey League. The practical significance of this is illustrated by the situation in 1922, the one year in all the 1920s when Toronto won the Stanley Cup.

Late in March 1922 the Toronto St. Patricks, NHL champions, defeated the Vancouver Millionaires in the Stanley Cup finals. The Millionaires were the champions of the Pacific Coast Hockey Association. They had earned the right to play the St. Pats for the Stanley Cup by defeating Regina, champions of the Western Canada Hockey League, in a western playoff.

A structure of this sort was complex and costly. It bred recurrent controversy over exactly where the Stanley Cup finals would be held, and exactly which champions of which leagues would play who, when. It would not last.

The early history of professional hockey nonetheless casts light on the nature of Canada, and Toronto, in the early 1920s. Why the *national* hockey league should only include teams from Ontario and Quebec, for example, is also a good question for those who wonder what Canada is all about.

A related wrinkle is that while the NHL at this point included only teams from Canadian cities, Seattle was represented in the Pacific Coast Hockey Association. In both 1919 and 1920 the Seattle Metropolitans competed in the Stanley Cup finals.

In 1922 there were four teams in the NHL, representing Montreal, Ottawa, Toronto, and Hamilton. The Hamilton franchise had earlier been in Quebec City, where it was known as the Quebec Bulldogs. The presence of a team with such a relentlessly British name in a city where the overwhelming majority of residents were so proud to speak French helps explain why Quebec has become what it is today. This sort of insensitivity probably also helps explain why the Quebec Bulldogs were never a successful hockey team.

IRISH LUCK

The 1922 Stanley Cup champions, the Toronto St. Patricks, wore green and white uniforms. In the press they were often nicknamed "the Irish." The local team was originally called the Toronto Arenas, but the name was changed in 1919 because, it is said, "Toronto wanted the luck of the Irish to descend on them."

All this points to another qualification of old Orange Toronto stereotypes. Since the middle of the nineteenth century the city had been home to a significant Irish Catholic minority. At Confederation, Catholics had accounted for as much as one-quarter of the population. Still earlier, liberal Protestants from southern Ireland had been prominent on the progressive wing of the old Upper Canadian elite.

In 1921 some 14 percent of Torontonians who regularly attended religious services were Catholics. Somewhat better than 21 percent of all city residents reported Irish racial origins. Reflecting yet another strain of the local irony and ambiguity, the "Irish" could also include Orangemen from the Protestant counties of Ulster.

In the summary tables of the official statistics, people of Irish descent were ultimately classed as "British." Yet when the Toronto Arenas were renamed the Toronto St. Patricks, the final struggles of the Irish independence movement in the United Kingdom were making recurrent headlines in Toronto newspapers. On December 6, 1922, about eight months after the St. Pats won the Stanley Cup in Canada, the Irish Free State was officially proclaimed across the ocean. The event marked the formal beginnings of the gradual unravelling of the British Empire that would take place over the next half-century.

BABE DYE AND LADIES' HOCKEY

The fifth and deciding game of the 1922 Stanley Cup finals, between the St. Pats and the Vancouver Millionaires, was held in Toronto on Tuesday, March 28, at "The Arena" on Mutual Street. The St. Pats defeated the Millionaires 5 to 1. Two great stars led the home team to victory. The first was Cecil "Babe" Dye, who could boast what the press called "a machine-gun shot." He scored four of Toronto's five goals. The second star was goalie John Ross Roach. Said the *Globe:* "Only a little fellow, weighing one hundred and twenty-five pounds, Roach never theless has shown that he has nothing to fear when competing against the best sharpshooters that professional hockey has produced."

Some local fans had suspected that "Vancouver were by far the better team," but in the end Dye and Roach made the difference for Toronto. In the last minutes of the game, the "ice was commencing to get sticky and it seemed a fitting climax that … a mist should slowly ascend and practically envelop Lehman," the Vancouver goalie.

In the opinion of the *Globe* reporter, the game was "not a brilliant affair," but Babe Dye's goals had at least "brought the crowd to its feet cheering wildly." When it was all over, the

A Fellow Needs Adams Black Jack

It doesn't much matter where a real boy is, he appreciates having Adams Black Jack Gum handy.

In a hard-fought game, it keeps him on his toes. Over home-work it helps him concentrate. When the weather is raw, or when he is rooting for Our Side, it eases his throat.

But best of all it is licorice!

What more could a youngster ask?

Most of them do ask for Adams Black Jack. At almost any store. In the blue package—5c.

—an Adams product, particularly prepared

Canadian Chewing Gum Co., Limited, Toronto, Winnipeg, Montreal

Girls (or ladies) also played hockey in Toronto during the 1920s, but it was boys who got into the ads. (January 1920)

St. Pats had "left not the slightest doubt in the world but that they are the best professional team in captivity."

Toronto in the early 1920s also had a vigorous amateur hockey scene. It attracted almost as much attention from the press as the NHL. In the 1921–22 season more than 4,000 players competed under the jurisdiction of the Toronto Amateur Hockey Association.

Following the early feminist currents of the era, organized hockey in the city, as elsewhere in Canada, was not restricted to men. According to a routine ad in the *Telegram*, on Saturday, March 4, 1922, there were two games of "Ladies' Hockey" at the Arena. The first featured "Alerts of Ottawa vs. North Toronto," and the second "Beaches vs. Trinity Methodist." Tickets could be purchased for 55¢, 80¢, and $1.10.

The local hockey scene of the day was the setting for another early milestone in the history of the sport. In March 1923 a teenage reporter with the pioneering Toronto radio station CFCA was assigned to broadcast a hockey game at the Arena between Kitchener and Parkdale. His name was Foster Hewitt.

SUNNYSIDE BEACH

It is no longer known how much Premier Drury liked hockey. Even in a more general way, there is little in Ontario today to remind us of his work. The most visible survivor of early 1920s populism in Toronto is probably the TTC, but while the TTC has been a recurrent winner of transit system awards on the North American continent, it has never been especially loved by the citizens of Toronto.

Until the middle of the 1950s there was one legacy of early 1920s populism in Toronto that a great many people in the city genuinely did love. Developed by the Toronto Harbour Commission, it officially opened on Wednesday, June 28, 1922, at 6 PM. Its proper name was Sunnyside Beach. Popularly, it was just known as Sunnyside – "the poor man's Riviera."

Even now there are more than a few aging Torontonians who remember Sunnyside, and still love it, and wish that they could visit the place again. Some small hint of its attractions can be gleaned from the newspaper ads that announced the official opening: "Ceremonies at Bathing Pavilion. Band Concerts – Afternoon and Evening ... 48th Highlanders, Royal

Grenadiers and Queen's Own Bands. Amusement Devices and Games, Supervised Bathing Facilities, Canoeing and Boating, Terraced Tea Gardens and Dancing, Lakefront Promenade and Boulevard Drive, 25 minutes by King Street Car from King and Yonge, 15 minutes by Automobile."

The things I remember most about Sunnyside from my own city childhood, in the late 1940s and early 1950s, are a giant roller coaster, an amazingly fast merry-go-round, the smell of french fries in white paper cones, pink candy floss on brown paper sticks, and a juke box that played "Toot Toot Tootsie, Goodbye" (a song that first appeared, I much later discovered, in 1922 – the year Sunnyside was born).

Sunnyside was located on the west-end Toronto waterfront, south of the Parkdale and High Park residential neighbourhoods, and west of the Canadian National Exhibition grounds. It took up the lion's share of some 197 acres of reclaimed land, between the Humber River and Bathurst Street.

Work on the project had begun in 1914, but it was set aside not long after the start of the First World War. In 1919 it began again. A dance pavilion was already in place, and once the landfill was completed, the boulevard for automobiles and a pedestrian boardwalk took shape. Then came "the continent's best bathing pavilion," the terraced tea gardens, the roller coaster, and the "adult" merry-go-round complex.

Once the place was officially opened, there were rides with names like Dodgem, Gadabout, Lover's Express, Red Bug, Scooter, and the Whip. There was also "the Auditorium Orthophonic Victrola, the world's largest in its day." It housed a gigantic record player in a nine-foot-high cabinet. The records it played could be heard as far as a mile away.

Lake Ontario was somewhat less polluted than it has subsequently become, but then as now, even in the summer it was cold. In 1925 a large swimming pool – 75 feet wide and 350 feet long – was added to the Sunnyside complex. Aficionados called it "the tank." By this point Sunnyside was also the scene of an annual Easter Parade, the Miss Toronto Beauty Pageant, a female impersonator's contest, touring acts like the Hopi Cliff Dwellers, and ladies' softball games, between the Cycles, Grottos, Lakesides, Marlboros, Parkdales, Pats, and the Supremes.

Announcing the opening of the second season at "the poor man's Riviera."
(May 1923)

SCARBOROUGH BEACH PARK

Despite the best efforts of the Harbour Commission, by the early 1920s Toronto's central Lake Ontario waterfront, just south of the downtown, was still an urban jungle of railway lines and docks. But there were beaches for the people at the eastern and western ends of the city. When it first opened, Sunnyside was a west-end analogue for the east-end public amusement grounds known as Scarborough Beach Park.

Both ends of the city hosted an assortment of waterfront athletic organizations. The east end could boast the Balmy Beach Canoe Club, the Beaches Athletic Association, and the Don Canoe Club. The Argonaut Rowing Club, the Parkdale Canoe Club, and the Toronto Canoe Club graced the west end.

Scarborough Beach Park had been created in 1907 at the eastern end of the Queen streetcar line. It was operated by William Mackenzie's old Toronto Railway Company. There are still one or two old Torontonians who especially remember a ride at the place called "the Chutes." On a hot summer day you could race down a steep water-slide in a small wooden boat and get drenched in a pool below.

Very quickly, however, Scarborough Beach Park was eclipsed by the fresh attractions of the poor man's Riviera at Sunnyside. The TTC didn't take over operation of Scarborough Beach in 1921, but a rump of the TRC continued to run the place for a few more years. It closed in September 1925, to make way for several lakefront residential streets dominated by fourplex apartments. These buildings remain part of the human physiography in the east-end Beaches district today, from Leuty Avenue east to Maclean.

Sunnyside would itself only last for a generation. In 1955 work began on the Queensway and on what would eventually be called the Gardiner Expressway. The roller coaster and the merry-go-round complex at Sunnyside were dismantled in the same year. Much of the Sunnyside amusement park was moved to the Canadian National Exhibition grounds.

Today only the old bathing pavilion survives. In 1979, at the close of a more recent burst of Toronto populism, city council approved plans for a $1.1-million restoration of this last remaining piece of Sunnyside Beach. The restored pavilion had its second official opening on June 14, 1980.

If you are prepared to travel, it is still possible to catch another vague glimpse of the glory that was Sunnyside in the Toronto of the 1920s. As the Gardiner Expressway reared its head in the middle of the 1950s, the main Sunnyside merry-go-round (a "real beauty ... made from hand-carved wood") was carefully taken apart and sent on a long journey south. You can see it today at Disneyland, in Anaheim, California.

CHINESE LAUNDRIES AND CHINESE RESTAURANTS

The strongest premonition during the 1920s of late twentieth-century multiculturalism in Toronto was "the Chinese colony," which local morality officers liked to regard as "the centre of the drug trafficking which has been going on in an extensive way."

According to the federal census, in 1921 Toronto was home to somewhat more than 2,100 people reporting Chinese "racial

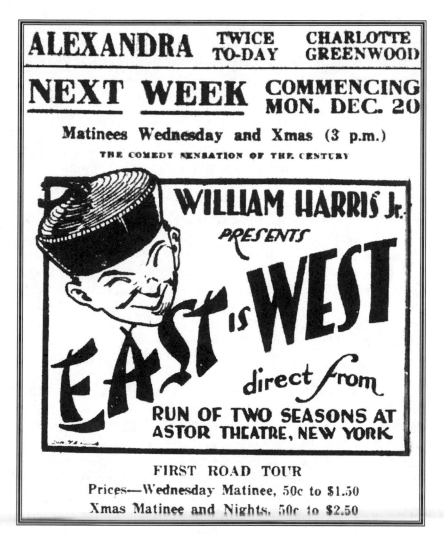

Probably not many (or even any) Chinese Torontonians went to see this "comedy sensation," and if they did they probably wouldn't have found it funny. (December 1920)

origins." In a place of more than half a million people, this amounted to less than one half of one percent of the total population. Nonetheless, there was already a "Chinatown" in the downtown area close to Yonge Street, between Queen and Dundas. The list of clubs in *Might's Directory* for 1920 includes a

Chinese Club at Elizabeth and Louisa streets and a Hong Kong Club on Queen Street West.

Legend has it that the origins of the Toronto Chinese community owe something to the 15,000 Chinese labourers who worked on the construction of the Canadian Pacific Railway in the 1870s and 1880s and then dispersed to various parts of the country.

While no doubt there actually were a few Chinese drug dealers in the city in the 1920s, by far the most common early occupation was operating laundries in the older residential districts. According to *Might's Directory*, two Chinese laundries had appeared in downtown Toronto as early as the late 1870s. By the early 1920s literally hundreds of them covered a much wider area. The 1922 directory lists more than 370 Chinese laundries in the city. The major concentration was on Dundas, Queen, and Yonge streets. Queen Street alone, east and west, could boast more than 50. But there were also significant numbers (10 or more on each) on Bathurst, Bloor, Church, College, King, Parliament, and Spadina.

By the early twentieth century, operating restaurants had emerged as another common occupation. Toronto's first Chinese restaurant, the Sing Wing, appeared in the early 1900s on Queen Street West, not far from Yonge Street. *Might's Directory* for 1921 lists more than eighty such places.

Some catered chiefly to Chinese customers. Most were for the people of the city at large. Those outside Chinatown served "Canadian-style" as well as Chinese food. Some apparently served very little Chinese food. The more than eighty restaurants enumerated in the 1921 directory were concentrated on Queen Street, but four were on Bloor, four on Church, three on College, two on Bathurst, and one each on Jarvis, Lansdowne, Pape, and Parliament.

THE SHING WAH DAILY NEWS

The extent to which Canadian public policy ought to encourage or discourage Asian immigration was a subject of much debate in the early 1920s. In June 1922 Toronto's *Mail and Empire* ran an anxious article headlined "CHINESE ANXIOUS TO ENTER CANADA." This was only the latest phase in a controversy that stretched back to the late nineteenth century. Its initial geographic focus was in British Columbia, the obvious point of entry for Asian migrants in the era before air travel.

Outside the province of Quebec, the Canada of the day still saw itself as a fundamentally British place. In 1885 the Canadian federal government had passed its first Chinese Immigration

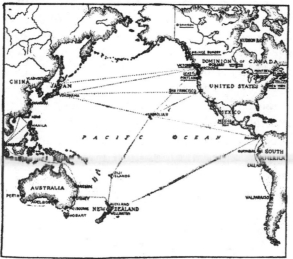

THE PACIFIC OCEAN
The Great Highway of Trade With the Orient

Canada, The United States, Mexico and Japan, China, Straits Settlements Australia and New Zealand, are among the countries which border its shores.

This *Bank* holds the *unique position* of having *branches* in all the *principal ports* on the *Pacific Coast* of *both Canada* and the *United States.* Its correspondents are the leading banks in those countries which border the far shores of the Pacific Ocean, and its equipment for handling the business of exporters and importers with the countries named above is thus unsurpassed.

The places underlined, in Canada, United States and Mexico, are branches of the bank.

THE CANADIAN BANK OF COMMERCE
HEAD OFFICE   TORONTO, CANADA

ESTABLISHED	Paid-up Capital $15,000,000
1867	Reserve Fund $15,000,000
508 BRANCHES	Total Assets $479,644,000

The "Pacific Rim" is not really a new concept. (January 1920)

Act. This placed a "head tax" of $50 on all Chinese entering Canada, except for government officials, merchants, students, and tourists. The tax was raised to $100 in 1900 and to an exorbitant $500 in 1904.

Despite the head tax, Chinese migrants kept arriving. According to Dora Nipp, a late twentieth-century student of Toronto's Chinese history, in comparison to Vancouver and Victoria, "here ... both the Chinese and the larger community made greater attempts to establish contact and interact with one another." In March 1922 the *Mail and Empire* nonetheless announced: "TO BAR ORIENTALS FROM THE DOMINION / AIM OF MOTION INTRODUCED AT OTTAWA BY MEMBER FOR NEW WESTMINSTER."

A year later, in March 1923, the Canadian federal government introduced legislation that effectively put a halt to Chinese immigration. Ironically, the legislation took formal effect on Dominion Day, July 1 – henceforth known to Chinese Canadians as "Humiliation Day," until the legislation was repealed in May 1947.

Ancient China itself was not known for generosity to its own cultural minorities. African students sometimes complain of unpleasant treatment in China today. It is an unhappy but plain historical fact that no race or culture has any monopoly on enthocentric passion and prejudice.

In 1921 there were 2,019 Chinese males in Toronto and only 115 females. Not all the males were bachelors in the strict sense: many had wives and families still living in China, to whom they regularly sent money. This was, in part, only a result of Canada's own harsh immigration laws, but it can also be read as a sign of tenuous (understandably) commitments to a longer-term future in the Dominion of Canada.

At the same time, by the early 1920s some Chinese people of Toronto had started to set down roots, and the community was even blossoming a little. Such public figures as T.C. Mark had begun to play a wider role in the life of the city. In 1922 the *Shing Wah Daily News,* a revival of an earlier aborted Toronto voice of the nationalist movement in China, commenced regular publication.

There were a number of "naturalized" Chinese families in the city by this point. In 1921 Toronto was home to thirty-one young girls and thirty-four young boys of Chinese background who had been born in Canada. In June 1920 the *Globe* reported that "Harry Leong, a Chinese boy" at York Street School downtown, had received a prize "for being the most enthusiastic over the Empire Day celebration."

The effective ban on Chinese immigration in 1923 stunted this early blossoming. In the later 1920s there would be yet another unhappy episode, but it hints at the future progress of the Chinese community in twentieth-century Toronto, despite the sordid obstacles that initially were put in its way.

At this point, the key Chinese-related issue in the city involved the difficulties of enforcing provincial legislation prohibiting Chinese employers from hiring "white women." The crux of the problem was that more than a few white women in the city were happy enough to have jobs in Chinese restaurants. Apparently, they did not think it was humiliating, or dangerous, to accept pay cheques from Chinese restaurant owners.

Howard Ferguson (front row, third from right) and his cabinet. (July 1923)

CHAPTER THREE

REALISM RETURNS

A week before the proclamation of the new Chinese Immigration Act in Ottawa, the October 1919 political revolution in Ontario had come to an end. E.C. Drury called a provincial election for June 25, 1923, and was soundly defeated.

The victors were Howard Ferguson's resurgent Conservatives. Ferguson's prophecy of Drury's demise, from more than two years before, had proved correct. Even Riverdale, the one Toronto riding that had elected a supporter of the Farmer-Labour coalition in 1919, turned decisively to the Conservatives in 1923. All nine other Toronto ridings went Tory as well.

Drury's regime had managed to accelerate the earlier mildly progressive agenda of the Whitney and Hearst Conservatives, and had introduced some new wrinkles of its own, including a provincial mother's allowance, a rural credit program funded by a provincial savings office, and a great new burst of highway building. The provincial budget doubled between 1919 and 1923.

Yet the revolutionaries had not managed to do away with the old game of politics. Nor had they managed to do away with the hard economic times that had helped get them elected just after the First World War. Drury's and Raney's high zeal for rigorous enforcement of the Ontario Temperance Act had offended their own Labour supporters. And within its own ranks, there was much other dissension about the aims and objectives of the government.

Alone among the Toronto newspapers of the day, the *Daily Star* supported Drury in 1923. At the other end of the local spectrum, the friends of Tommy Church at the *Evening Telegram* had been looking – from the instant Drury had formed his cabinet – for a hard issue with which they could tirelessly assail the new government. Early in 1922 they found it.

At the close of the 1921 legislative session, there had been a festive gathering at Queen's Park. Apparently, liquor was served, in violation of the OTA and in the presence of several attractive women. According to reports, some members of the Farmer-Labour coalition were present – perhaps even including a few members of Drury's cabinet.

If true, the story demonstrated the monstrous hypocrisy of a government that claimed to be devoted to "moral uplift" and to the ending of all the old games. By the early months of 1922 the *Telegram* was righteously demanding an investigation into the "WINE-WOMEN-AND-SONG ORGY IN THE LEGISLATURE." It ran news stories with such headlines as "ONTARIO HAS DISCREDITED AND WILL DEFEAT 'ERNIE' DRURY."

The morning *Mail and Empire* picked up on the theme. It reported "BOOZE PARTY INVESTIGATION RESTS WITH LEGISLATURE" and carried the salacious imagery into still newer fields with such headlines as "BIG DEFICIT FOR ONTARIO ... ORGY OF SPENDING." Drury denied that cabinet ministers had been present at the degrading affair; the *Star* implied that the entire discussion was low-minded and foolish; but the wine-women-and-song orgy was a key issue in Drury's defeat in June 1923.

CASA LOMA AND THE HOME BANK

It seems clear that more than a few Torontonians who voted against the Drury regime in 1923 hoped the Conservatives could at last dispel the stubborn postwar economic bust in the city. The victorious Tory candidate in Riverdale, George Oakley, had run as "a successful businessman, who [would] help to make a success of the business of this province."

The connections between politics and economics, however, are not direct. In the immediate wake of Drury's defeat, in August 1923, the Home Bank of Canada failed, after a long

Original Dixieland "Jazz" Band

JAZZ!

Yes! you must have a few Jazz numbers in your collection. Here are two of the latest, played by none other than the Original Dixieland "Jazz" Band.

Home Again Blues—Fox Trot
Crazy Blues—Fox Trot

On His Master's Voice Record 18729 16-inch D.S. $1.90

All these new selections are on

"His Master's Voice" Records

Make Believe—Fox Trot	Rega Orchestra	216272
Now and Then—Fox Trot	Rega Orchestra	
I'm a Lonesome Little Rain Drop—Fox Trot	Diamond Trio	216274
Kiss a Miss—Waltz	Diamond Trio	
My Mammy—Fox Trot	Diamond Trio	
Coral Sea—Fox Trot Intro. "Allah's Holiday")		216275
	Martucci's Venetian Garden Orchestra	
Mazie—Fox Trot		18738
Answer—Fox Trot All Star Trio assisted by their Orchestra		
My Mammy Male Quartet	Peerless Quartet	18730
Underneath Hawaiian Skies Albert Campbell-Henry Burr		
Rose I Call Sweetheart (Tenor)	William Robyn	18741
Mother of Pearl (Tenor)	William Robyn	
Turkey in the Straw (Piano Accordion)	Pietro	18743
Russian Rag (Piano Accordion)	Pietro	

All on 10-inch Double-sided Records $1.00

Sally—Medley Fox Trot		35706
Lady Billy Medley Fox Trot Joseph C. Smith's Orchestra		
Why Don't I but?—Marimba—Medley Fox Trot		35707
	All Star Trio and their Orchestra	
Siren of a Southern Sea—Medley Fox Trot		

On 12-inch Double-sided Records $1.65

Ask to hear them played on the

Victrola
at Any "His Master's Voice" dealers

Manufactured by Berliner Gram-o-phone Co., Limited, Montreal 21251

*This ad appeared in May 1921 – a little more than two years before
G. Howard Ferguson moved into the premier's office at Queen's Park.
According to one newspaper wit of the day, "Fergie"'s goal was "to take the
Conservative harps off the willows and give the boys some political jazz."*

period of increasing financial difficulty. This would be the last failure of a major Canadian financial institution until the collapse of the Canadian Commercial and Northlands banks in the 1980s.

One of the Home Bank's major shareholders was Sir Henry Mill Pellatt, gentleman of Toronto. The bank's failure put the finishing touches on difficulties in Sir Henry's financial affairs that had been accumulating for several years. Or, on some accounts, accumulating difficulties in Sir Henry's financial affairs put the finishing touches on the Home Bank.

Pellatt the Plunger was still a shrewd operator. Even so, though he managed to extricate a tidy enough income for himself from his collapsing empire, he could no longer afford the vast expense of maintaining Casa Loma with its ninety-eight rooms and 5,000 electric lights. By the end of 1923 he had moved to less demanding quarters. The king of Casa Loma had occupied his house on the hill for only a decade. Now it was a vacant symbol of broken dreams.

HEMINGWAY IN TORONTO

The defeat of the Drury regime, the federal ban on Chinese immigration, and Henry Pellatt's flight from Casa Loma all mark 1923 as a year when the mood of Toronto swung in new directions.

There had been several kinds of dreamy idealism in the city in 1920 and 1921 and 1922. In 1923 they were set aside. People went back to an earlier "real" world. (Or so, at least, it seemed.)

The new realism in Toronto affected the fate of a young journalist from Chicago. The background to this story began in January 1920, when Ernest Hemingway was only twenty years old. Already he had literary ambitions. He had worked on the *Kansas City Star*, had been wounded in the First World War, and for the moment was at a loose end. His mother was friendly with the wife of Ralph Connable, another Chicago native, who in 1915 had moved to Toronto to take charge of the F.W. Woolworth stores in Canada. The Connables wanted a temporary companion for their nineteen-year-old son, who had been lame since birth. Ralph Connable offered Hemingway the job. Hemingway liked the idea, partly because he wanted more experience as a journalist and knew Connable had contacts at the *Toronto Daily Star*. In the middle of January 1920 Hemingway moved into the Connables' mansionesque house at 153 Lyndhurst Avenue, just north of Casa Loma. Ralph Connable introduced him to the diminutive sportsman Gregory Clark and others at the *Star*.

Hemingway began an association with the Toronto paper that would play an important part in his career over the next four years. In the middle of May 1920 he left the Connables' house and returned to his parents' summer place in northern Michigan, but he continued to send articles to the *Star* in Toronto. Towards the end of 1921, when he went to live in France, he struck a shrewd deal to act as the paper's European correspondent.

Between February 1920 and January 1924 the *Star* printed more than 170 Hemingway items. His eventual New York publisher, Charles Scribner Jr., would describe Hemingway's association with the paper as one of his "most fortunate opportunities ... For a writer, there is no substitute for being published and read. The *Star* gave him an appreciative readership and kept him writing on a regular basis."

At first, Hemingway himself must have appreciated the opportunity, but he would eventually develop a great contempt for Toronto. This had at least something to do with a bitter personal experience he had in the city in 1923 (the year his first book, *Three Stories and Ten Poems*, was published). There are earlier signs, however, of a somewhat different attitude. In June 1920 he wrote to Harriet Connable, thanking her for his stay on Lyndhurst Avenue. He was even polite enough to say "I miss Toronto."

There may have been a hint of sincerity in the remark. When in the summer of 1923 Hemingway's first wife, Hadley Richardson, became pregnant, Hemingway conceived the scheme of leaving France and returning to Toronto. Hadley would have her baby in North American safety (as Hemingway explained to his friend in Paris, Ezra Pound, Toronto was "the right place to have a baby because that is the *specialité de ville*"). The young family would then stay in the city for about two years, while Ernest worked for the *Star* to provide them with some initial security.

At the end of August 1923, Hemingway was back in town. He looked up Ralph Connable and Gregory Clark, and rented

East or
West
Eddy's
Best
--since 1851!

If he eats
them

Don't worry ~

Since Jan. 1, 1915, all Eddy matches have been
NON-POISONOUS!

EDDY FACTS

Eddy matches for every use
are sold by
— *364 Department stores and*
    5-10-15c stores.
--*14175 General stores.*
--*16847 Grocers.*
-- *6339 Hotels.*
-- *3957 Restaurants and Cafés.*
-- *2951 Tobacconists.*
-- *1433 Clubs.*
      Not including railway
      stations, trains, steam
      ships, etc.
--*120,000,000 matches a day!*

Eddy's everywhere!

Time was when matches *were* poisonous. Time
was when there *was* danger to health of employees
in the match-making process.

But Eddy enterprise put a full stop to both risks
—and that was long before the Government wisely
made it illegal to manufacture poisonous matches.

There are people who still believe matches are
poisonous. How welcome the assurance of the Eddy
Company that in all their 35 different kinds of
matches there cannot be found a single match-
head harmful to health!

What a relief to every mother to have the positive assurance that on his joyous explorations baby
cannot be harmed by stray matches encountered
on his prowl, if he puts them in his mouth.

Isn't it good also to know that the care taken by
the Eddy Company for the health of their employees makes for safer, cleaner matches, perfectly
adapted to every consumer use?

Eddy's is the Canadian word for matches—safe
in manufacture, safe in use.

EDDY'S MATCHES
THE E.B. EDDY CO. LIMITED
Canada

Ernest Hemingway's first wife had her first baby in Toronto because that
was "the specialité de ville." (March 1922)

an apartment at 1599 Bathurst (in what is now a co-op apartment building, known as "The Hemingway"). On September 10 he started a regular job at the *Toronto Daily Star*, at the then princely salary of $125 a week. From 1599 Bathurst he reported to Gertrude Stein, another of his writer friends in Paris, that "contrary to my remembrance the cuisine here is good," especially at some "Chinese places." Yet nothing could match the life of an American in Paris after the First World War.

Hemingway wrote to his father, asking, "Is business as bad in the States as it is in Canada? Here there have been bank failures and businesses dropping off right and left. A country with a busted boom is most depressing."

More to the point was Hemingway's dissatisfaction with his employer. His earlier Toronto journalism had been mediated by J.H. Cranston of the *Star Weekly* and John R. Bone, the managing editor of the *Daily Star*. In 1923 he was reporting directly to the daily paper's city editor, Harry Hindmarsh. On Hindmarsh's view, Hemingway had become a "prima donna" in Paris and needed to be bent to the demands of a daily newspaper machine in North America. According to the later testimony of Cranston, Hindmarsh could sometimes be "a sadist" who "took delight in humbling or breaking men's spirits."

Harry Hindmarsh did his best to break Ernest Hemingway into his new job, but Hemingway did not want to be broken – even for $125 a week. By the Christmas of 1923 he had had enough. He abandoned his plans to stay in Toronto for as long as two years, and on December 27 submitted his resignation to John Bone, with "regret" and "no rudeness implied." By the end of January 1924 Ernest and Hadley and their new, born-in-Toronto son (nicknamed "Bumbi") were back in France.

THE YOUNG MORLEY CALLAGHAN

Despite Harry Hindmarsh, the more than 170 articles in the *Star* gave Hemingway's early professional career a significant push. He owed someone something for one of his most fortunate opportunities.

He would repay the debt in his own way. During his short and unhappy second appearance in Toronto, he made a new friend. Morley Callaghan was somewhat younger than Hemingway. He had been born to a local Irish Catholic family in 1903. In the autumn of 1923, when he too was working for the *Star*, he met the rising young author who had just arrived from Paris.

Callaghan had his own literary ambitions. Hemingway read his early stories and commented: "You're a real writer. You write big-time stuff. All you have to do is carry on." Just before he left for Paris again in 1924, Hemingway gave Callaghan a copy of *Three Stories and Ten Poems*. He inscribed it "To Callaghan with best luck and predictions." He told the young Toronto writer: "Whatever you do, don't let anyone around here tell you anything."

Callaghan kept in touch with Hemingway after Hemingway returned to Paris. "As soon as you get anything done," the older young man had said to the younger one, "shoot it to Paris. I'll tell them about you."

FERGIE

Some of Hemingway's early writing masterfully captures the lure of the same northern North American wilderness that fascinated Tom Thomson and the Group of Seven. The "Big Two-Hearted River" stories are a good example. They are set in the upper peninsula of Michigan, just south of Lake Superior, but if you know the country east and north of Georgian Bay, they have a familiar taste. There is some slight literary as well as professional logic to Hemingway's brief Toronto period.

Yet Ernest Hemingway was too new for Toronto in the 1920s. And so was Morley Callaghan. Callaghan would help pioneer a movement in his native city that would become more important in the future, but he was not at all typical of Toronto in 1923 or 1924 or 1925. A much more representative figure was G. Howard Ferguson, who had led the provincial Tories to their decisive victory in 1923.

Like E.C. Drury, Howard Ferguson did not come from Toronto. He was born in 1870 in Kemptville, in the old United Empire Loyalist heartland of eastern Ontario. But when Drury lost the 1923 election, he returned to his farm in Simcoe County; when Ferguson finally left Ontario politics, in the 1930s, he would settle into the upscale Toronto suburb of Forest Hill, north of St. Clair and east of Bathurst. And he would eventually die in Toronto, in 1946.

Like Tommy Church, "Fergie" was an Orangeman, as well as an Ontario Tory and an Empire Loyalist. He was also a rambunctious character. He fit the new mood of 1923. A satirical piece in the newspapers captured the new premier's state of mind: "We want the old-time political religion ... I'm not running a Sunday school class or a standard hotel. I've got to take the Conservative harps off the willows and give the boys some political jazz. They've had about enough moping by the waters of Babylon."

At the same time, even more than Tommy Church, G. Howard Ferguson had a subtle and ambiguous vision. He was attracted to the old local Tory ideological rhetoric, but he had an instinct for its limitations. The new conservative realism he brought back to Queen's Park was a genuine defeat for the agrarian idealism of E.C. Drury. In other ways it was only a mask for carrying on with changes that the failed political revolution of 1919 had inadvertently helped to crystallize.

LONDON AND NEW YORK

Fergie had a genuine taste for the noble imperial civilization of the British Empire. By the end of the 1920s, well over half a century after the formal beginnings of the Dominion of Canada, he would introduce the practice of calling Ontario's expanding, but still rather rugged, provincial roads "King's Highways."

He also served as his own minister of education. From this height he boosted the dosage of imperial indoctrination that local schoolchildren had been receiving since the late nineteenth century. *The Ontario Readers Third Book*, "Authorized By The Minister of Education" and published by the T. Eaton Company of Toronto in 1925, is a case in point. Its first page was taken up by a colour illustration of the Union Jack, accompanied by the motto "ONE FLAG, ONE FLEET, ONE THRONE."

Like Hemingway, however, Fergie also found the busted boom in Canada depressing. He had a practical grasp of regional economics and could appreciate some subtle commercial facts. The English-speaking business community in Montreal had close financial ties to the imperial metropolis in London, England, but while there was a side to Toronto connected in this direction as well, its dominant financial ties were with New York.

By the mid-1920s Torontonians could "ride, hike, paddle, fish or just loaf"
at holiday spots deep in the northern wilderness that fascinated both
Hemingway and the Group of Seven. (June 1923)

In 1867 William McMaster and others had established the
Canadian Bank of Commerce in Toronto. Much later, the pio-
neer geographer of the city's economic development, Jacob
Spelt, would explain that the board of directors of the
Commerce "was closely connected with the import and export
trade via New York."

By the early 1920s the Canadian Bank of Commerce was
Toronto's leading financial institution. Its aging president, Sir
Edmund Walker, had warm feelings for the British Empire. It
was a shield against fatally aggressive overtures from an increasingly muscle-bound New York financial sector. The Empire also
played a strategic role in the growth of the southern Ontario
automobile industry that would eventually help dispel the hard
economic times. Shields and strategy aside, however, in the
early 1920s those who worried most about Toronto's prosperity
were leaning more towards the United States than towards the

British Empire. As early as February 1920 an editorial in the *Globe* reported that the international financial centre of New York now "claims to be larger than London."

Later observers have noted two apparently contradictory trends in the life of the city after the defeat of the Farmer-Labour government. There was a fresh engagement with the commerce of the continent, but also a fresh engagement with the romance of the Empire. In Ontario's ambiguous capital city both trends made sense. Not the least of Fergie's talents was that he could keep both in mind, without getting confused.

TOMMY CHURCH'S FIRST DEFEAT

Only six months after Howard Ferguson's triumph over the Farmer-Labour government, Toronto life exhibited some hard evidence of the ambiguities of the new Tory realism. On the morning of Wednesday, January 2, 1924, the front page of the *Globe* carried the headline "TORONTO'S 'TOMMY' MEETS FIRST DEFEAT AT HANDS OF HILTZ." That evening the *Telegram* unhappily conveyed the same news: "W.W. HILTZ ELECTED MAYOR, T.L. CHURCH'S FIRST DEFEAT."

After Church had moved from municipal to federal politics in 1921, C. Alfred Maguire had served two terms as mayor of Toronto, in 1922 and 1923. By late 1923 it was clear that Maguire would not run again. Meanwhile, Toronto's Tommy had found he did not cut much of a figure in Ottawa. He decided to enter the 1924 mayoralty contest.

Had he won, it seems, he intended to serve simultaneously as mayor of Toronto and MP for North Toronto in Ottawa. But this particular twist of the kaleidoscope did not stop at Tory Toronto. This time Tommy Church lost. The man who defeated him, William Wesley Hiltz, was described by the *Globe* as "a builder living at 682 Broadview avenue." He was a seasoned municipal politician who had supported prohibition in the past. The Liberal *Globe* was pleased.

The *Telegram* reacted bitterly to the first defeat of Church's political career. It pictured Hiltz as "the billion dollar corporation candidate." It stressed that, on re-entering the municipal arena after two years of serving the people of Toronto in the federal Parliament, "Mr. Church had no organization and had to depend on friends to help him get the vote out." The "downtown vote, as always, went against T.L. In the foreign sections, Mr. Hiltz captured by far the greatest of the ballots."

THE PRESS

Followers of the local press could have predicted these divergent reactions. By 1923 there were four daily newspapers in Toronto – two in the morning and two at night. Throughout the 1920s the price of all four remained a modest two cents each.

The newspapers' initial cost structures had leaned on income from political sources. By the late nineteenth century revenues from large-scale commercial advertising were more important. Yet the Toronto papers of the 1920s still showed unmistakable signs of their traditional political markings.

The *Globe* was the most venerable of the group. George Brown had established it in 1844, and had himself eventually become the effective founder of the modern "Grit" or "Liberal" or "Great Reform" party, in what became the province of Ontario in 1867.

Even under Brown's tutelage the *Globe* had been more than a Toronto paper. Part of its original commercial success flowed from its popularity among the wider "rural population, the reading population" beyond the city limits. By the 1920s, with what was elsewhere increasingly viewed as typical Toronto arrogance, it was already calling itself "Canada's National Newspaper."

The initial Ontario regional establishment of the late nineteenth century had also been built around the party that Brown bequeathed to his followers. Beyond its partisan political convictions the *Globe* remained Toronto's establishment journal and newspaper of record. Of all the Toronto papers, it tended to have the smallest circulation in the 1920s (just over 90,000 in 1923), but it claimed that its readers more than made up for their numbers by their political and economic influence in the city, the province, and the country at large.

The *Globe's* morning competition, the *Daily Mail and Empire*, traced its origins back to a paper called the *Mail*. It had been established in 1872 as a Toronto voice for John A. Macdonald's faction in the federal Conservative Party. Subsequently, the editors of the *Mail* strayed from the true path. In 1887 the Macdonald Conservatives set up another Toronto paper, the *Empire*. Four years after Macdonald's death, the two

The **Globe** *was Toronto's oldest and most-established newspaper in the 1920s. Its readership was comparatively small, but influential. (December 1924)*

Conservative morning papers in the city merged, to form the *Mail and Empire*, in 1895.

The *Mail and Empire* was still a Conservative paper in the 1920s, but in its layout and style it was a more convivial and reader-friendly journal than the *Globe*. According to my own family legends, some readers who were not attracted by the *Mail and Empire*'s political slant nevertheless appreciated its mass appeal. In the eyes of some self-consciously ordinary people, only unapologetic snobs, aspiring high financiers, and incurable political junkies regularly read the *Globe*.

It is clear enough from reading the Toronto newspapers of the 1920s today that the *Mail and Empire* was not usually as rabid about its underlying politics as the friends of Tommy Church at the *Evening Telegram* were about theirs. The *"Tely"* had been established in 1876 – during Henry Pellatt's youth – by the local antiquarian John Ross Robertson. In the 1920s it was still cultivating the Toronto of its birth: an overwhelmingly British colonial city of less than 90,000 people. It also paid special attention to the more than one-quarter of 1920s Torontonians who were born in the United Kingdom.

In 1923 the front page of the *Tely*'s first section was still covered with want ads. These continued as the reader moved on, only gradually interrupted by notoriously slanted articles on the imperial, dominion, and local news of the day. The old *Tely* had a studied contempt for anything that was not British, conservative, Protestant, and humble in the face of the grandeur of the Empire. Yet if you can find enough retrospective charity to overlook its archaic tribalism, it was a lively paper.

The journal that gave Ernest Hemingway's career a boost in the early 1920s, the *Toronto Daily Star*, was the youngest of the lot. It had been started by striking printers in 1892 as the *Evening Star*, with the backing of the local labour movement. In 1899 it was reorganized by progressive businessmen. Under the name *Daily Star* (as of January 24, 1900), it became a voice for the federal Liberal government of Wilfrid Laurier, among the Toronto masses who would not read the *Globe*.

The *Star*'s origins were reflected in its support for the post-war Drury regime. By this point it was the most slickly North American of the four city papers in layout and style. It also enjoyed the largest circulation (almost 135,000 for the *Daily Star* in January 1924, and 155,000 for the popular *Star Weekly*).

Though its ownership has changed, the *Star* is the only Toronto newspaper whose corporate identity has survived intact from the 1920s down to the present. The *Globe* and the *Mail and Empire* would be merged in 1936, to form today's *Globe and Mail.* The *Telegram* ceased publication in 1971, and a rump of its staff formed the *Toronto Sun.* The *Star* of the 1920s saw itself as a people's paper, as it still does today. Following the habits of the early twentieth-century Liberal Party in Canada, however, it showed more admiration for the United States than it tends to now. And it stood up staunchly for the principle of Canadian-American free trade.

THE STANDARD ELECTRIC HOME

By the end of 1923 many in Toronto were growing impatient with tough financial times. Unrest over the city's still-sluggish economic base was heightened by a buoyant recovery already under way south of the Great Lakes. The "steady influx of United States business firms into the Canadian field" noted by the *Mail and Empire* in March 1922 was apparently not helping much. A few restless participants in the Canadian labour force had begun to move in the opposite direction.

In a January 1924 editorial on the subject the *Globe* tried to reassure its readers. The Canadians heading south were only part of a "passing phase that will come to an end as the fevered industrial pulse of the Northern industrial states slows down to normal." Several months later, in May, the *Globe* ran a more detailed article on "THE EXODUS TO THE UNITED STATES." It ended with a similar "Comforting Conclusion," but stressed that more had to be done to create new opportunities in Canada itself.

Like those who went south, the great majority who stayed in Toronto were enthused about a rising, urban, consumer lifestyle. This new lifestyle flowed from the concept of a mechanized mass household, touted in Toronto Hydro newspaper ads of the 1920s as the "Standard Electric Home." The concept had been evolving for at least a generation, but it began to blossom brilliantly after the First World War.

Throughout North America this was the new realism's answer to the fading prospects of the old idealism epitomized by the independent family farm. Among house-proud Torontonians it had a special appeal. Toronto could not

By the time John Boyd took this photograph in January 1924, automobiles and new work-saving devices had started to transform domestic life, but horses were still delivering blocks of ice to keep perishable foods cold in city homes.

realistically aspire to the heights of power and influence of such places as New York and Chicago. Shortly before he left the city in December 1923, Ernest Hemingway observed in the *Star Weekly* that though it was "easy to make money ... in Canada," it was "hard to get rich." Nevertheless, the ordinary people north of the lakes could at least begin to cultivate the new mechanized mass household with a unique enthusiasm and panache.

In the middle of January 1920 the *Globe* featured a special section on "new devices to save work." It included an ad for an exotic-looking "1900 Cataract electric washer." During the 1920 Christmas season the Toronto Hydro Shop promoted electric curling tongs, an electric shaving cup, and "a Hydro coffee percolator." In April 1921 ads for Premier vacuum cleaners in the *Daily Star* stressed that "the housewife with a Premier has leisure ..." In May, ads for "a refrigerator without ice" appeared in the *Mail and Empire.*

The promotional tide carried on throughout 1922 and 1923. By 1924 it had reached new heights. A casual sampling for the month of May reveals ads for a "gas range" (with such advantages as "less work, well-cooked food, no dust and dirt, more rest for mother, meals on time"); assorted ads for "McClary's electric range" (promising, "oh that freedom"); assorted ads for electric washers ("Is wash-day drudgery making your wife old before her time?"); and still more ads for a complex-looking system of "automatic electric refrigeration."

During the first half of the 1920s the sluggish regional economy thwarted assiduous Toronto cultivators of the new lifestyle. One problem was that the price of virtually everything was apparently too high. Price reductions on all manner of products were a regular feature in local newspaper advertising of the day.

The cost of the single-family houses that dominated the local real estate market began to decline as well. According to a January 1925 article in the *Star*, almost 65 percent of Toronto householders owned their own dwellings – a figure "probably not equalled by any other large city." By this point it was becoming easier to purchase even this essential framework for the mechanized mass household. Early in 1927 the city of Toronto assessment commissioner would report on some recent anomalies in the tax assessments on residential property. The crux of the problem, he urged, was that there "had been a general lowering in the sale prices of housing during the past three or four years."

By the middle of the 1920s trends of this sort would at last help spark a short but unusually sweet boom in Toronto. The new lifestyle would take off. Soon enough, however, the assiduous local cultivators would be thwarted again by the Great Depression of the 1930s. In this regard, as in others, the 1920s merely started things that would only begin to reach fruition a great many years later.

Yet even the sluggish local economy of 1920–24 spawned some impressive underlying progress. Electricity was a crucial prerequisite for the Standard Electric Home. In 1930 *Might's Directory* would review the progress of the "Toronto Hydro-Electric System." In 1916 the system had served some 40,000 meters in the city. This had increased to more than 93,000 meters by 1922, and to more than 141,000 meters by 1924. More than 175,000 meters would be served by the end of the decade.

ALL ALONE BY THE TELEPHONE

The new urban lifestyle involved more than new devices to save work. It also featured a potent new array of communications machinery.

By the start of the 1920s the early technology of the silent movie was already established in local theatres. Mary Pickford, born in the city in 1893, had become Toronto's first great gift to the emerging dream factory in Hollywood, California. Early in March 1923 the *Daily Star* carried ads for a silent movie called *Satan's Paradise*. It was "the first feature production to be made in Toronto, a wholly Canadian picture." On Monday, March 5, the film started a run at the Allen Theatre, at the corner of Richmond and Victoria streets downtown.

The title *Satan's Paradise* is vaguely reminiscent of the successful Canadian movies David Cronenberg would make in Toronto a half-century later. The city's first feature production, however, was apparently not too popular. It had its final showings at the Allen on Saturday, March 10, 1923.

The telephone was the first major new communications device based in the home (and the office). Torontonians, like other Canadians, embraced it with unusual enthusiasm. This may have had something to do with the claim that Scotsman Alexander Graham Bell had discovered the principle of the telephone in 1874 at his parents' house in Brantford, Ontario – not in Boston, Massachusetts, in 1875. On January 6, 1921, an editorial in the *Daily Star*, entitled "IT'S CANADIAN, NOT AMERICAN," tried to set the record straight.

Claims about the Canadian origins of the telephone have rarely impressed citizens of the United States. By the early 1920s Bell's invention had nonetheless begun to establish itself as part of the mainstream in Toronto life. According to *Might's Directory*, there were only 7,242 telephones in the city in 1900. By 1910 there were 32,515; by 1915, 58,260; by 1920, 95,749; and by 1921, 101,531.

In January 1920 all the Toronto papers carried ads touting "the 1920 phonograph ... the Brunswick." In August 1922 a wide array of Victrola phonographs were advertised, at prices ranging from $37.50 to $615.00. Prices for different kinds and sizes of phonograph records in the early 1920s ranged from 65¢ to $1.65.

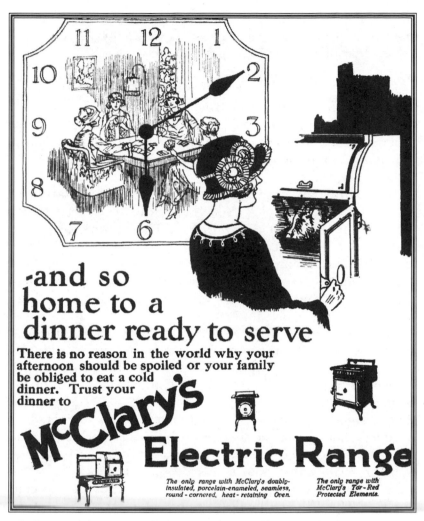

Today we take electrical kitchen appliances for granted. In the 1920s they were still liberating innovations. (May 1924)

Thomas Edison had invented the phonograph in 1877, just after Bell invented the telephone (and this time clearly in the United States, not Canada). The particular commercial version on sale in the early 1920s was descended from products that had first appeared in 1906. You had to wind up the machines, and the sound quality was abysmal.

Between 1919 and 1924 the Bell Telephone Laboratories in the United States developed a new process of electrical recording.

In 1925 the Victor and Columbia labels issued the first commercial electric recordings. The Brunswick Company began to market the first all-electric phonograph in the same year.

THE RADIO CROSSES BOUNDARIES

Phonograph records, silent movies, and telephones broadened their markets enormously in the 1920s. But they had all been around earlier. Radio was the decade's almost unique communications innovation. In some ways it was the most potent of all the new machinery.

On Thursday, June 22, 1922, the first radio station in Toronto (and Ontario) – CFCA – began to broadcast from a plant in the offices of the *Daily Star*. The station was owned and operated by Toronto's most popular newspaper. In early June 1922, to prepare its readers for the new technology, the *Star* had included a "radio department" page in its daily edition. The page provided a convenient vehicle for advertising early radio sets.

The June 1922 ads reflected the novelty of the new machines. A radio was not yet just something you put in your living room, to receive programs from stations on the dial; it was also a mysterious link to assorted strange noises from the cosmos. One Toronto ad in the summer of 1922 had stressed that a radio was "ideal for the summer vacation." Some older products tried to take advantage of the rising market of radio listeners, in ads that stressed such possibilities as "recording radio messages with – Waterman's ideal fountain pen."

As in the case of the telephone, house-proud Torontonians quickly took up the radio. On March 1, 1923, the *Star* claimed: "RADIO ADVERTISING QUEEN CITY ABROAD, STAR BROADCASTING STATION IS MAKING TORONTO KNOWN EVERYWHERE." Only a day later Foster Hewitt made his first hockey broadcast. The *Star* reported: "ICE BATTLE BY RADIO KEPT THE FANS ON EDGE." In December 1923 the unhappy but still youthful Ernest Hemingway observed that, judging by the people he had come to know in the queen city, "Canadians ... are all in a hurry to get home to supper / And their radio sets."

Again, as in the case of the telephone, Canada could claim some role in the invention of radio technology. On Christmas Eve 1906 Reginald Fessenden, who in 1866 had been born in what became the province of Quebec in 1867, made the world's first public radio broadcast of music and voice.

Canada's first experimental radio station began broadcasting in Montreal in 1919. For a while in the 1920s Toronto newspapers carried program listings for Canadian stations as far away as Vancouver. By 1924 the recently established Canadian National Railways had begun a primitive programming service in both English and French. (Its Toronto outlet was known as CNRT.) By the late 1920s there would be five local radio stations in Toronto itself.

KDKA, however, was the world's first commercial radio broadcasting station. It started in Pittsburgh in November 1920. New stations proliferated rapidly south of the Great Lakes, and radio sets in Toronto easily received their signals.

The local newspapers had begun to carry program listings for U.S. stations even before the *Star* established CFCA, and advertising began to appear on U.S. radio stations in 1922. In November 1926 David Sarnoff established the National Broadcasting Company in New York. Its initial nine-station network soon had thirty-one affiliates.

Like the silent movies, radio quickly became a vehicle for disseminating the popular culture of English-speaking North America in Toronto. Howard Ferguson worried about how this might blur the aggressive promotion of British imperial civilization in the public schools. A generation later, Harold Adams Innis at the University of Toronto would explain that "the radio crosses boundaries which stopped the press."

THEIR ADOPTED COUNTRY

The lifestyle of the mechanized mass household was open to anyone who could pay for it. The federal ban on Chinese immigration, however, also played a key role in the new realism of 1923. It reasserted the cultural dominance of the Anglo-Protestant majority.

Even so, a new global industrial culture was rising on the back of the new communications machinery, spawning new social forces. A continent like North America, or especially a country like Canada, or even more especially a city like Toronto, might try to regulate the speed at which it dealt with these new forces, but even in the 1920s it could not make them disappear.

In 1921, according to federal census statistics, 15 percent of those living within the official city of Toronto boundaries – or

*Northern Electric was the forerunner of today's Canadian hi-tech enterprise
Northern Telecom, now headquartered in the Toronto-region city of
Mississauga. (November 1923)*

almost 77,000 people – had one form or another of non-British ancestry. Even among the British groups in the census statistics, already more and more were starting to see themselves as Canadian first.

The first people to call themselves *Canadien* had not been Anglo-Saxon Protestants. Though few had even begun to think the subject through, it was beginning to be recognized that if people of reputed British ancestry could choose to call themselves Canadian, so could anyone else. The *Globe* explained in a September 1924 editorial: "The Canadian" was simply "the man or woman who desires to be a Canadian, who takes pride in the name, and who is devoted to the interests of Canada."

All this had particular implications for one non-British group in the city, already some four times larger than "the Chinese colony." On July 2, 1920, the *Mail and Empire* carried an article headed "MARRIED MEN WON THE TUG-OF-WAR / ITALIAN COMMUNITY CELEBRATE DOMINION DAY ..." It noted that the "Italian community of Toronto celebrated the natal day of their adopted country at the ninth annual picnic held yesterday afternoon at Exhibition Park."

Italians had begun to arrive in Toronto in the late nineteenth century. According to federal census statistics, by 1921 there were more than 8,200 Torontonians of Italian ancestry. Many had originally come to Canada via the United States. They were recruited by local *padroni,* or labour agents, for construction and other labouring jobs. Like other early Italian Torontonians, the *padroni* often operated fruit stores.

In June 1922 the *Mail and Empire* reported that "the last American immigration law has practically closed the United States to Italians." As a result, the Italian government had "asked the British government to facilitate Italian emigration to Canada, Australia, and New Zealand."

According to the pioneering urban historian Robert Harney, Italian immigration to the city slowed dramatically after 1924. The federal census nonetheless indicates that Toronto's Italian population increased by more than 5,000 people between 1921 and 1931.

The great majority came from the rural areas of southern Italy. They were especially attracted to three Toronto neighbourhoods. One was the downtown "Ward" – bounded by

Yonge, Queen, University, and College – an early magnet for
many different groups of non-British migrants to the city. The
others were the near west-end district between Dundas and
College, west of Manning Avenue, and the more northwesterly
area west of Dufferin Street, between Bloor and Davenport.

MINISTER FOR MULTICULTURALISM

The Italian community of the 1920s established a foothold for
the Italians who would play a leading role in the great migrations to Toronto that followed the Second World War. In 1921,
however, Torontonians of Italian ancestry only accounted for
some 1.6 percent of the population in the city at large. This was
virtually identical to the proportion reporting French racial origins. The great majority of this group were born in Canada, not
France, many having migrated to Toronto from elsewhere in
the country. From their standpoint, it was not the French but
the British who were the new Canadians. The Germans were
the city's next-largest European national group. Many of them
had not migrated from Europe, but from other parts of
Ontario or from the United States.

According to census statistics, the most rapidly growing non-
British groups in the city during the 1920s were none of the
above. This honour fell to the Ukrainians and the Poles. There
were just over 1,000 Torontonians of Ukrainian descent in
1921; by 1931 there would be more than 4,400. In 1921 more
than 2,600 city residents reported Polish ancestry; by 1931
there would be more than 8,200. In spite of this rapid increase,
in absolute numbers Italian Torontonians would still be more
numerous in 1931 than Poles and Ukrainians combined. But
already some of the kaleidoscopic cultural variety that would
blossom so boldly in the 1960s had begun to germinate.

On March 4, 1923, Peter and Josephine Haidasz, a Polish
couple who lived in the west end of the city, had a son whom
they named Stanley. In the late 1950s Stanley Haidasz would be
elected to represent the Toronto riding of Parkdale in the
Canadian federal Parliament at Ottawa. In the 1970s he would
become the minister responsible for multiculturalism, in the
government of Pierre Elliott Trudeau.

*Many different kinds of Torontonians wanted to get rich in the mid-1920s.
Yet, according to this June 1923 ad, out of every 100 twenty-five-year-old
men only one would be "wealthy" and only four would be "well-to-do"
by age sixty-five.*

Frederick Banting and his new bride. (June 1924)

CHAPTER FOUR

WOOING GOOD TIMES

By the middle of 1924 Torontonians' enthusiasm for buying all kinds of new products had brought fresh respect for the craft of making money. It was not easy to get rich in Canada, as Hemingway had noted, but in a modest way, it was not impossible. During the early twentieth-century economic take-off, astute observers of the wider British Empire had already judged Toronto's ruling elite "a nice sensible plutocracy."

The political revolution of October 1919 had temporarily dimmed the light on this side of the local scene. The failure of the Home Bank prolonged the effect. Now, however, there were signs that the busted boom was coming to an end. On June 5, 1924, the Laura Secord Candy Shops ran a public service ad headed "BUSINESS IS GOOD" and claiming that "every day" was starting to show "definite sustained progress."

THE MASSEYS AND THE MASSES

The city's most prominent plutocratic dynasty in the 1920s owed a lot to the democratic family farmers who had done so much to elect the Drury regime in 1919. The Massey-Harris Company could trace its origins back to 1849, when Daniel Massey began to manufacture agricultural machinery in Newcastle – some seventy kilometres east of Toronto.

Where Toronto's Wealth is Greatest
The Circulation of
THE TORONTO STAR
DAILY AND WEEKLY
Exceeds that of any THREE PAPER COMBINATION

The Star *had supported E.C. Drury's populist government in the 1923
Ontario election. Through this ad, which appeared in June 1924, the paper
hoped to show that it also had more plutocratic readers.*

Reprinted with permission – The Toronto Star.

This Daniel Massey was the son of a Daniel Massey who had
moved from upstate New York in 1802. Unlike Howard
Ferguson's family, the Masseys were not Loyalists. They had
merely been migrants on the Anglo-American frontier. They
were also strict Methodists, with a politically radical streak. In
the 1830s the Daniel Massey who started the Newcastle factory
in 1849 was a staunch supporter of William Lyon Mackenzie.

The son of this "second Daniel," Hart Massey, dramatically
expanded the family's agricultural machinery business in the
1860s and 1870s. In 1879 the Massey Manufacturing Company
moved to "the largest and best equipped factory ever built in
Canada," in the west end of Toronto.

In 1891 the firm merged with its main regional rival, the A.
Harris, Son & Company of Brantford. Massey-Harris, headquartered in Toronto, became the largest manufacturer of agricultural machinery in the British Empire. It dominated the
Canadian market and was also Canada's first home-grown
multinational corporation. It could boast that in "England,
Scotland, Ireland, France, Germany, Belgium, Russia, Asia

Minor, South Africa, South America, the West Indies, Australia, our machines are at work."

In December 1921 Hart Massey's favourite grandson, the thirty-four-year-old Vincent, became president of Massey-Harris. The job was not too demanding, and Vincent Massey would keep it until October 1925. According to his biographer, Claude Bissell, these were "crucial years during which policies of retrenchment and preparation were skillfully blended so that in 1925 the company was prepared to take full advantage of improved conditions."

Vincent was the last Massey to play an active role in the business. Lawren Harris – from the other end of the 1891 merger – had already cast his lot with the Group of Seven. In the autumn of 1925 Vincent Massey joined Mackenzie King's cabinet in Ottawa. He began the new career that would culminate with his appointment as the first Canadian-born governor general of Canada, in 1952.

The Massey family had made three great gifts to the people of Toronto. The first was Massey Hall, opened in 1894 at the corner of Shuter and Victoria streets. Next came the Fred Victor Mission at Queen and Jarvis – a memorial to the strong Methodist social conscience of Hart Massey's youngest son. Then there was Hart House at the University of Toronto, completed in 1919.

As relief from his duties at Massey-Harris, Vincent Massey spent much of the early 1920s working in the Hart House theatre. Some of its sets were designed by Lawren Harris and his friends. Hart House itself aspired to bring the gentleman's life of the English university undergraduate to the pioneer shores of Lake Ontario. Despite his professional relationship with William Lyon Mackenzie's grandson, Vincent Massey worshipped the British Empire as much as Henry Pellatt did.

Vincent's younger brother, Raymond, would become a Hollywood actor, famous both for his craggily authentic movie portrayals of Abraham Lincoln and for his late-career success as Dr. Gillespie in the television series "Doctor Kildare."

CANADIAN BRANCH PLANTS IN THE UNITED STATES

Vincent Massey's departure from Massey-Harris in 1925 marked the end of the firm's gradual transition from a Canadian family business to an impersonally run global corporation. In 1911 Massey-Harris had purchased the Johnson Harvester Company of Batavia, New York. By the First World War, Massey-Harris had begun to sell agricultural machinery in the United States. In 1928 it would buy the J.I. Case Plow Works Inc. in Racine, Wisconsin.

This was the other side of the influx of American branch plants into the Canadian field. Other businesses in Toronto were involved as well. One of the earliest was the Moore Corporation, best known for its business forms (distributed for many years through an entity called the American Sales Book Company). Established by S.J. Moore in 1879, the firm had opened a U.S. branch in Buffalo as early as the 1880s. By the late 1920s the Moore Corporation in Toronto would be operating branch plants in the states of California, Minnesota, New Hampshire, New York, and Washington.

In 1890 the local pharmacist John J. McLaughlin began to manufacture "Belfast Style Ginger Ale" for thirsty Torontonians. In 1907 he introduced "Canada Dry – the Champagne of Ginger Ales." In 1922 Canada Dry opened its first U.S. bottling plant, on 38th Street in New York City. The Canadian Bank of Commerce was already operating banks in Oregon and California. In 1925 its Oregon operations took over the Pacific Bank of Portland.

ON GREAT SLAVE LAKE

Even nice sensible plutocrats do not have a monopoly on economic interests. In the summer of 1924 Harold Adams Innis, an economics lecturer at the University of Toronto, embarked on a trip that would show another kind of respect for the craft of making money in Canada.

With his friend John Long, Innis set out from the northern Alberta town of Peace River in the middle of June. Innis and Long paddled an eighteen-foot, canvas-covered canoe down the river that gave the town its name, following it into the Slave River. On July 6 they reached Fort Resolution on Great Slave Lake, in the Northwest Territories.

Innis wrote to his wife in Toronto: "I am looking out over Great Slave Lake, through a maze of tents and teepees. The Indians are all over the place – they are coming in for 'Treaty Money.' And of course they all have dogs so that you can imag-

The Toronto-based J.J. McLaughlin enterprise started to make "Belfast Style" ginger ale in 1890 and "Canada Dry" in 1907. In 1922 it opened its first branch plant in New York City. (June 1922)

ine what the place is like. We are hoping to go to Hay River as soon as a motor boat comes along."

The motor boat came along two days later. On the Hudson's Bay Company vessel *Laird River*, Innis and Long cruised across Great Slave Lake to the Mackenzie River. They then followed the Mackenzie all the way to Aklavik and the Arctic Ocean.

In the 1920s the Mackenzie Valley was the last frontier of the Canadian fur trade. In 1924 the age of the airplane and the bush pilot, which would transform northern Canada as surely as new devices to save work would transform Toronto, had just begun. By this time, Harold Innis had started to write the book that would be published in 1930 as *The Fur Trade in Canada: An Introduction to Canadian Economic History.* He believed in field work. He wanted to see with his own eyes the final phases of what he was writing about.

Innis had a native son's interest in Canada. The British Empire would not disappear for another half-century, but he could see that it would end. He wondered about Canada's future when it did, and began to look for answers in the distant past. In 1924 the Group of Seven were sketching the Rocky Mountains. What Lawren Harris was to painting, Harold Innis was to history – and to anthropology, economics, geography, and political science as well.

THE FUR TRADE IN CANADA

Innis was not quite thirty years old when he and John Long embarked on their Mackenzie Valley adventure. He was born in 1894 on a "strict Baptist" family farm in southwestern Ontario and had attended Ontario's Baptist college, McMaster University. The college was a bequest of William McMaster, the most prominent founder of the Canadian Bank of Commerce. At this point it was still on Bloor Street in Toronto (in the building occupied today by the Royal Conservatory of Music).

After graduating from McMaster, Innis was wounded in the First World War. He came back to Toronto and completed his M.A.; then he went to the University of Chicago, where he took a Ph.D. in economics. His thesis was on the history of the Canadian Pacific Railway. By 1924 he had become obsessed by the similarities between the transcontinental Canadian economic union that the CPR had forged in the 1880s and 1890s and the east-west unity pioneered by the "Indian and European" fur trade between 1497 and 1821.

There had also been a fur trade in parts of the United States, but because of the rugged geography in what Innis liked to call "northern North America," this phase in the modern economic development of the continent had left much deeper marks on Canada. In northern North America, you could travel from the Atlantic to the Arctic to the Pacific oceans along interior water routes, via the indigenous Indian transportation technology of the canoe and portage. The transcontinental railways that consummated the Confederation of 1867 economically had only imitated these aboriginal pathways.

In 1924 many still imagined that, were it not for the British Empire, Canada (with the possible exception of the historic French-speaking majority in Quebec) could only become part

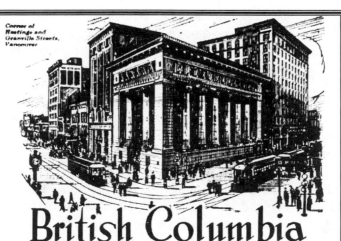

British Columbia
Is a Solid Corner-Stone in
National Prosperity

IT MATTERS not what corner of Western Canada is asked to tell its story, there is an immediate response in language and figures that encourage the brightest hopes for increasing prosperity.

Here are some illuminating British Columbia trade figures for the year 1923:

> The revenue from Timber alone was around $70,000,000, Agriculture $60,000,000, Mines $41,000,000, Fisheries $22,250,000, a total of $193,000,000.

> *British Columbia has demonstrated her ability to pay her public debts with a sinking fund reserve towards payment of over $12,000,000. This is equal to $23.14 per head of population.*

On top of this comes a despatch dated London (Eng.), October 24th, describing a *"Sweeping Victory for British Columbia apples in the fact that the Province captures 14 first honors and one second at the Imperial Show, and that the gold challenge cup given by the agents-general of British Columbia, Nova Scotia, Ontario and Quebec has been awarded to British Columbia."*

The sister Provinces of Manitoba, Saskatchewan and Alberta are still leading the Dominion in per capita wealth, and have more money to spend from this year's harvest than in any year in the history of these Provinces.

Detailed, reliable information from any well-equipped advertising agency or direct from the publishers.

The Big Western Canada Daily Newspapers offer you the one selling force that effectively covers this whole field, quickly, inexpensively, with results that are never in doubt from the first step in the campaign.

The Big Daily in Each City

Winnipeg:	Free Press	Lethbridge:	Herald
Brandon:	Sun	Medicine Hat:	News
Regina:	Leader & Post	Calgary:	Herald
Moose Jaw:	Times & Herald	Edmonton:	Journal
Saskatoon:	Star & Phoenix	Nelson:	News
	Vancouver: Province		

Even before the railways the unique geography of the northern fur trade had taken Canadian national ambitions all the way to the Pacific coast – in modern British Columbia. (November 1924) of the United States. On the fresh view of the past that Innis was pondering, Canada had not remained geographically separate from the United States because it remained part of the British Empire; it had remained part of the British Empire because it was geographically separate from the United States.

Innis would go on to become the first Canadian-born chairman of the Department of Political Economy at the University of Toronto. His attention would finally turn to the complex problems of communications in world history. The often mysterious media writings of "the later Innis" would inspire Marshall McLuhan in the 1950s and 1960s. By this point Innis himself would have evolved into – in the later whimsical characterization of the *Times Literary Supplement* in the United Kingdom – "Canada's first and perhaps only genuine intellectual." Not long before his death in November 1952, he would be elected president of the American Economic Association.

In the middle of the 1920s "the early Innis" was in the middle of his patriotic project. As the geographer Cole Harris would much later explain, Harold Innis argued that Canada's "southern boundary is not a geographical absurdity."

Innis was too good at his job to ignore the concurrent importance of north-south cultural and economic ties in North America, from the beginnings of the Canadian fur trade down to the present. He was also too shrewd an observer of current events to miss the force of the new realism after the First World War. In the 1930s he would note that "Canada is facing to an increasing extent the effects of a contrast between two systems. An old system linked her to Europe ... The new system links Canada to the United States."

Yet by 1924 Harold Innis had begun to try telling a kind of romantic truth about Canada. It did not have to remain part of the British Empire. It did not have to become part of the United States either. Canada was its own open-ended geographic adventure. It had started with a multiracial collaboration in the unique vast wilderness between the Great Lakes and the North Pole.

As the conclusion to *The Fur Trade* would somewhat cryptically explain: "It is no mere accident that the present Dominion coincides roughly with the fur-trading areas of northern North America ... 'The lords of the lakes and forest have passed away' but their work will endure in the boundaries of the Dominion of Canada and in Canadian institutional life ... We have not yet realized that the Indian and his culture were fundamental to the growth of Canadian institutions. We are only beginning to realize the central position of the Canadian Shield."

Fly to Fort Norman

In absolute safety and comfort for what it costs to hire guides and buy outfit. Flying time about eight hours each way.

Two six-passenger Flying Boats of a stable, safe type, approved by the British Air Board, to be placed in schedule service between Peace River and Fort Norman the first day of May.

Capt. Fred Robert McCall, D.S.O., M.C., D.F.C., in charge of actual flying.

Bookings in Order Received
No Deviation From This Rule

Wire **W.R. Gayner,** 5 Thompson Block
8th Avenue, Calgary, Alta.

Harold Innis and John Long travelled the Mackenzie Valley by boat in 1924. If they'd wanted to try the latest technology, they could have taken an airplane. (February 1921)

COME TO THE FAIR

Harold Innis and John Long's own geographic adventure in the summer of 1924 was part of a wider enthusiasm of the day. On Thursday, September 4, shortly after they had returned to Toronto, the *Globe* ran a travel article by a journalist called John Nelson. It was headed "THE PEACE RIVER COUNTRY IS AN EMPIRE IN ITSELF."

Two days later, on Saturday, September 6, the Canadian National Exhibition closed for another year. On the following Monday the *Globe* printed a notice in a box at the top of the front page, declaring that "1924 registered a new record attendance" for Toronto's annual late-summer fair – the largest event of its kind, it was sometimes said, in the entire world.

The notice went on to add that "this week the Western Fair at London and the Central Canada Exhibition at Ottawa throw open their gates. Scores of other fairs – big and little – in all parts of the country follow in their wake. The *Globe* urges the good people of every community and district to make this a year of records ALL DOWN THE LINE."

According to the notice, attending such fairs was "a homely and practical way of wooing 'good times' in which every citizen can help. Cheerful crowds and gratified exhibitors everywhere do much to stimulate business and spread the heartening flavor of confidence which heralds prosperity."

THE COLORED MEN'S BUSINESS CLUB

Not all citizens of Toronto could be expected to heed this appeal altogether gladly. Today one striking feature of Harold Innis's writing on the collaboration of Indians and Europeans in the early fur trade is how it shows the Canadian precedents for the metropolitan multiracial society of the late twentieth century. Like Morley Callaghan and Ernest Hemingway, however, Harold Innis was too new for Toronto in the 1920s.

Innis's book on the fur trade would not even be published until 1930. In the meantime, the 1923 federal ban on Chinese immigration helped to reassert the dominance of the Anglo-Protestant majority in the life of the city. For Torontonians of African descent the new realism had a repressive edge.

Though there were not many black Torontonians at this point, the 1920 edition of *Might's Directory* did list a "Colored Men's Business Club" at 161 Adelaide Street West. The 1921

federal census reported some 1,230 residents of Toronto whose
racial origin was "Negro." This amounted to less than one-quarter of one percent of the city's total population. But the local
black community made up for what it lacked in size with a long
and somewhat ironic past.

Some of the British colonial officials and Loyalist refugees who
established the town of York in 1793 had brought black ser-
vants and slaves. In the same year "An act to prevent the further introduction of slaves, and to limit the term of contracts
for servitude in this province" was passed in the fledgling colonial legislature. Similar laws were passed in some northern U.S.
states. But the ruling Tory oligarchy of old Upper Canada liked
to stress that in British North America even black people were
free, and it refused to acknowledge U.S. fugitive slave laws in
Canadian courts.

The abolition of slavery throughout the British Empire in
1834 reinforced "the free-soil sanctuary of Canada." In terms of
the local political spectrum, by the late 1840s George Brown
and his brother Gordon had added a progressive dimension to
the cause. Toronto became a modest haven for black refugees
travelling on the Underground Railroad. In the 1850s free
blacks constituted as much as 3 percent of the city's population. On September 10, 1851, a historic "North American
Convention of Colored Freemen" was held at the recently con-
structed St. Lawrence Hall on King Street East.

Most of the early, self-described "coloured citizens of
Toronto and vicinity" were even more "loyal and dutiful sub-
jects of Her Majesty's just and powerful government" than the
rabid white Tories. A few were rewarded with unusually successful careers.

Wilson Ruffin Abbott had settled in Toronto with his family
in 1835. He was a small businessman who showed a talent for
real estate speculation. By the time of his death in 1876, he
owned more than seventy-five properties. His son, Anderson,
would become the first Canadian-born black medical doctor.

The American Civil War put an end to the early active
phase of Toronto's black history, but an increasingly small community of African descent remained in the city. Toronto's first
black alderman, William Peyton Hubbard, was elected in 1894.
Hubbard lived on into a ripe old age, in a large house on

Broadview Avenue, just south of the Danforth. In January 1927 the *Star* would run a feature article on Hubbard on his eighty-fifth birthday.

William Peyton Hubbard's son, Fred, married Grace Abbott, daughter of Dr. Anderson Abbott, and pursued a career in public transportation. It started with the old Toronto Railway Company and ended with the TTC. During his time with the TRC Fred Hubbard acted as manager of Scarborough Beach Park. When the park gave way to a new streetscape in the late 1920s, Hubbard Boulevard was named in his honour. It still runs parallel to Lake Ontario, between Balsam and Wineva, in the east-end Beaches.

CARIBBEAN CONNECTIONS

In the Toronto of the 1920s, the Abbotts and the Hubbards were legends from the city's black past. On December 15, 1920, a dim view of the future surfaced. The Canadian Bank of Commerce opened a new branch in Barbados, in the British West Indies. Soon it would open another branch in Kingston, Jamaica.

In the meticulous log of his work that he kept, John Boyd called this 1926 Toronto photograph "Jamaican Wedding."

Canadian banks in the Caribbean would help introduce people of African descent in the West Indies to northern North America. Banks headquartered in Halifax and Montreal had already moved in this direction. The Bank of Nova Scotia had established a branch in Jamaica as long ago as 1889.

Broader concepts that linked Toronto with the Caribbean Sea were in the air throughout the 1920s. In May 1921 the *Mail and Empire* ran an article headed "FEDERATION OF BRITISH AMERICA SAID TO BE UNDER CONSIDERATION." The piece explained that "establishment of a Confederation of British America, to include Canada and the British colonies of the Bahamas, Barbados, Bermuda, Jamaica, the Leeward Islands, Trinidad and Windward Islands, and possibly British Honduras and British Guiana" was "under consideration in the British Dominions and possessions of North, South and Central America."

In September 1924 the *Globe* announced: "WEST INDIES TRADE IS OPEN TO CANADA." In February 1925 a deputation from Canada toured the West Indies, "bringing an invitation from the King government to discuss trade relations." A Canada–West Indies trade conference, held in Ottawa during the later part of June 1925, would sign a formal trade agreement. Some two and a half years later, in December 1927, the *Daily Star* would urge: "EMPIRE BEING CREATED IN CARIBBEAN." According to a March 1928 *Star* article, "BRITISH GUIANA SEEKS CANADIAN ANNEXATION."

In Toronto, as in other parts of the country, this sort of news raised the same anxieties that had prompted the ban on Chinese immigration in 1923. In the 1921 federal census, the exact number of city residents with Negro racial origins was reported as 1,236 – more than two and a half times larger than the 472 reported in the 1911 census. When the 1920s began Toronto's black population was showing a sudden surge of growth. Census data imply that this growth owed something to the earliest beginnings of black migration from the West Indies. Between 1911 and 1921 the number of Torontonians originally from the West Indies more than doubled. According to the Canadian black historian Daniel Hill, "West Indian and American Blacks ... were recruited and brought to Canada during the First World War by railroad and industrial interests."

But the city's black community expanded hardly at all between 1921 and 1931. In 1931 the number of Torontonians with Negro racial origins was reported as 1,344, and in that year the number of Torontonians who had been born in the West Indies was exactly the same as it had been in 1921. Between 1921 and 1931 Toronto's black population grew at a slower rate than its Chinese population, even though there was an official ban on Chinese immigration.

Here as elsewhere, the 1920s saw only the bare beginnings of changes that would not reach fruition for a great many years. More than a generation would elapse before black West Indians began to arrive in the city in significant numbers. Meanwhile, the Abbotts and the Hubbards and their kith and kin carried on with their lives. They remained witnesses to the stubborn fact that there had been some Torontonians with ancient African roots ever since the founding of the British North American town of York.

SIXTY-TWO PERCENT

A month after the *Globe*'s September 1924 report on Canada–West Indies trade, another chapter in the saga of prohibition in Ontario began to unfold.

Especially in Toronto, the Farmer-Labour government's ruthless enforcement of the Ontario Temperance Act had done much to elect Howard Ferguson's Tories. The local wets had danced in the streets of the city to celebrate Ferguson's victory on June 25, 1923. Fergie was aware that many supporters expected him to bring back the demon rum. Yet he had his own roots in rural Ontario. He knew that the grand old cause of 1916 and 1919 and 1921 was still in bloom. On the rules of the old game of politics, caution was the key to success.

So there was yet another popular vote. This time it was called a plebiscite, not a referendum. Thus, Queen's Park would not be bound by the results. It was held on Thursday, October 23, 1924. Voters were asked to choose between two options: either to carry on with the OTA or to replace it with a government-controlled system of legal liquor marketing. Systems of the latter sort had already been introduced in other English-speaking Canadian provinces.

In Toronto a decisive 62 percent of the active electorate voted for "Government Control," but some 52 percent in

Ontario at large opted for the OTA. This was a smaller prohibition majority than in either the 1921 or 1919 contests. But it was still a majority.

Fergie's initial reaction adumbrated the policy he would pursue over the next few years. On the one hand, as the *Telegram* in Toronto reported with disappointment, " 'THE MAJORITY MUST PREVAIL'/GOVERNMENT ENFORCES OTA"; on the other, the premier of Ontario slyly observed, "The fact that the majority, as compared with the vote of 1919, has been much reduced may make it more difficult to properly enforce the Act."

CHURCH UNION SPELLS BETTER ECONOMIC LIFE

Another great moral event was in the Toronto air during the autumn of 1924. Today few would likely agree with the late 1920s *Globe* editorialist who argued that one key difference between Canada and the United States was the United Church of Canada. The argument flows from an aspect of the past that has become profoundly mysterious.

Organized religion had more meaning for more people in the early twentieth century. The ambiguous and ironic Toronto the Good was still a "city of churches." The creation of the uniquely Canadian United Church was a big event in the life of the city. In 1923, 1924, and 1925 its progress was carefully traced by the local press. A December 1924 headline in the *Daily Star* declared: "SCOTTISH PASTOR CALLS UNION DIVINE COMMAND ... CANADA SETTING EXAMPLE TO THE WORLD."

Old Upper Canada had been periodically convulsed by intense religious discord, fomented by a failed scheme for a constitutionally established Anglican Church. By the early twentieth century, the city of churches was noted for its denominational pluralism. The phenomenon was reflected in the structure of Toronto's leading university, with its Trinity College for the Anglicans, Victoria College for the Methodists, St. Michael's College for the Catholics, and University College for other dissenters, agnostics, atheists, and Jews.

There had been related trends towards denominational pluralism throughout English-speaking Canada, and they would all become grist for the union mill. The United Church has, in fact, been called "the most self-consciously Canadian of all churches." In one of its several aspects, the Protestant

City of Toronto Archives SC 266-5561

The first Toronto service of the new United Church of Canada was held at the Arena on Mutual Street, June 10, 1925. The crowds here are waiting to get in.

church union movement of the 1920s reflected the growth of early English-speaking Canadian national sentiment after the First World War.

The movement brought together the Congregational Churches of Canada; the Methodist Church in Bermuda, Canada, and Newfoundland; the Presbyterian Church in Canada; and a transitional group called the General Council of Local Union Churches, based in Saskatchewan. Both the Methodist and Presbyterian churches had played important roles in Toronto life. Since the early 1870s, the Metropolitan Church at the corner of Queen and Church streets had been "the Cathedral Church of Methodism in Canada."

As elsewhere, not all members of the Toronto congregations involved supported the new scheme. After much discussion, the formal unification process began with a private member's bill in the federal Parliament. On May 1, 1924, the front page of the *Globe* reported: "PARLIAMENT IS BESIEGED BY CITIZENS INTERESTED IN CHURCH UNION."

As the process evolved, church members acquired democratic rights to vote on the issue. Headlines from the *Star* in December 1924 sketched the resulting controversy: "WHO WILL HAVE VOTE ON QUESTION OF CHURCH UNION?"; "ANTI-UNION LEADERS ASSURE RALLIES THAT STRONG NUCLEUS WILL REMAIN"; "1,307 OF 1,603 PASTORS ENTER UNITED CHURCH"; "CHURCH ELDERS SIT VERY LATE ON VOTER'S LIST."

The voting, scheduled to take place over a six-month period, began early in December. Finally, on June 10, 1925, the United Church of Canada was officially established. It held the first meeting of its General Council at Toronto's Metropolitan Church.

The new denomination was the largest Protestant sect in the country. Had all the Presbyterians joined, it would have been the largest in the capital city of Ontario as well. A substantial body of the old Scottish "Kirk," however, saw the union movement as a form of Methodist imperialism and remained aloof. In the late 1920s, the Anglican Church – truest spiritual home of Tory Toronto – was still the single largest religious group in the city.

In the middle of the 1920s a further dimension to the union movement became evident. This was a local variation on the Protestant ethic and the spirit of capitalism – yet another approach to wooing good times. A January 1925 headline in the *Daily Star* declared: "CHURCH UNION SPELLS BETTER ECONOMIC LIFE."

TORONTO DURING THE FRENCH REGIME

While the church union issue was grabbing headlines, another academic figure was quietly working on a book that, like Innis's, would not be published until the 1930s. Percy Robinson taught Latin at St. Andrew's private school for boys in Aurora. But he had more ardent avocational interests in painting and local history.

He was a good enough amateur painter to exhibit on a few occasions with the Group of Seven. His local historical interest concerned the Toronto region before the establishment of the British North American town of York.

In his view the era began with Samuel de Champlain's adventures west of the Ottawa River in 1615 and ended with the arrival of John Graves Simcoe on the northwestern shore of Lake Ontario, in the summer of 1793. The title of Percy Robinson's eventual book would be *Toronto during the French Regime*.

Robinson's historical research would make clear that there had been far more Huron, Iroquois, Mississauga, and Ojibwa

Though Toronto's own French Canadian population was not large in the 1920s, everyone in the city knew that Quebec was a different part of Canada. (November 1924)

than French and *Canadiens* in the Toronto region during the French regime. In fact, his book-in-progress might have been more accurately called "French and Indian Toronto." It would trace the same multiracial themes that Harold Innis was uncovering in the Canadian fur trade.

Yet the city's French history had not ended with the British town of York. Especially since the late nineteenth century, substantial numbers of French Canadians had migrated from Quebec. By the end of the First World War, Toronto's French Canadian population was as large as its Italian community.

Ontario and Quebec had also lived through an exotic collective experience during the quarter-century before the Canadian Confederation of 1867. One result was that Toronto in the 1920s had a Catholic separate school system, partly supported by public funds. Catholic Torontonians with Irish, Italian, Polish, and other backgrounds took advantage of the separate schools. So did descendants of the French Canadians whose electoral strength had won the schools in the first place, when Ontario and Quebec were a single province in the middle of the nineteenth century.

In some Ontario separate schools of the 1920s, French-language education had become an issue of the day. The issue flowed from the prohibition of French as a language of instruction beyond the third year of elementary school, as prescribed in the Ontario Department of Education's "Regulation 17" of 1912. In January 1924 the *Globe* ran an editorial on "FRENCH IN THE SCHOOLS."

In June 1924 the *Canadian Forum*, a high-minded journal of opinion founded at the University of Toronto in 1920, published an article on the "possibility of a Separatist movement in French Canada." It reviewed a recent book from Quebec that advocated "a sovereign American French state" after the inevitable eventual fall of the British Empire.

The authors of the book envisioned that the geography of the new French state would include the Maritime provinces. Elsewhere, as Quebec separatists saw it, "Ontario and the West are progressing steadily and surely, consciously or unconsciously, toward annexation to the United States."

HOLY BLOSSOM AND ITS HEIRS

After June 1925 Roman Catholics made up the fourth-largest religious group in Toronto – following the Anglicans, the new United Church members, and the dissident Presbyterians. After the Catholics the fifth-largest group was the Jewish community.

In the eyes of census statisticians, "Jewish" – like "Chinese" – was both a religious orientation and a "racial origin." In the federal census of 1911 the racial origin of what Stephen Speisman's much later book would call *The Jews of Toronto* had been identified as Jewish; for some reason this was changed to "Hebrew" in the censuses of 1921 and 1931.

However it was officially described, in 1921 Toronto's Jewish community included almost 35,000 people. By 1931 it would have grown to more than 45,000. This amounted to somewhat less than 7 percent of the total population in 1921, and rather more than 7 percent in 1931. Except for the 1930s, the relative demographic weight of the city's Jewish community in the 1920s was greater than it has ever been since. It was also greater than it had ever been before.

The early twentieth-century history of the Jews of Toronto is notable in another sense. It foreshadowed what would happen to the wider population of the metropolis throughout the rest of the twentieth century. By the 1920s the Jewish community in the city of churches had become the largest and most influential pioneer of cultural diversity in the old Toronto the Good.

There had been some Jews in the city since the first half of the nineteenth century. Most members of "the old community" had roots in the United Kingdom. A few early German and other continental Europeans quickly blended in. In the beginning, the Jews of Toronto were British, like almost everyone else.

The old community's main institutional arm was Holy Blossom Synagogue, though the congregation did not officially adopt the name Holy Blossom until the early 1870s. The synagogue had started in the middle of the nineteenth century, over a drugstore at Yonge and Richmond. By the 1920s it was housed in an impressive structure on Bond Street, with vaguely Middle Eastern turrets and façade.

Historically, the old community was concentrated almost entirely between Yonge and Parliament, south of Bloor. A few of its members were unusually prosperous. Most were merchants and small businessmen. According to Speisman, the Jewish image they projected to the city at large was "English-speaking and Anglophile, cultured and middle class."

All this had helped give Toronto's earliest Jewish history benign overtones. Holy Blossom Synagogue seemed a natural complement to the city's British colonial culture. "The relationship between the old community and non-Jews was nothing less than cordial," Speisman tells us. "Whatever anti-semitism existed in Toronto ... remained latent so long as the principal Jewish image was projected by Holy Blossom."

By the 1920s, however, the benign cast of local Jewish life had changed, and the community was emerging from a generation of culture shock. In the late nineteenth century, Toronto had become a destination for Jewish refugees from eastern Europe, especially from Poland and Russia. In the first two decades of the twentieth century their numbers had increased, dramatically and suddenly. Often they did not speak English when they arrived in Toronto. They were not Anglophiles. With roots in the ghettoes of eastern European cities, they were not middle class either. The old Jewish community of Toronto had some trouble adjusting to "the new community." The Anglo-Protestant majority had still more.

Like other early non-British groups, at first the new community was attracted to the downtown Ward area between Yonge and University, north of Queen and south of College. As it became more established, it began to move west. By the 1920s the historic Toronto Jewish scene, with its heartland in the Spadina Avenue and Kensington Market areas, was in full bloom.

Where possible, new-community Jews preferred to work for themselves or for other Jews. The early garment industry in Toronto, a kind of branch plant of similar businesses in both Montreal and New York, owed much to Jews from eastern Europe. The new community's working-class culture helped bring continental European conceptions of socialism to the city as well.

New synagogues, quite different from Holy Blossom, took root. Goel Tzedec, erected on University Avenue as early as 1907, signalled that the new community had begun to arrive in style. As Toronto's Jewish population grew by leaps and bounds in the early twentieth century, there would be many more such institutions. After the opening of Beth Jacob in 1922, a notorious headline in the *Telegram* bemoaned "ANOTHER NEW SYNAGOGUE."

The increasing demographic weight of the new community prompted a flowering of other Jewish institutions. Toronto's

The Nordheimers were old-community Jews who had settled in Toronto in the 1840s. Samuel Nordheimer married into the city's Anglican elite in the 1870s. Eventually he became, as Stephen Speisman has put it, "so assimilated ... that he was regarded as a Gentile." (November 1923)

original "Jewish Y" – the YM/YWHA – was established in 1921. In 1922 the Standard Theatre, a Yiddish playhouse that succeeded the earlier Lyric Theatre in the Ward, opened on Spadina Avenue. The Mount Sinai Hospital – "the only kosher hospital in Canada" – started up the same year (though it would not actually borrow its name from the original Mount Sinai Hospital in New York City until 1923). In December 1925 the Brunswick Avenue Talmud Torah opened its doors. It was the city's first major Hebrew educational centre. And it was housed in an impressive new building.

THE KU KLUX KLAN

By this point the old community had more or less made its peace with the new one. The sheer demographic weight of the east European Jews left no real choice. The Anglophile Holy Blossom could no longer be the prime exponent of Judaism in Toronto.

In the wider city the new community's increasing demographic weight triggered a sad symbiosis between anti-Semitic sentiment and the new realism of the 1923 Chinese Immigration Act. Toronto's Jewish population had almost doubled between 1911 and 1921. Throughout the 1920s there would be well over four times as many Jews as Italians in the city. For the Anglo-Protestant majority, this was unprecedented.

A new kind of hostility gained a new degree of public acceptance. In September 1924 the *Telegram* actually proposed a Jewish poll tax, to discourage further immigration. The *Star* attacked the proposal as a "Gross Libel" that "does not represent Toronto opinion." But the controversy did not end. In 1925 a local group that called itself the Ku Klux Klan organized to combat the "propaganda" both "of the Roman Catholics and of the Jews."

Rabbi Brickner of Holy Blossom correctly predicted that "the good sense of our Protestant neighbours in Toronto" would turn a deaf ear to the likes of the Ku Klux Klan. But the old cordiality between Jews and non-Jews had been severely strained by the dramatic increase in the Jewish population. In Speisman's diplomatic language, a new "latent anti-semitism and subtle discrimination" took root and "continued to exist ... despite all attempts to eradicate them."

Am I My Brother's Keeper?

The Tragic Story
of the Jewish Children of Europe

Hundreds of Thousands of Jewish Children Are Starving

Their sunken eyes, distended stomachs, their pipe-stem legs, are evidence of the final stages of starvation.

They cry for food—cry in the monotone voice of a starving child, repeating BREAD, BREAD, BREAD, BREAD, until those who hear them are driven almost to distraction.

These children are loved as are your own children—

Children who are just as precious to their parents as are yours to you—

We fathers and mothers who are blessed with happy, healthy children—

We sons and daughters who have never suffered the pangs of hunger—

Are We to Let These Children Die?

Would we let them die if they were in Canada?

NO!—A thousand times NO!—comes the answer like a roar from thousands of voices.

Then let us send this answer back across the water to those unfortunates who, for the past twelve years, have suffered and starved as at no other time in their history.

The United Jewish Campaign—Oct. 18 to 23

TORONTO'S SHARE:
One Hundred Thousand Dollars

HEADQUARTERS:
78 Queen Street West, Toronto, Ont.

I hereby subscribe to the UNITED JEWISH CAMPAIGN OF TORONTO the sum of .... Dollars ($)

Payable as follows ....

Signed ....

Business Address ....

Residence ....

Cheques are made payable to Edmund Scheuer, Treasurer, United Jewish Campaign, 78 Queen St. West, Toronto, Ont.

SIR WILLIAM MULOCK, K.C.M.G.
Honorary Chairman

EDMUND SCHEUER
Treasurer

ABRAHAM COHEN
Secretary

CHARLES DRAIMIN
Chairman

M. H. EPSTEIN
Associate Chairman

RABBI FERDINAND ISSERMAN
Provincial Secretary

The chancellor of the University of Toronto, Sir William Mulock, who was not Jewish, served as honorary chairman of this 1926 campaign.

In other ways, Toronto the Good remained at least not too bad. By the 1920s the new Jewish community had begun to make inroads into local political life. In this as in other respects the east Europeans abandoned an earlier *noblesse oblige*, as practised by the Anglophiles at Holy Blossom.

The city's first Jewish alderman, Joseph Singer, had been elected in the revolutionary year of 1919. Nathan Phillips made his first youthful appearance as an alderman in 1924 – the year of Tommy Church's first defeat. After a long seasoning, he would become "the mayor of all the people" in 1955 (and the first mayor of Toronto I actually remember from my own youth). In 1925 Mount Sinai Hospital began to receive funding from Howard Ferguson's Ontario provincial government.

In all this, there were some subtle – but positive – forms of discrimination at work. In a new strand of the traditional local ambiguity and irony, the new community had cut its first political teeth in the old Orange political machine of Tory Toronto. Despite the reservations of his friends at the *Telegram*, the east European Jews in the near west-end wards three and four were among the voters Tommy Church could count on. In 1929 E.F. Singer would win the Toronto riding of St. Andrews for Fergie's Conservatives, becoming the first Jewish member of the Ontario Legislative Assembly. Much later, the same ironic tradition would take Allan and then Larry Grossman to the highest places in Ontario provincial politics. Though Toronto has never been perfect, for anyone, in the end even the new-community Jews would become part of the mainstream in the city's public life. They were new pioneers, on a new frontier.

Starting a race at the Broadview Y. (May 1925)

CHAPTER FIVE

THE BOOM BEGINS

Luck was with Toronto in the middle of the 1920s. Just as conflict over the new east European Jewish community was taking on dark edges, the rising young metropolis was distracted by brighter events.

On Monday, November 3, 1924, less than two months after the *Telegram*'s Jewish poll tax proposal, the James Fisher advertising agency ran a buoyant ad in the *Globe*. It showed a sun rising above the confident caption: "The dawn of better times." At last a new boom was at the door – brief, as it turned out, but resounding.

Many of the new elements in the life of the city had begun to chafe against one another by the end of the First World War. There was much potential for fresh forms of conflict. Hard economic times helped cultivate diverse feelings of cultural, political, and social grievance – among minorities and majorities alike.

In November 1924 the appeals of a local Ku Klux Klan group still lay ahead, but as Rabbi Brickner predicted, most Torontonians would ignore them. On February 26, 1925, the *Globe* ran an editorial headed "KKK NOT WANTED." For the time being, the city's most troubling new problems would drown in a flood of economic growth.

NEWSPRINT AND WHEAT

The boom had been approaching for some time. January 1924 headlines had proclaimed: "LARGE NEWSPRINT EXPORTS CREATE HEALTHY CONDITION IN BIG CANADIAN INDUSTRY." Much of the newsprint came from the forests of the Canadian Shield, and most of it was going to the United States. The increasingly buoyant U.S. economy was starting to pull Canada along.

Another event early in 1925 boosted a part of the Canadian economy that did not depend on the United States. Towards the end of January the price of wheat on international markets skyrocketed to record levels. This was good news for the still quite new Prairie provinces of western Canada. It was good news too for central Canada; prosperous wheat farmers in the West had fresh appetites for the agricultural machinery manufactured by Massey-Harris in Brantford and Toronto.

In February 1925 Maple Leaf Mills in Toronto arranged to sell over 1.6 million barrels of Canadian flour to the new government in the Soviet Union. A few days before, an article in the *Globe* had clarified the general point. According to experts in the imperial metropolis, "CANADA HAS TURNED TOWARD EXPANSION." British authorities were stressing the "recovery of the West," which "naturally opens up better prospects for the industrial East."

More headlines in the press for the first two months of the new year began to fill the story out: "GEO. WESTON SALESMEN SEE OPTIMISTIC TREND"; "BOOT, SHOE INDUSTRY IN HEALTHY STATE"; "BUSINESS MACHINE MEN SEE GREAT YEAR AHEAD"; "STEEL OF CANADA MOVES UP SHARPLY"; "GOOD TIMES AHEAD IS CHEERFUL WORD TO HARDWARE MEN"; "FINANCIAL FORECASTER SEES BOOM FOR DOMINION THROUGHOUT YEAR."

MCLAUGHLIN-BUICK

Toronto's immediate hinterland had its own powerful engine of recovery. As early as 1922 the new mass-production automobile industry had begun to drive the boom in the United States. Southern Ontario had acquired a Canadian share of the business, and after something of a false start in 1922 and 1923, Canada joined in on the U.S. auto boom in 1925.

A few strictly indigenous Canadian automobile manufacturers had appeared during the late nineteenth and early twentieth centuries. "The Russell," for instance, was produced in

Toronto before the First World War. Geographically, however, Ontario was only a northern extremity of the manufacturing belt south of the Great Lakes. In the end, it would not be able to resist the new industrial power in Detroit.

In August 1904 Gordon MacGregor, president of the

THE · BUILDING · OF · THE · DOMINION

DO YOU KNOW That through its organization and services on land and sea, the Canadian Pacific probably took a larger share in the Great War, and in more various ways than any other Corporation outside Great Britain itself, and proved its supreme value as an Imperial line of communication between East and West.

Battlements of Business–TORONTO

HERE is the focal point, the very heart of the industrial, commercial and financial activities of the wealthy Province of Ontario.

Here, in concrete and steel, is expressed the spirit of progress which typifies this great business centre.

More than half the manufactured products of the Dominion, and 26 per cent of Canada's field crops come from the Province of which Toronto is the political and commercial capital.

The stately Queen City, under the friendly spur of competition from a score of flourishing Ontario cities, affords a fine example of efficiency in manufacturing and trading.

Toronto is a distributing point of more than provincial importance. Her commerce extends to those vast territories, East and West, reached by the Canadian Pacific. The products of her factories go beyond Canada's shores to markets of the world. So widespread are her activities that Transportation that "spans the world" has become a vital factor in Toronto's future. There is a bond of common interest linking the activities of the Queen City with the greatest of the world's carriers — The Canadian Pacific.

CANADIAN PACIFIC
It Spans the World

By the middle of the 1920s Toronto was polishing its image as a business city. (February 1925)

Walkerville Wagon Company, signed an agreement with Henry Ford. MacGregor's firm was just outside Windsor, Ontario, across the river from Detroit. In October 1904 the Ford Motor Company of Canada started to manufacture cars in the Walkerville Wagon plant. This was only the beginning of a potent trend. By the 1920s the Canadian automobile industry had become the most comprehensive expression of the U.S. branch-plant syndrome extant.

As it evolved over the two decades after the founding of Ford Canada, the industry did retain some strictly Canadian content. Probably the best-known and longest-lived case was the McLaughlin-Buick, produced in Oshawa, Ontario, and recurrently advertised in the 1920s as "Canada's Standard Car." In 1908 the McLaughlin Carriage Company of Oshawa had established the McLaughlin Motor Car Company. It began to build Canadian automobiles using Buick engines, by arrangement with the U.S. interests that were establishing General Motors. In 1915, the McLaughlin family enterprise in Oshawa began to produce Chevrolets in Canada as well. In 1918 the enterprise was reorganized as a full-fledged subsidiary of General Motors in the United States, and renamed General Motors of Canada, with R.S. "Sam" McLaughlin as president.

General Motors of Canada would continue to produce the "ever popular" McLaughlin-Buick until the Second World War. Legend has it that one of the Canadian vehicles was once left standing outside the parent company's New York office. When GM executive Alfred P. Sloan saw it, he commanded that it be sent back to Canada: "It's gathering crowds, and it's no more like one of our Buicks than a St. Bernard is like a Daschund."

The Toronto service sector gained a lot from the branch-plant automobile industry in southern Ontario, even though much of the raw production was in the Windsor region, close to Detroit. Oshawa, on the other hand, fell under Toronto's more immediate urban shadow. While Ford Canada's main facilities were in Windsor (originally in a Windsor suburb known as Ford, Ontario), the company opened a Toronto assembly plant in October 1923. And throughout the 1920s Durant Motors of Canada Ltd. – the Canadian branch of a new firm established by the ousted original founder of General Motors in the U.S. –

produced cars in the new suburban town of Leaside.

One reason for locating some production in Ontario's capital city was the growth of its local automobile market. According to *Might's Directory*, there were some 32,000 cars and 6,200 trucks in Toronto in 1921. By the end of 1925 this had jumped to more than 63,000 cars and 8,500 trucks. By the end of the 1920s there would be more than 104,600 cars and 14,200 trucks in the city.

By the early months of 1925, aggressive efforts to expand the size of the market through price reductions were afoot. Overland, Packard, Studebaker, and Willys-Knight all advertised major price reductions during January and February. Duggan Motors at 619–623 Yonge Street offered a Ford Coupe for $760.88, or $257.88 down and $43.50 a month.

At the end of February the *Globe* ran a special automobile feature. It began: "With winter on the wain and the advent of the long, bright sunshiny days, one's thoughts naturally turn to the great open spaces along the broad highways – the long, swift, invigorating drive to the country with the picnic basket – visits to the babbling brook and pleasant evening drives about town." To help pay for the broad highways that made visits to the babbling brook possible, Howard Ferguson's Ontario government introduced the province's first gasoline tax in 1925.

The Canadian federal government had established a subsidy program for highway development in 1919, but money was running out. Fortunately, as reported by the *Globe* on Wednesday, February 25, 1925, Ottawa "WILL EXTEND TIME FOR HIGHWAY WORK / TWO YEARS IN WHICH PROVINCES MAY EARN SHARE OF HIGHWAY UPKEEP." Canada was doing what it could to keep up with the Joneses south of the border. Two weeks earlier, the *Globe* had announced: "DELUGE OF DOLLARS IS POURED OUT IN U.S. FOR AUTO HIGHWAYS."

In 1918 there had been less than 80 miles (130 kilometres) of hard-surfaced roads in Ontario. By the late 1920s the figure would rise to some 2,400 miles (or 3,800 kilometres).

Inside Toronto, pleasant evening drives about town could be dangerous. According to a report in the *Star*, in 1924 "55 people were killed or died from injuries received from automobiles on the streets" of the city. To help keep the number of accidents down, Toronto's first traffic lights were installed at

The new boom was in sight but not quite in progress when this ad for "Canada's Standard Car" ran in September 1924.

the intersection of Bloor and Yonge streets, on August 8, 1925. Less than a month later, George Henry, provincial minister of highways, announced that all motorists in Ontario would soon be required "to take out licenses to drive."

IMPERIAL PREFERENCE

Historically, a key political ingredient in the Canadian branch-plant auto industry had been a 35 percent tariff on automobiles imported into Canada. By producing for the Canadian market at branch plants in Canada, U.S. firms could avoid the Canadian tariff. This was a legacy of the "National Policy" of Canadian economic development established by John A. Macdonald in the late nineteenth century. Though Mackenzie King's federal Liberals made some adjustments to the policy in the 1920s, its essential principles remained intact.

Given the country's small population and vast geography, it cost more to produce automobiles in Canada than in the United States. The lion's share of the production was in southern Ontario. To residents of Vancouver or Winnipeg or Halifax or even Montreal, it was all too easy to see the National Policy as a scheme by which the rest of Canada paid artificially high prices for such things as automobiles – to provide southern Ontario with a more affluent lifestyle than it deserved.

All this helped heighten feelings of regional grievance in the wider Confederation. The June 1924 issue of the *Canadian Forum* that reported on early separatist rumblings in Quebec also discussed prospects for a secessionist movement in western Canada.

Yet if the small Canadian market had been all that the Canadian automobile industry could rely on, the industry would not have played so strong a role in the Toronto boom. Another key ingredient in the development policy that had evolved by the end of the nineteenth century was "Imperial Preference." This was a different sort of tariff instrument intended to promote privileged access for Canadian-made products in the global markets of the British Empire. When Ford Canada was established in 1904, its mandate was to produce automobiles for sale not just in Canada, but in "the rest of the British Empire" as well. Other U.S. branch plants would have similar mandates. As Harold Innis would explain in the concluding sections of his book on the fur trade, Canada "participated in the industrial growth of the United States, becoming the gateway of that country to the markets of the British Empire."

On Thursday, May 1, 1924, the *Globe* in Toronto reported that in the most recent past "HALF OF AUTOS PRODUCED WERE FOR BRITISH MARKET." Several months later, in September, another headline stressed: "MOTOR CAR EXPORTS SHOW MARKED GAIN ... ALMOST EVERY PART OF THE BRITISH EMPIRE IS REPRESENTED IN THE LIST OF DESTINATIONS OF CANADIAN CARS."

This economic fact was an element in the logic behind Fergie's 1920s textbooks for Ontario schools that so ardently stressed the virtues of British imperial civilization. It also helped give residents of southern Ontario a material interest in the domestic politics of the United Kingdom.

Ramsay Macdonald's early British Labour government was a particular concern, since it did not share the enthusiasm for imperial preference shown by its Conservative opponents. On Thursday, October 30, 1924, the *Evening Telegram* in Toronto had an extra reason for being pleased to announce that "SOCIALISM SWEPT FROM POWER BY BRITISH ELECTORS." It made the point explicit in another headline: "TORY VICTORY IN BRITAIN TO REVIVE PREFERENCE TALK."

As the boom gathered strength, the combination of Canadian and British Empire markets took the Canadian branch-plant auto industry to new heights. The General Motors of Canada track record suggests the wonders that were worked. The firm had produced somewhat less than 35,000 automobiles in 1924. This would rise to some 45,000 in 1925, 57,000 in 1926, 91,000 in 1927, 102,000 in 1928, and 104,000 in 1929.

In 1929 the Canadian automobile industry as a whole would produce "a phenomenal 262,000 passenger cars and trucks." This made it the second-largest automobile industry in the world – well behind the United States, but ahead of each of France, the United Kingdom, and Germany.

NORTHERN MINING

On Saturday, January 31, 1925, another powerful regional engine of growth was hinted at in the *Star*. An anonymous columnist known as "The Observer" (in fact the progressive

Today Canadians may purchase cars built by General Motors of Canada at lower prices, which are largely the result of an ever increasing export trade.

Totalling over $65,000,000 for the past five years, these exports absorb a substantial proportion of General Motors of Canada production.

They swell that production to a point far beyond the possible demands of our home market alone.

They permit volume-buying that would otherwise be out of the question.

They justify large-scale methods that could otherwise not be employed.

They allow efficiency economies that could otherwise not be practiced.

They have reduced the cost of the luxurious Cadillac, which stands the unchallenged leader of all fine motor cars.

They have reduced the cost of Canada's standard car, the prized McLaughlin-Buick, a worthy memorial to the great Canadian industrial pioneer whose name it bears.

They have reduced the cost of the Canadian Oakland . . . winning and holding good will.

They have reduced the cost of the Oldsmobile built in Canada . . . the car that asks no favors—fears no road.

They have reduced the cost of the Pontiac, Chief of the Sixes.

They have reduced the cost of the astonishing Canadian-built Chevrolet . . . so smooth, so powerful.

A dollar here, a dollar there . . . hundreds from this, hundreds from that . . . thousands saved in materials, thousands in operating costs . . . millions and millions in all—millions gained by exports . . . millions saved for You!

GENERAL MOTORS of CANADA, LIMITED, OSHAWA, ONTARIO

The Millions *Gained* by Export are Millions *saved* for You!

CADILLAC CHEVROLET
McLAUGHLIN-BUICK
OLDSMOBILE
OAKLAND PONTIAC

GENERAL MOTORS *of* CANADA *Limited*

Malta and Bombay, India, were parts of the British Empire where these Canadian-made automobiles were sent in the 1920s. (September 1926)

United Church clergyman Salem Bland) published a short piece entitled "THE GROUP OF SEVEN AND THE CANADIAN SOUL." It declared: "Probably there is in Canada a larger proportion of people than in any other country of modern civilization who delight in the wilderness."

There were economic as well as aesthetic motivations mixed in with the delight. They could be witnessed on the floor of Toronto's Standard Mining Exchange. On Saturday, January 3, 1925, the *Star* announced: "BIG DOINGS SEEN ON STANDARD EXCHANGE." The place was one of two stock exchanges in the Toronto of the 1920s. It had been established in 1908; its older brother, the Toronto Stock Exchange, had its origins in the middle of the nineteenth century. Mining investments, however, were highly speculative. Their promoters thrived on big risks. They had their own financing habits and their own financial institution. In the last half of the 1920s the Standard Mining Exchange helped bring the high adventure of prospecting in the northern wilderness into Canada's second-largest city.

During the late nineteenth century, Queen's Park had begun to promote a new agricultural settlement frontier, on the Clay Belts of the Canadian Shield in northern Ontario. Northern farming would never amount to much, but the Shield proved to be a treasure house for virtually every known economic mineral, with the exception of coal and tin. Copper, gold, nickel, and silver were especially abundant.

While the work of prospecting and constructing new mines took place in northern Ontario, the major financing and servicing for the enterprise was in Toronto. Mining in northern Ontario would turn Toronto into a financial centre with sophistication and depth.

On Tuesday, February 10, 1925, the *Globe* reported: "NORTHERN ONTARIO MINES OPEN YEAR AT PACE WHICH PROMISES TO OUTDISTANCE CONSIDERABLY FORMER YEARS' RECORD." On February 17 sales on the Standard Mining Exchange set "a new high record for the year to date, and also for some years back." On February 18 it was announced that "KIRKLAND LAKE MINES PROFITS ARE HIGHER." Before 1924 "the net profits from the Kirkland Lake field never reached $1,000,000 for a single year." Activity during the early part of 1925 was proceeding "at a rate which exceeds $2,750,000 a year."

In 1923 the annual value of mineral production in Ontario had amounted to some $72 million. By 1929 the figure would have risen to $117 million. Though some of the biggest financial action went to New York, Toronto was the channel through which most of the extra dollars flowed. Many got stuck – and fuelled the local boom.

BONNE ENTENTE

The optimistic mood of early 1925 helped turn the city's attention to some higher-minded concerns. The Ontario government's Regulation 17, which limited the use of French in the province's schools, had been a sore point in Quebec – ever since its introduction in 1912.

Conscription for service in the First World War had roused ancient passions among French Canadians. Then there were the early rumblings of Quebec separatism in the June 1924 *Canadian Forum.* More practically, a controversy had recently arisen over mining development along the border between northern Ontario and Quebec.

Late in January 1925 Howard Ferguson led a delegation of "churchmen, statesmen, business men and leading citizens" from "all parts of Toronto" on what the press described as "another bonne entente pilgrimage" to the lower St. Lawrence valley. The objective was to "GO FAR TO REMOVE POSSIBILITY OF FRICTION" between the two "sister provinces" of central Canada.

The leadership of French-speaking Quebec extended a warm welcome. Several French-language newspapers printed greetings in English. Premier Taschereau allowed that there were "differences of opinion and points of view between our provinces," but "Who will deny that on fiscal policy we stand on the same ground?"

In spite of all these good intentions, little immediate progress was made on substantive issues. Fergie stressed that "during the past five years" Queen's Park had spent "nearly half a million dollars" on French-language education, but he would not promise to abolish Regulation 17. (Before the new boom had run its course, however, Regulation 17 would disappear.)

At the January 1925 meeting, some members of the Toronto press were struck by the ability of leading francophone Quebecers to speak English. Among all 200 Ontario delegates only the Roman Catholic archbishop of Toronto, Neil McNeil, managed to address the leading Quebecers in more or less fluent French.

Early in February 1925 A.E. Kirkpatrick asked a meeting of the Toronto East Liberal Association to "imagine what fine position Canadian business men would be in 20 years from now if Canadians spoke French and English with the same facility that Quebec public men now speak the two languages." Yet, for the most part, imaginings of this sort would remain only pious aspirations (as they still are, albeit to a lesser degree, even in Toronto today). Two days after Kirkpatrick's talk, the *Globe* ran an article headlined "RADIO WILL MAKE ENGLISH LANGUAGE THE UNIVERSAL TONGUE."

BRAZILIAN TRACTION AND THE CNE

The brightest hopes of late 1924 and early 1925 were not immediately gratified. Yet by early September 1925 there could be no doubt that a big new boom had arrived.

One indicator was a bold revival in the fortunes of what had become the leading survivor of Sir William Mackenzie's old empire. The Brazilian Traction Light and Power Company had been created in 1912. It was an amalgamation of assorted energy and transportation enterprises in Brazil that Sir William had been assembling since 1899. Under new management, it had weathered both the collapse of his personal career in the early 1920s and his death in 1923.

By the late summer of 1925 Brazilian Traction had become the brightest star on the local business scene. On Labour Day – Monday, September 7 – the *Globe* enthused: "BRAZILIAN SHARES CONTINUE TO CLIMB." The stock had risen "to new heights since 1914 when it sold for up to 74 3/4 in extremely brisk trading during the Saturday session on the Toronto Stock Exchange."

On the same day some 204,500 people attended the Canadian National Exhibition. It was the biggest Labour Day crowd the Ex had ever known. A record 18,000 automobiles were parked on the grounds – said to be "the largest assembly of cars ever gathered together at one time in Canada." An enterprising reporter counted "license plates of 36 states in the Union and of every province in the Dominion, except British Columbia and Prince Edward Island."

Other early September headlines confirmed the message: "CANADA BETTERS TRADE BALANCE BY $59,575,374 IN 12 MONTHS";

Mining in northern Ontario also created jobs at financial enterprises like Nesbitt Thomson in Toronto. (May 1926)

"PURCHASING POWER GREATER THAN EVER / ONTARIO FINANCIERS RETURN FROM PRAIRIES WITH GLOWING REPORTS"; "GREAT STRIDES MADE BY MOTOR INDUSTRY"; "GRAIN CAR LOADINGS ECLIPSE ALL RECORDS."

FERGIE'S FOAM

By now G. Howard Ferguson had already made the first gentle but specific move in his subtle and cautious strategy for abolishing prohibition in Ontario, without abolishing his government at the same time.

As Fergie had implied earlier, the slender provincial majority favouring the Ontario Temperance Act in the October 1924 plebiscite raised some enforcement problems. More to the point, an important part of his political base – which Drury had thought he could do without – leaned on the Torontonians and their counterparts in other Ontario cities who wanted a government-controlled liquor-marketing system.

In the middle of January 1925 an editorial in the *Star* flagged the plot that was afoot. Queen's Park was conducting experiments, "laboratorical and otherwise." These would apparently demonstrate that beer with a somewhat limited 4.4 percent alcoholic content was not really intoxicating. Less than a month later, Fergie announced that, in the government's judgment, a proposal for marketing 4.4 percent beer legally was in the "interest of temperance."

Even some OTA supporters were coming to acknowledge that the act had absurd side-effects. Despite the Drury regime's repressions, more than a few doctors had continued to prescribe quart bottles of liquor generously. On February 20, 1925, the *Globe* ran an editorial on "THE YOUNG DOCTOR'S KEEPER." It revealed the case of one youthful physician whose "medical practice had returned him $345 in three months, whereas his prescription issuance in the same period had netted him $1,200."

In the early spring of 1925 Queen's Park took practical action. On May 2 a happy headline in the *Telegram* declared "BREWERIES HUSTLING ON 4.4." The new beer was put up for sale, legally, on May 21. To appease temperance advocates, the regulations for public consumption of the beverage prohibited the stand-up bar in Ontario. This would still be in effect when I started drinking beer publicly in Toronto, in the 1960s.

At first, Fergie's appeasement strategy worked well enough. On June 4, 1925, the *Mail and Empire* ran an article headlined "TEMPERANCE WORKER DEFENDS NEW BEER." By late summer, however, there were signs that legal 4.4 beer was only a halfway house on a road to grander schemes. The attorney general, W.F. Nickle, had introduced the product with great restraint. Government permits to sell it were only granted to a select few. Late in August Ferguson himself announced an end to this introductory policy.

On September 1 the *Globe* declared: "WILL ISSUE PERMITS FOR 4.4 BEER SALE TO ALL AND SUNDRY." In the premier's view, the new drink had proved "harmless." He was now ready to "wipe out Nickle's cautious restrictions." Yet concerned consumers were in all too much agreement about the harmlessness of the compromise product. It whetted the appetite without slaking the thirst. Fresh pressures for more substantial fare began to mount. In Toronto, as in other parts of Ontario, experienced drinkers took to deriding 4.4 as "Fergie's foam." By the end of 1926 it would be clear that the compromise could not endure forever – or even for very long.

MAPLE LEAF STADIUM

Only a few days after Fergie announced his determination to wipe out Nickle's restrictions on 4.4 beer, news of another imminent big change in Toronto life was in the air. On Saturday, September 5, 1925, the headlines in the newspapers declared: "MAPLE LEAF STADIUM ASSURED."

Once upon a time the city's leading summer sport had been lacrosse a kind of ice hockey without ice. According to Morley Callaghan in the 1950s, in an earlier Toronto the Minto Cup in lacrosse was "as important as the Stanley Cup is now in hockey." Yet, as Callaghan would also explain, by the 1920s lacrosse "had lost its hold on the imagination of the young." The "whole pattern of sport in Toronto had changed and got set again in those few years before the first world war. The big spectator games had become the games played most often by the school boys. Rugby in the fall, hockey in the winter, and baseball in the summer."

In baseball Toronto had a team in the International League, known as the Maple Leafs. After an early false start in the 1880s, the club had a more enduring beginning in 1895.

Beauty contest finalists at Sunnyside, August 1926 . This was the year the
baseball Leafs enjoyed their first season at the new Maple Leaf Stadium.
Like the poor man's Riviera, the new stadium had been built on "made"
land created by the Toronto Harbour Commission.

Montreal would join the league in 1928, after several earlier
false starts in the late nineteenth and early twentieth centuries.
Much later, when I was growing up in the late 1940s and early
1950s, the Havana Cubans added a more cosmopolitan dimension. Ottawa was briefly represented as well, from 1951 to 1954.

For most of the 1920s the Toronto Maple Leafs were the
only team that made the league international. There were
seven other clubs – from Baltimore, Buffalo, Jersey City,
Providence, Reading, Rochester, and Syracuse. Even then the
baseball Leafs in Toronto were mostly citizens of the U.S.A.

Until 1926 they played their home games at Hanlan's Point,
on the Toronto Island. Morley Callaghan would remember that
"those days at Hanlan's Park during the first world war and on

through the twenties" had "a warmth about them ... Riding the ferry boats across the bay was a beautiful adventure." At the Island Stadium everything was "so happy and relaxed."

By 1925 the city was ready for something new. On September 5 the *Globe* reported that "next season the Leafs will play their games in a magnificent $300,000 stadium on the mainland at the foot of Bathurst Street, on 'made' land acquired from the Toronto Harbor Commission."

In Callaghan's view this was a great mistake. The baseball Leafs ought to have stayed on the Island. Judgments of this sort depend on when (or perhaps where) you grew up. One of my own vivid memories of Toronto in the early 1950s is my first night baseball game at Maple Leaf Stadium, between the Leafs and the Havana Cubans. It was dark in the stands. The field was brightly lit. The Cubans were exciting. The place seemed magical to me.

Nothing I have experienced at today's state-of-the-art SkyDome has quite lived up to this first thrill. Maple Leaf Stadium was an early flower of the boom in the last half of the 1920s. It would be demolished in 1968. I think it, like Sunnyside, deserved a happier fate – a judgment that only shows when I grew up myself.

THE ADVERTISING AGE

Two days after the announcement of Maple Leaf Stadium's imminent construction, on Monday, September 7, 1925, an ad headed "Open Letter No. 19" appeared in the local newspapers. It was addressed to "W.L.M. King," prime minister of Canada, from "J.J. Gibbons, President, J.J. Gibbons, Advertising Agents."

The ad was part of a series whose underlying theme was the importance of strong tariffs for Canada's economic growth. The series reflected a wider trend. By the middle of the 1920s Toronto was becoming the centre of Canada's English-language advertising industry.

Montreal would remain the undisputed Canadian economic capital until after the Second World War. The first advertising agency in the country had opened there in 1889. Yet, though the old Montreal business community worked in English, it lived in a society where the majority spoke French. Since

Ontario had the largest anglophone market in Canada, as an English Canadian advertising industry began to take root, it logically gravitated towards Ontario's capital city.

In May 1924 the James Fisher agency had run an elegant-looking newspaper ad in Toronto, addressed "TO MANUFACTURERS LONGING FOR NORMAL TIMES." This was part of another extended series, culminating with the buoyant "DAWN OF BETTER TIMES" in November. In February 1925, at the height of the year's first wave of optimism over the new boom, the Fisher agency took out a full-page ad in the *Globe*. It presented photographs of the firm's leading staff, under the forthright headline "READY TO SERVE BIG BUSINESS."

James Fisher and J.J. Gibbons were not alone. Toronto's first full-service professional firm, the Mason Advertising Agency, was established in 1892. According to *Might's Directory*, in 1920 there were ten advertising agencies in the city. The number would increase to thirty-four by 1929.

A few of these were Canadian branches of U.S. firms. Most Toronto advertising agencies of the 1920s, however, were indigenous Canadian organizations. They had a vested interest in an enterprise that would be described in an October 1928 *New York Sun* editorial entitled "CANADA BUILDING A NATION."

The Toronto advertising industry of the 1920s was even a force of sorts for early English Canadian cultural nationalism. It helped support the city's graphic arts industry and paid some bills for the Group of Seven. It helped support the city's printing and publishing industry, including magazines like *Maclean's* and *Saturday Night*. It also helped support early Canadian radio. In 1920, when Harold Innis was trying to explain Toronto to his future wife from Wilmette, Illinois, he told her it was "the literary centre of Canada if not the industrial centre." The city's advertising business did a lot to give this distinction economic muscle.

Geographically, the industry of the mid- to late 1920s was concentrated on the fringes of the downtown business district. The most popular office locations were Richmond, King, Bay, Adelaide, Victoria, and Wellington streets. By the late 1920s several agencies that would have important subsequent histories had appeared. Along with James Fisher and J.J. Gibbons, the list included Clark E. Locke Ltd., Cockfield, Brown & Company Ltd., and F.H. Hayhurst & Company. The cultural weight of the

Toronto advertising industry of the day is also reflected in a Morley Callaghan novel set in the city of the early 1930s. A fictional agency called Hillquist and Aikenhead appears in *They Shall Inherit the Earth*, first published in 1934.

The "Canadian market" advertising industry in Toronto, hard at work promoting itself. (September 1925)

MURRAY-KAY'S GOODBYE TO KING STREET

The resurgent economy was good news for advertising agencies. It also ought to have been good news for the local retailers who sold new products for Standard Electric Homes. For many it was. But just as a fresh burst of prosperity was at last taking hold, Toronto's oldest big department retailer disappeared.

The Murray-Kay Dry Goods Store, at King and Victoria streets in the heart of the old downtown, had roots in the era extending back before Confederation. In the 1920s it was still calling itself "the shopping 'Mecca' of fashionable people."

In the nineteenth century, King Street had been the city's main retail strip. By the twentieth century, downtown Toronto's retail centre of gravity had begun to march northward. King was being transformed into a moderately cavernous office district, to accommodate the city's local variation on the rising corporate culture in North America.

In the late fall of 1924 Murray-Kay declared that it would be leaving its King Street store for a new location. It launched a great "Goodbye to King Street" sale. Then, quite suddenly, on January 6, 1925, the management announced that "on account of prospective excessive costs of building," it had "decided not to proceed with its plans for the erection of a new store."

Financial troubles were apparently not an issue. The business was still turning a profit, and on January 22 the press reported that Murray-Kay shareholders were likely to receive as much as $37 a share from the dissolution of the enterprise. At the end of the month the shopping Mecca of fashionable people closed down, selling its remaining stock to smaller retailers in the city. It had been part of the Toronto of Henry Pellatt and Casa Loma, William Mackenzie and the TRC, the cordial dominance of the Anglophile, old-community Jews at Holy Blossom, and baseball at the Island Stadium. By the middle of the 1920s all this was ending forever. The Murray-Kay Dry Goods Store seems to have decided that it would end forever too.

SHOPPING AT SIMPSON'S

Murray-Kay's final goodbye to King Street in the middle of the 1920s left Toronto's downtown department store scene to two enterprises established just after the Confederation of 1867. Both were north of the old King Street strip, at Queen and

Yonge. Simpson's was on the southwest corner, Eaton's on the northwest.

In 1923 the local historian J.E. Middleton had observed: "In outward semblance Toronto is an American city ... The shop windows are all dressed in the alluring New York manner." The resemblance was more than on the surface alone: in the last half of the 1920s Eaton's and Simpson's carried on a miniaturized version of the rivalry between Gimbel's and Macy's in New York.

In several respects Simpson's was the obvious lesser light. Despite additions in 1923 and 1928, its downtown Toronto complex would never quite match Eaton's. Both Eaton's and Simpson's developed chains in other parts of Canada, and here as well Simpson's would never quite equal the Eaton empire.

Simpson's had started as a small dry-goods outlet, established by the Scottish-born Robert Simpson in 1872. Over the next twenty-five years it evolved into a major department store. Unlike Eaton's, it did not remain a family business. When Robert Simpson died in 1897, the operation was sold to three Toronto magnates of the day – A.E. Ames, J.W. Flavelle, and H.H. Fudger.

Despite its smaller magnitude, Simpson's had a more upscale image than its rival. Its architecture was more impressive. Hopes for a new boom led to the addition of 1923, and booming business in 1925, 1926, and 1927 would lead to the "Greater Simpson's" enlargement of 1928. This took the store all the way from Yonge Street west to Bay, between Richmond and Queen (in the premises occupied today by the Hudson's Bay Company, which would have no stores at all in Toronto until well after the Second World War).

Like Eaton's, Simpson's published catalogues. It also offered home delivery service. Both catalogue purchases and items bought at the store could be delivered to your home. Until 1928 Simpson's deliveries were handled by horse-drawn trucks. All the horses were stylish dapple-greys. They lined up smartly with their vehicles every workday morning, on the north side of Richmond Street, just west of Yonge.

THE EATON EMPIRE

Timothy Eaton, born in Northern Ireland in 1834 (the year that the old town of York became the city of Toronto), had established his first Toronto dry-goods outlet in 1869. By the time of his death in 1907 Eaton's was more than the city's largest department store: it was doing an extensive mail-order business with the family farmers of Ontario and western Canada; it had opened a major store in Winnipeg in 1905; it manufactured many of the products it sold; and its downtown Toronto operations, including stores, offices, mail-order department, stables, and factories, dominated the area due east and north of what is now the old city hall.

City of Toronto Archives SC 266-6981

Newsboy at King and Yonge, January 1926. By this time Murray-Kay had vanished and all the big retail action was at the Queen Street intersection, three blocks north.

Eaton's was still a family business in the 1920s (as it remains even today). Timothy's son, John Craig, had taken over when Timothy died. John Craig Eaton shared Henry Pellatt's passion for the romance of the British Empire. He was knighted in 1915 as a reward for outfitting a unit known as the Eaton Machine Gun Battery in the First World War.

In 1909 John Craig purchased land near Pellatt's Casa Loma site. Here he erected a mansion called Ardwold ("high green hill" in Gaelic). Not as vast as Casa Loma, it had a mere fifty rooms, fourteen bathrooms, an indoor swimming pool, and a hospital. It would be demolished in 1936. The Eaton family, however, unlike the Pellatts, would continue to thrive economically, down to the present.

John Craig died prematurely, in his mid-forties, on March 30, 1922. His son, John David Eaton, only thirteen years old at the time, would not take official command of the T. Eaton Company until 1942. During the two decades immediately following John Craig's death, R.Y. Eaton, the son of Timothy's brother, John, acted as regent. By this point John Craig's wife, the former Flora McCrea, a nurse from Omemee, Ontario, had settled comfortably into the role of "Lady Eaton." Even after R.Y. Eaton's regency, she would serve as an influential dowager queen.

With the establishment of the Winnipeg store, Eaton's had begun to add dreams about the transcontinental Canada of Harold Innis's fur trade to John Craig's passion for the British Empire. The complete cross-Canada structure would not be completed until John David's regime in the 1940s and 1950s, but decisive steps were taken under R.Y. Eaton's regency, in the last half of the 1920s.

R.Y. began by establishing a store in Montreal in 1925. In 1926 an Eaton's store opened its doors in Regina, Saskatchewan. Stores were added in Hamilton, Ontario, and Moncton, New Brunswick, in 1927, and in Halifax, Nova Scotia, and Saskatoon, Saskatchewan, in 1928. In 1930, before it was certain that the 1929 stock market crash implied a new bust of cosmic proportions, Eaton's opened stores in Calgary and Edmonton, Alberta.

Meanwhile, back in Toronto, Eaton's had been running an annual Santa Claus Parade since 1905. As early as 1914, John Craig had purchased land on the southwest corner of Yonge and College streets. The plot was to build a new flagship store there when Toronto's retail centre of gravity moved still further north. With the boom in the last half of the 1920s, plans for a new Eaton's College Street store sprang to life.

Just as this project was under way, the 1929 crash hit. Eaton's College Street, as the business journalist Ian Brown has explained, "was halted by the Depression at a fraction of its planned magnificence." After the Second World War some would say that John Craig Eaton had misjudged just how far north the downtown retail centre of the city would move. He ought to have bought land at the corner of Yonge and Bloor, not Yonge and College.

In the 1970s, Eaton's discontinued its catalogue service. It masterminded the new Eaton Centre, which now dominates the Toronto Yonge Street corridor between Dundas and Queen. It also changed its marketing philosophy. Today it aspires to be urban Canada's upscale department store.

In Toronto during the 1920s Eaton's was a different kind of place. Its eyes were fixed on the mass market, and it had a populist edge. If you had pretensions to finer things, you could shop at Simpson's. Eaton's catered instead to cheerful, plain citizens. It was the headquarters for assiduous cultivators of the mechanized mass household.

The place had at least a few populist edges for its employees as well. Though old Timothy was a dictator, he had shown some principled concern for the welfare of his staff. The management style that had evolved by the 1920s featured a rigorous but benign paternalism. Though Eaton's was not noted for high wages, it was loyal to its employees. It pioneered local Saturday holidays. It had paid married enlisted men full pay and single enlisted men half pay during the First World War. A job at Eaton's would be a ticket to survival during the Great Depression.

In the nineteenth century, Timothy Eaton had led the family into the Methodist faith. In his time, John Craig Eaton established Timothy Eaton Memorial Church on St. Clair Avenue. (It became part of the new United Church of Canada in 1925.) Yet the T. Eaton Company demonstrated an equal appreciation for the early stirrings of cultural diversity in the city. In the 1920s it was a logical refuge for many recent migrants from the United Kingdom. It was also the largest non-Jewish employer of the increasingly numerous Jews of Toronto.

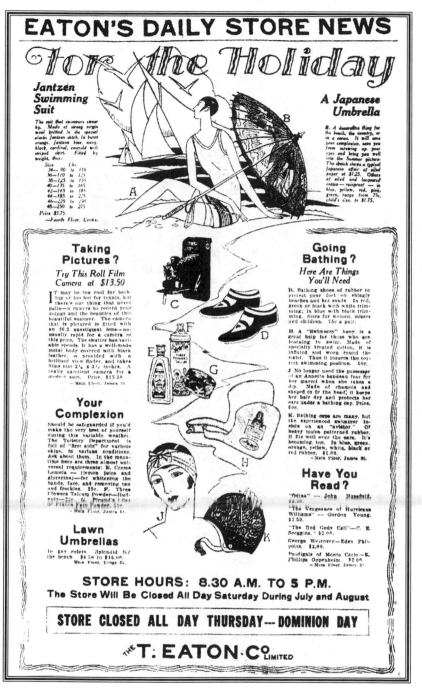

The schoolchildren's longed-for summer holidays were about to begin when this Eaton's ad ran, Tuesday, June 29, 1926.

Courtesy of the Eaton's Archives.

Toronto adding-machine staff on election night. (September 1926)

CHAPTER SIX

NATIONAL ANTHEMS

Rapid change can be upsetting, even when it's good. It can prompt a reaching back for tokens of the past. Along with early mutlicultural conflicts in the fall of 1924, this may help explain why the start of the new boom in Toronto was accompanied by a return of Tommy Church's old Orange political machine to city hall.

Church himself did not come back, but on New Year's Day 1925 twenty-five of thirty-three different municipal candidates recommended by the Orange Lodge were voted into office. The *Daily Star* gloomily announced: "ORANGE ORDER PROVED ITS REAL GOOD PICKER."

For mayor in 1925 the *Star* itself had recommended William Wesley Hiltz – the man who had handed T.L. Church his first defeat the year before. The man who won the election, however, was Thomas Foster, "the dean of city council." Hiltz became only the second chief magistrate of the city in sixty-seven years who did not win at least a second term from the voters. Foster would be elected mayor again, in 1926 and 1927.

Foster was seventy-three years old in 1925. He stressed a conservative "policy of economy and the lowest possible taxation consistent with good government, efficient operation of the civic services, and providing for the city's real needs." But his conservatism did not have any fierce ideological spirit. In his last successful mayoral campaign, he was supported by the *Globe* as well as the *Evening Telegram.* Though he had the backing of the Orange Lodge, Thomas Foster was no Tommy Church.

THE JAZZ AGE

Despite Mayor Foster's seventy-three years, the new boom helped bring the full musical sweep of "the Jazz Age" to Toronto during his regime. In September 1925 the papers were running ads for "Romanelli and his celebrated King Edward Hotel Radio Syncopaters."

Today jazz is appreciated ardently by only a few. It has even become, according to one U.S. critic, "a persecuted chamber music." Jazz in the 1920s and 1930s was much more like rock n' roll in the 1950s and 1960s – a controversial new phase in North American popular music. Another September 1925 item in the Toronto papers noted that a New York pundit "CALLS 'JAZZ' MUSIC ABOMINABLE RUMPUS." Yet even during its formative period, there was some recognition that jazz could be marking the start of a more highbrow trend. As early as March 1922 the *Mail and Empire* ran an editorial under the headline "AUTHORITIES DIFFER ON JAZZ QUESTION."

For Toronto's most popular morning paper, jazz could "contain the germ of a discovery which may develop into the national music of this continent." Whatever else, it was "an attempt to combine in one piece the tom-tom incantations of the Congo, the whine of the Orient, the squeak of the Chinese pipes, the sensuous purr of Iberia, the intoxicating syncopations of the gypsy, the plectret pep of the negro's banjo, the skirl of the highlander's pipes, the Irish breakdown and the hilarious dances of the American western frontiers or the Canadian logging camps."

The *Mail and Empire* editorial also recognized that, at bottom, "jazz has been the work of the negroes." Both the small size of its black population in the 1920s and the local black community's ironic British Tory past put Toronto at a disadvantage.

Some Torontonians nonetheless bought copies of the great Hot Five recordings that Louis Armstrong made in 1925 and 1926 (with titles like "Oriental Strut" and "King of the Zulus"). Others would visit New York to see Duke Ellington at the

Get into the Swim
in an Aberley

ABERLEYS are just made to swim in ! Their snug, elastic fit allows perfect muscle freedom for every stroke. Doubles the thrill of water sports.

Aberleys are 100% pure wool, made in all sizes and in one and two-piece styles for men, women, boys and girls, in a variety of pleasing shades.

Swim in an Aberley this summer. You'll see a lot of them at the popular beaches. Ask your dealer to show you Aberleys. Aberley Knitting Mills Limited, Toronto.

Aberley

100% PURE WOOL

Form Fitting
SWIMMING SUITS

The Jazz Age was also about "Form Fitting Swimming Suits." (June 1926)

Cotton Club in Harlem, in 1927, 1928, and 1929. Black enter-
tainers from the U.S. had been visiting Toronto since the end
of the American Civil War. Morley Callaghan's first novel,
Strange Fugitive, is set in the city in the middle of the 1920s. Its
climax includes a party at a downtown hotel, with a "negro
orchestra" that "played lively jazz."

There was another, non-musical side to the Jazz Age. The
phrase symbolized a new footloose attitude to old customs,
especially among young people. It was popular parlance for a
trend summarized in more cultivated circles by "the lost generation" (a phrase put to Hemingway in Paris by Gertrude Stein).
  Toronto's local variation on the trend had already been
flagged in a *Globe* headline of January 1924: "AMENITIES OF
SOCIAL LIFE SEEM TO HAVE DISAPPEARED FROM CODE OF YOUNGER
FOLK." Apparently, "Toronto hostesses" were "discouraged by
lack of courtesy and destructive disregard for fittings of fine
homes shown by smart young society people." The Canadian
historian Donald Creighton, born in Toronto in 1902, has
reported that in the 1920s some "young men and women fell in
love" and entered into "unions unauthorized by church or state
… called 'companionate marriages.'"

ROMANELLI'S RADIO SYNCOPATERS

Live jazz in Toronto in the middle of the 1920s was mostly made
by white men who emulated black musicians from other parts
of "this continent." From a present-day purist's standpoint, it
was usually just popular dance music. But it put some smart
continental tunes into the heads of Torontonians, including
"'Aint She Sweet," "Always," "Baby Face," "Bye-Bye Blackbird,"
"Tea for Two," and "The Best Things in Life Are Free."
  In the U.S.A. Paul Whiteman – the so-called King of Jazz –
was the most successful white exponent of sanitized black
music, mixed in with the likes of "Aint She Sweet." He
appeared in Toronto in May 1924. Luigi Romanelli, who
presided over the Radio Syncopaters serenading at the King
Edward Hotel (along with his brother, Don), was strictly a local
name. He would not become as famous as Guy Lombardo and
the Royal Canadians, from London, Ontario, who started making records in the United States in 1924.
  The Romanellis did find steady local work in the booming

last half of the 1920s. In the warmer weather they made music on the pleasure boats that plied Lake Ontario off Toronto Bay. A June 1925 ad in the *Star* noted that for the "first moonlight excursion on the ss *Cayuga*" there would be "dancing to Romanelli's Orchestra." A June 1926 ad in the *Tely* announced: "Moonlight excursion tomorrow night, Romanelli's Orchestra."

A May 1927 ad in the *Mail and Empire* reported that the "season's first illumination cruise" would have "Romanelli's Orchestra on board for dancing." Now the boom was really booming. Young Torontonians were dancing in the pavilion at Sunnyside Beach. They were dancing at the "casino on the beach, Centre Island, every night ... the real smart place." And they were dancing at the Silver Slipper, on Riverside Drive in the west end – "the snappiest place in town."

THE NEW SYMPHONY

In May 1925 there were ads in the press for "Raymond Fagan and his Symphonic Dance Orchestra ... the band that all Toronto loves." By this point the city was also beginning to build its muscles for performing European classical music. A fledgling symphony orchestra had formed in 1908 but had disbanded during the First World War. Efforts to launch a successor reached fruition with the dawn of better times, late in 1924. All Toronto seems to have loved this enterprise somewhat less than Raymond Fagan's symphonic dance band. A January 1925 headline in the *Star* reported: "A FEW THOUSAND DOLLARS IS NEEDED FOR 'OUR' ORCHESTRA."

The "New Symphony Orchestra," as it was described in a February 1925 ad in the *Globe*, performed at Massey Hall and was conducted by Luigi Von Kunits. It had its limitations. According to the city's old resident historian George Glazebrook: "Only twilight concerts were given ... making it possible to enlist musicians who in the evening played in theatres."

There would be another reorganization in 1932. Even when I was growing up after the Second World War, however, Toronto was not famous for its symphony orchestra. When my high-school music teacher tried to sell us season's tickets in the early 1960s, he allowed that the Toronto Symphony was less than perfect. But he urged that going to the concerts and listening shrewdly for imperfections could still contribute to our musical education.

DANCING
TO-NIGHT

On the 5.25 p.m.
Niagara Boat

The grand opening of the dancing season starts to-night. Bring
your best girl and enjoy a real
treat among the fresh lake
breezes.

ROMANELLI'S ORCHESTRA

and the splendid steamer Chippewa dance floor are an unbeat-
able combination. Refreshment
booth on board. $1.00 fare in-
cludes a 6-hour sail and all the
dancing you like.

$1

RETURN

Sunday Trips

                        A.M. A.M. P.M. P.M.
Boats leave Toronto Sunday - 8.15 9.15 2.15 4.30
(Daylight Saving Time)

By Special Request
A Special Programme will be given by the S.S. Chippewa

Symphony Orchestra
Under the Direction of Dan Romanelli

On
The **4.30 p.m. Boat** Return
Fare **$1.25**

PHONE ADELAIDE 4201
FOR FULL INFORMATION

Canada Steamship Lines, Limited
46 YONGE STREET

*In the summer in the booming city young Torontonians took boat rides on
Lake Ontario and danced to Romanelli's Orchestra. (June 1926)*

A much smaller group would become more eminent. The Hart House String Quartet, which played its first concert in 1924, began with Geza de Kresz and Harry Adaskin on violin, Milton Blackstone on viola, and Boris Hambourg on cello. Boris Hambourg was one of three brothers who had come to Toronto from Russia in 1910 and had formed the Hambourg Conservatory of Music.

The Hart House Quartet's early local triumphs were as interpreters of Beethoven. In January 1925 even the *Star* acknowledged that "HART HOUSE PLAYERS DO GREAT BEETHOVEN." In 1928 the group would introduce new music by Maurice Ravel at a concert in New York. Throughout the last half of the 1920s it performed regularly on the early CNR radio network in Canada. It would go on to establish an international career with Victor records.

Another successful local group, the Mendelssohn Choir, had been organized during the late nineteenth century. By the 1920s its concerts with U.S. orchestras had broadened its reputation. In May 1924 the *Globe* announced: "PRIDE CITY HOLDS FOR NATIVE CHOIR GAINS EXPRESSION." Toronto could also boast a classical music celebrity at this point. As the *Star* explained in May 1927: "EDWARD JOHNSON MAY BE WORLD'S GREATEST TENOR."

By the end of the 1920s the city had an enriched infrastructure for European classical music in place. Glenn Gould, who would become one of the world's most accomplished interpreters of the music of Bach, was born in the east-end Beaches in 1932. By the late 1960s the local symphony orchestra would still be less than perfect, but Glenn Gould had shown that Toronto could nurture high musical talent.

MILITIA REGIMENTS AND MILITIA BANDS

The 1920s and 1930s were a high-water mark for another stream in the city's musical life. In early September 1924 the *Globe* had noted "BANDS AT EXHIBITION HAVE STRENUOUS DAY." The article singled out the band of the "Governor-General's Body Guard."

In early September 1925 the same paper announced: "TWENTY THOUSAND THRILLED BY GRANDSTAND SPECTACULAR ... INSPIRING ACCOMPANIMENT OF MASSED BANDS"; and "QOR WINS CLASS A IN STIRRING CONTEST FOR CANADA'S BANDS" ("QOR" was short for "Queen's Own Rifles"). In June 1926 the *Tely* informed its readers about a "Canada Day" event held by the largest city in neighbouring Ohio. The headline proclaimed: "CLEVELAND CHEERS FRIENDLY INVASION BY TORONTO SCOTTISH."

All these items involved the bands of Toronto's militia regiments. Since the early nineteenth century, militia regiments had been potent elements in the city's British imperial mass base. In the 1920s all the leading regiments had military bands. The bandsmen were not full-time professional musicians – they had day jobs at factories, garages, offices, and stores – yet many developed real skill on their clarinets, drums, flutes, French horns, saxophones, trombones, trumpets, and tubas. They rehearsed every week, went to army camp in the summer, and received militia pay.

They played in the Garrison Day Parade, the Labour Day Parade, the Santa Claus Parade, and the Warriors' Day Parade. They played at the Canadian National Exhibition, Hanlan's Point, Sunnyside Beach, and (until it was torn down in 1926) Scarborough Beach Park. They played at hockey games in the Arena on Mutual Street, at winter concerts in assorted auditoria, at summer concerts in city parks. And they played for their monthly regimental parades at the Armouries on University Avenue.

The old Armouries, at the corner of University Avenue and Osgoode Street, made a fitting headquarters for Toronto's militia regiments in the 1920s (and for many years after as well, until it was torn down in 1963).

The building, erected in 1891, was a somewhat gigantic version of similar structures in other parts of the country. Adorned with several medieval towers, it looked a lot more like a suitably feudal fortress than the nondescript box at the corner of Queen and Jarvis streets that serves as an armouries in downtown Toronto today. Like the militia bands, the old Armouries was an artifact of Toronto's British colonial culture.

There was also a military band tradition in the United States. Its most famous creation, under the direction of "Lt. Commander John Philip Sousa ... The March King," gave two concerts at Massey Hall, on September 19, 1925.

American bands were more flashy and dazzling than the militia bands of Toronto. They wore garish uniforms and played boisterous and brassy musical arrangements. The Canadian musicians in such collections of comrades as the Forty-Eighth Highlanders, the Governor-General's Body Guard, the Mississauga Horse, the Queen's Own Rifles, the Royal Canadian Regiment, the Royal Grenadiers, and the Toronto Scottish favoured Old World military tailoring, and a robust but civilized march and concert repertoire, more steeped in the European classical tradition. They aspired to the august grace and grandeur of the British Empire, on which the sun never set.

MY GRANDFATHER AND HIS PALS

Throughout the 1920s the bandmasters of the city's militia regiments were listed prominently at the front of *Might's Directory*. The lists bear witness to the significance of the militia bands in the life of the city. I can't resist noting that they bear witness as well to my one family connection with the known public realm of Toronto in the 1920s.

Starting in 1922, the listed bandmaster for the Governor-General's Body Guard was Warrant Officer Sidney White. He was born on Barnwell Road in Brixton, in London, England, in 1884, and had received his early musical education with the Kennington Lane Salvation Army Band.

In 1904 he immigrated with his family to Ontario. As required at the time, he spent a year working as an agricultural labourer, on a farm in York County. In 1905 he moved to Toronto and took a day job at Eaton's, where he would work for the rest of his life. He would remain bandmaster of the Governor-General's Body Guard and its successor, the Governor-General's Horse Guard, until his death in 1950. (As an economy measure during the Depression, the Body Guards were amalgamated with the Mississauga Horse.)

Sidney White's greatest significance for my own earliest childhood in Toronto was that he was my grandfather. I was too young to understand very much during the last few years of his life, but I did know that he liked me, and I liked him.

According to my father, my grandfather was all too immersed in Toronto's British colonial culture. He was not at all as interested in becoming a Canadian as he ought to have been. He could not forget that he was one of the more than one-quarter

of 1920s Torontonians who had been born in the United
Kingdom.

As I look through the roster of the band of the Governor-
General's Body Guard in the mid- to late 1920s, I can see much
evidence of British or at least Anglo-Protestant influence at
work. The surnames tell the story: Armstrong, Barnes, Bulmer,
Callaway, Egley, Geary, Higginson, Jones, and on and on. Even
among these emissaries of British imperial civilization, however,
the cultural diversity of Toronto had already made a token
appearance. The roster includes a drummer known as H.W.
Organ, my great uncle-in-law. He was from a German family.
Having lived in Toronto through both world wars, he thought
it more prudent to say he was Irish.

The Band of the Governor-General's Body Guard, mid- to late 1920s.
Top row, from left: E.T. Callaway, B. Brake, H.W. Organ, J.L. Barnes,
J.E. Jones, H.F. Jeffs, G.T. Jones, C. Egley, E. Higginson, T. Aspinall,
M. Henderson. Middle row, from left: I.O. Stephenson, R. Lodge,
R. McLachlan, P. Wilson, J. Guerriere, J.B. Robertson, G. Wright,
H. Cross, C.D. Latrullo, R.J. Bradfield, A.L. Watson. Front row, from left:
R. West, J. Birch, G. Jenner, G. Armstrong, W.H. Cornell, S. White,
D. Bulmer, H. Clarke, D. Newbigging, E.W. Clarke, C.R. MacClanathan,
S. Geary.

I remember from my youth as well the legend of the old Body Guard's incomparable French horn player, Cosmo Latrullo. In the photograph of the bandsmen in full formal dress that accompanies the roster of the mid- to late 1920s, "C.D. Latrullo" does look to be an incomparable person. And both the roster and the photograph include a clarinet player called "J. Guerriere."

I also can't resist adding an account of the group's appearance in the May 1927 Garrison Day Parade, from the *Mail and Empire* for Monday, May 23: "Resplendent in their magnificent uniform and white plumed silver helmet the band of the Governor-General's Body Guard created a stir of excitement all down the solid walls of humanity which lined the route of the march."

THE CASE OF EDWARD JACKSON

On Saturday, June 19, 1926, the *Evening Telegram* published another kind of commentary on the evolving fate of British colonial culture and cultural diversity in Toronto. The first page of the second section carried a photograph of a sign in the window of Edward Jackson's fish and chip store on Danforth Avenue. The sign read: "I go to gaol Friday June 25th. Why? Because I'm not a Greek or Chinaman. 5 Greeks, 3 Chinamen, 1 Italian have restaurant or refreshment licenses between Broadview & Carlaw. I a British subject cannot obtain one."

Jackson had come to Toronto from London, England, in 1913. As the *Tely* explained, he was "a high type of Britisher" (or an arrogant snob from the old country, as others might say). He had run fish and chip stores in several other parts of the city, before locating on the Danforth. The Board of Police Commissioners would not explain why his request for a licence had been denied, but he was going to jail because he had been operating without one. (He had declared he could not pay an alternative fine.)

According to the *Tely:* "One explanation is that an alderman has been active on behalf of a neighbouring property owner." Jackson's landlord, "Charles Cira, an Italian owner of 414 Danforth avenue," had "been assisting in Jackson's behalf, even engaging his own lawyer to fight for the license."

KING AND BYNG

Even if it was not always friendly to individual Britishers of a high type, the Toronto that was booming in the last half of the 1920s still remembered that it had some special reasons for cherishing the British Empire. In October 1925 the local press reported: "HUGE GAINS SHOWN FOR DOMINION TRADE IN PAST 12 MONTHS." Another headline in March 1926 declared: "CANADA'S EXPORTS INCREASE BY 216 MILLIONS IN YEAR."

In fact, by this point the importance of imperial markets was already diminishing. In 1910 some 56 percent of Canadian exports had gone to the British Empire; only 37 percent had gone to the United States. By 1930 a considerably smaller 35 percent would be destined for the Empire; a full 45 percent would be going to the U.S.A.

There was some irony in the trend. In 1911 the Canadian electorate had formally rejected the free trade, or "reciprocity," agreement between Canada and the United States negotiated by Wilfrid Laurier's Liberal government in Ottawa. Voters in Toronto had played a decisive role in the rejection. Fifteen years later a September 1926 headline in the *Daily Star* would explain: "CANADA GETTING CLOSER TO U.S. IN EVERY SENSE BUT POLITICALLY."

Yet for Toronto, and many other parts of southern Ontario, automobile exports to the British Empire were still a driving force behind the new prosperity that had crystallized in 1925. The early twentieth-century Toronto business community had sharp instincts about its own fragility. Even local Liberal magnates with continental sympathies felt a need for some protection against the predatory advances of an increasingly mighty American colossus.

The Empire was the only shield at hand. The "Toronto Eighteen" – prominent Liberals who broke with their party on free trade with the U.S. – had helped defeat Laurier in the reciprocity election of 1911. They had included Sir Edmund Walker of the Canadian Bank of Commerce and Sir John Craig Eaton. Sir John had withdrawn, for a time, his department store's advertising from the *Daily Star* when the paper insisted on following Laurier's free trade line.

Similar concerns influenced Toronto's role in the landmark Canadian federal elections of 1925 and 1926. By the autumn of

Take a Kodak
on Your Vacation

Put Kodak at the top of your vacation list. For there's no other part of your vacation equipment that you'll have occasion to use so often. Kodak *keeps* the happy days for you and brings them home for the folks to see.

Your dealer has a wide range of Kodaks from which to make your choice.

Autographic Kodaks
$5 *up*
At your dealer's

Canadian Kodak Co., Limited, Toronto

This ad ran in Toronto on June 12, 1926, less than two weeks before Mackenzie King lost control of the Canadian House of Commons in Ottawa, on June 25.

1925 the rather shaky first Liberal government of Mackenzie King in Ottawa had decided to face the people once again. The contest was held on Thursday, October 29.

The Progressives, who had taken 64 federal seats in 1921, fell back to a mere 24 seats in 1925. As in Ontario, the populist revolt of the early 1920s was withering on the vine in Canada at large. But Mackenzie King's Liberals won only 99 seats in 1925, and though Arthur Meighen's Conservatives won 116, this was still 7 seats short of a bare governing majority. The much-reduced Progressive block held the balance of power in the new parliament.

King decided to carry on, hoping for support from the Progressives. Even though he had fewer seats than Meighen's Conservatives, under British parliamentary rules this was his right. By late June 1926, however, it had become clear that King could no longer command the support of a Liberal-Progressive majority. He advised the governor general, Lord Byng, to dissolve the legislature and call a fresh election.

Lord Byng declined King's advice. He asked Arthur Meighen to form a new government and see if it could command a majority in the house. Meighen gladly accepted the challenge, but his government proved even less successful than King's. It lasted only three days. Now Meighen advised dissolution and a fresh election. This time Lord Byng took his prime minister's advice. Another federal election was called for September 14, 1926.

Mackenzie King was secretly delighted. He could not believe, he confessed to his diary, that Lord Byng "wd deliver himself so completely into my hands ... Spent the last hour tonight singing hymns ... I go into the battle of another election – believing we have a great issue – that the people will respond to – that is the making of our nation."

The great issue – as King saw it – was that Lord Byng, by refusing to grant Mackenzie King the election he had asked for in June 1926, had undemocratically interfered in the politics of the self-governing Dominion of Canada. As subsequent Liberal advertising explained, the governor general had "put Canada back into a Colonial Status."

Technically, Lord Byng had done nothing wrong. The Canada of the day had a British parliamentary government; Lord Byng was the representative of the Sovereign in Canada; and the

Sovereign retained the right to do what Lord Byng had done.

The problem was that Lord Byng was not a Canadian. He was an English aristocrat, appointed by the government of the United Kingdom. Meighen harboured pro-imperialist sentiments. Mackenzie King did not. Lord Byng's actions showed an imprudent insensitivity towards the aspirations of a rising Canadian democracy. Railing against them helped give Mackenzie King a working majority of 128 seats in the federal election of September 14, 1926.

TORY TORONTO AT HIGH TIDE

On the morning of the 1926 federal election the *Globe* carried a boxed announcement on its front page: "Stereopticon slides of election returns will be thrown on canvas from The Globe office tonight for the accommodation of the public. The Dominion Bank has kindly consented to the use of the Melinda Street side of its King and Yonge skyscraper for this purpose."

Standing in a noisy downtown darkness on the night of Tuesday, September 14, 1926, assorted Torontonians watched the slide show. Tommy Church was among them. At one point the results for Toronto and York were flashed on the canvas. A reporter asked Church what he thought. He just smiled his tight, narrow smile and pointed to the slide. He was so happy he could not speak.

In the 1926 federal election William Lyon Mackenzie King, grandson of the first mayor of Toronto, raised the voice of the new Canada whose rugged wilderness geography the Toronto-based Group of Seven had begun to promote with such success. He raised the voice of the new Canada whose most ancient history Harold Innis was starting to write about at the University of Toronto.

King raised the voice of the new Canada that could boast such men of science as Banting, Best, and Collip; that Agnes Macphail wanted to turn into a better place for low-salaried workers; that the Toronto advertising industry was helping to build; and that the Toronto-based T. Eaton Company was starting to fill with a national chain of department stores.

Yet in both the elections of 1925 and 1926 the voters of Toronto did not return even one supporter of Mackenzie King's Liberal government to Ottawa.

"Stereopticon slides" of the 1926 federal election results were shown on canvas, draped across the back of "the skyscraper" illustrated in this May 1924 Dominion Bank ad. The building still graces the southwest corner of King and Yonge today. Its interior continues to evoke the grandeur of high finance in an earlier era.

The local federal ridings had been rearranged and enlarged since the 1921 election. For the so-called region of Toronto and York, there were now a full dozen federal seats – nine in Toronto and three in the adjacent rural and suburban parts of York County. Mackenzie King himself had won a version of York North in 1921. In 1925 he was defeated in York North. In 1926 he retreated to the riding of Prince Albert, in the solidly Liberal province of Saskatchewan.

Back in Ontario's capital city, in both 1925 and 1926 York North and all eleven other Toronto and York ridings returned Conservative supporters of Arthur Meighen – by strong margins. In both 1925 and 1926 Tommy Church, still smarting from his defeat in the 1924 mayoralty contest, was among the victors. So he smiled when he watched the local results on the stereopticon slides.

It would be wrong to read too much philosophical conviction into this Tory Toronto high tide. In a late 1923 *Star Weekly* article Ernest Hemingway had already put his finger on one key point. Before he came to Canada, Hemingway wrote, he had thought that "all Canadians are in a wild political ferment about the Dominion's status in the Empire, and are either ardent Imperialists or anxious to break loose altogether." He subsequently discovered that this was "not true." People in Toronto were "almost uninterested" in the issue. "For one Torontonian who could explain what Imperial preference means there are ten who could tell you the score of the Argos-Queen's game."

An item in the *Globe* on Monday, September 5, 1926, underlined the argument. It stressed "the apathy and general appearance of disinterestedness which has marked this election." Among the factors promoting apathy were yet another record-breaking season at the Canadian National Exhibition and "the astounding pennant climb of the Leafs baseball team."

Exactly one day before Mackenzie King won the 1926 election, the Leafs had clinched the International League pennant. The team's first season at the new Maple Leaf Stadium would be crowned by still more glory: the Toronto Maple Leafs finished 1926 by defeating the Louisville Colonels in what the local press liked to call "The Little World Series."

I can deduce another point from what I know about my own family history. One reason Toronto cast so many votes for the Conservative imperialist Arthur Meighen in 1926 was that more than one-quarter of its residents had been born in the United Kingdom.

My grandfather thought the Liberal nationalist Mackenzie King was a damned fool. My grandfather thought that progress in Canada meant that Canada should become more like the imperial metropolis in England. His son thought (and still thinks) that progress in Canada means Canada should become more Canadian.

Tory Toronto in 1926 also drew on some particular local economic grievances. Especially after 1925, Mackenzie King knew that to survive he would have to attract support from the Progressives, who were strongest in western Canada. One approach was to tackle the tariff issue, since western Canadians tended to see high tariffs as a regional relief program for Ontario. One achievement of Mackenzie King's extremely shaky minority government of 1925–26 had been to reduce the Canadian tariff on automobiles from 35 percent to 20 percent.

The reduction was not great enough to thwart the great leap forward in the Canadian branch-plant automobile industry between 1926 and 1929. And to placate imperialists, Toronto Liberal campaign advertising in 1925 and 1926 stressed that the King government had "negotiated trade agreements with Australia and the British West Indies." Still, to many local business partisans all this was only happenstance and hollow rhetoric. In June 1926 the *Telegram* complained that the city was not growing as rapidly as it ought to in the new boom. The crux of the problem was the King government's "pro–United States anti-Canadian industrial policy."

These economic arguments imply a final, more strictly political point. Some Conservative imperialists of the day claimed to be the most authentic Canadian nationalists as well. On this view, the real threat to Canadian national development was not the United Kingdom and the British Empire. It was the increasingly mighty republican colossus, south of the Great Lakes.

THE MAKING OF OUR NATION

In the Canadian version of British parliamentary democracy (as in the original model), the numbers of geographic ridings won in elections often reflect highly skewed approximations of broad popular support. Thus, on September 15, 1926, the *Globe* could carry an article headlined "IN JUBILANT MOOD TORONTO LIBERALS CELEBRATE VICTORY." The article referred to the "city's leaven of Liberalism." It explained how, after the Tories had finished honking their automobile horns and dancing up and down Yonge Street over their undoubted local triumph, the Grits had raised a great cheer for the electoral result that really counted – in the country at large.

Along with popular apathy, the competing attractions of the Leafs baseball club and the CNE, and transient senses of local economic and political interest in the British Empire, the results of the 1926 Canadian federal election also signalled what Mackenzie King had earlier confessed to his diary. Even in Tory Toronto the train of events marked an important beginning for "the making of our nation."

"I believe that *this country can have no greater destiny than as one of the free self-governed nations of the British Empire.* That is the highest destiny we can have."

From a speech by Rt. Hon. Mr. King,
Vancouver, August, 1926

Is this Loyalty?

The Liberals hold that the Governor-General bears the same relation to his Ministers that His Majesty the King bears to his Ministers. The Conservatives by their actions say No! and would put Canada back into a Colonial Status.

The Constitutional issue is made by the Conservatives.

They are ashamed of it but cannot excuse their acts.

In their greed to seize power which they could not and cannot hold, they have embarrassed His Excellency the Governor-General. They have violated British Parliamentary Practices. They formed an illegal government. They insulted the electors by defying the rules upon which the Constitution is based.

What they did could never have been done in the British Parliament.

No wonder they seek to place the blame elsewhere.

Your vote will condemn or endorse these acts.

Can any true Britisher condone them?

THE TORIES—
have degraded the flag by making it a party emblem.

Again and again they have attacked the Crown behind a smoke screen of feverish Loyalty.

THE TORIES—
In 1838 execrated the Governor-General, the Earl of Durham, when he advised the Crown to give Canada responsible Government.

THE TORIES—
In 1842 attacked the Governor-General, Sir Chas. Bagot, when he put Self-Government into practice.

THE TORIES—
In 1849 stoned and rotten-egged the Governor-General when he assented to measures they disliked.

THE TORIES—
In 1860 when the visiting Prince of Wales refused to be their partisan, burnt the Governor-General, Sir Edmund Head, in effigy.

THE TORIES—
In 1896 through Sir Chas. Tupper, attacked the Governor-General, Lord Aberdeen, for refusing to sanction appointments made after his Government's defeat.

THE TORIES—
In 1926 tried to draw Canada's revered and beloved Governor-General into Party Politics.

✦ THE PRESENT ✦
Mr. Meighen, leader in 1919, placed upon the statute book legislation permitting the deportation of British born citizens without trial. A Conservative Senate refused the Liberals the right to remove it.

No Liberal Government has ever attacked the Crown. They have always fought to uphold our Constitution of, which the Crown is the head.

Meighen can't Win! If you want Stable Government Give King a Working Majority.

If you believe Canada is a self-governing Nation within the British Empire,

Vote Liberal

The majority of Torontonians did not pay much attention to this Liberal election ad, run in city newspapers on September 3, 1926.

In the middle of the 1920s the local papers ran articles and editorials on a controversy over a distinctive Canadian flag. It would not be resolved until the middle of the 1960s. In 1927 a federal-provincial conference began the long struggle over patriation of the Canadian constitution from the United Kingdom. It would not be resolved until the early 1980s.

In the last half of the 1920s, even the three largest issues of the early 1990s Canadian constitutional debacle were already in the air. In September 1925 the *Globe* published a letter from a C.E. Donkert of Hanover, Ontario, on "THE SENATE PROBLEM." Donkert urged that "each Province, regardless of the size of its population, should be equally represented in the Upper House."

Another 1925 headline announced: "SIX NATIONS WARNED CANADIAN LAW RULES." In December 1927 the *Star* advised: "INDIAN SIX NATIONS RESERVE EQUALLY DIVIDED ON QUESTION OF SELF-GOVERNMENT," and then, a day later: "GOVERNMENT STANDS PAT ON RULE OF SIX NATIONS."

In the 1925 federal election the Conservatives in Quebec ran as an almost independent entity, under the quasi-nationalist E.L. Patenaude. Toronto newspapers referred to Patenaude's "parti quebecois." In 1927 the Dominion of Canada celebrated its sixtieth birthday. In May the *Star* in Toronto made clear that the French-speaking majority in Quebec was snubbing "the Jubilee Year." Nonetheless, "FRENCH IN ALBERTA WILL CELEBRATE DESPITE A SUGGESTION FROM QUEBEC."

Two more-immediate events set up signposts that would mark the road from the 1920s down to the present. In 1926 Mackenzie King appointed Toronto's own Vincent Massey as Canada's first ambassador to the United States. The interests of the Dominion of Canada would no longer be represented in Washington, D.C., by officials of the British Empire.

In London, England, an Imperial Conference held late in 1926 began the process of clarifying that Canada and the other self-governing dominions of "the British Commonwealth of Nations" were in no way beholden to the government of the United Kingdom or its appointees. The clarification would be completed by the Statute of Westminster in 1931.

YOUTH OF ONTARIO REVOLT

Not long after the second federal election in less than a year, Howard Ferguson decided to call another Ontario provincial election, for Wednesday, December 1, 1926. In many parts of Toronto the great issue here was more to the popular taste than the status of self-governing dominions in the British Empire.

Fergie had at last resolved to get rid of prohibition and the Ontario Temperance Act. The wets of the province were still deriding 4.4 beer. According to an early November 1926 head-line in the *Globe,* "YOUTH OF ONTARIO REVOLT AGAINST LAW ASSERTS FERGUSON / SPIRIT BEHIND O.T.A. DOES MUCH TO BRING ABOUT THAT CONDITION ..." Ontario was now ready to convert to a system of government-controlled liquor marketing, on the model already in place in several less-populous Canadian provinces.

This time there would be no popular plebiscite or referen-dum. Regional economic interests, new pressures from south of the Great Lakes, and new waves of non-British immigrants from other parts of the world were all serving to stiffen the Ontario majority's sense of its 135-year-old *British* North American iden-tity. Fergie had conveniently concluded that plebiscites and ref-erendums were foreign to the true genius of British parliamen-tary democracy.

The government at Queen's Park announced that if it won the election on December 1, it would repeal the OTA and intro-duce a system of "Government Control." If the people of Ontario wanted to keep prohibition, they could defeat the gov-ernment at the polls.

When the results were in, Fergie's Conservatives had won 74 of 112 seats in the provincial legislature. They took a deci-sive 56 percent of the popular vote – the highest percentage won by any party since the start of Ontario provincial politics in 1867. The Liberals, under the fanatical prohibitionist William Sinclair, won a mere 21 seats. The United Farmers, now calling themselves Progressives and under the equally fanatical W.E. Raney, won 16 seats. Labour won one seat – in Waterloo South. The Conservative who had managed the OTA for Howard Ferguson from 1923 to 1926, W.F. Nickle, ran as a prohibition-ist Independent in Kingston and lost his seat.

As in the federal arena, the provincial ridings in Toronto had been adjusted and enlarged since the last election. There were now fifteen provincial seats in the city, narrowly defined: Beaches, Bellwoods, Bracondale, Brockton, Dovercourt, Eglinton, Greenwood, High Park, Parkdale, Riverdale, St. Andrew, St. David, St. George, St. Patrick, and Woodbine. Once again, in 1926 every one of these seats returned a Conservative member.

According to the *Globe* on the morning of December 2, "TORY ORGANIZATION IS GIVEN THE CREDIT FOR TORONTO SWEEP." This signals another feature of Tory Toronto in the last half of the 1920s. The Conservatives had the best-organized and most affluent political machine in the city – in an era when the etiquette of even British parliamentary democracy was still more rough, ready, and robust than it is today.

THE LONG LINE-UPS

On Friday, December 3, 1926, the local papers featured such headlines as "DISTILLERY STOCKS MAKE SHARP RISE FOLLOWING VOTE" and "U.S. BORDER GUARDS FEAR WET ONTARIO." Thirsty Torontonians, however, could not even obtain the required permits to buy liquor legally until Wednesday, May 18, 1927.

On the evening of May 16, 1927, the *Star* announced: "SEVEN POINTS IN CITY FOR LIQUOR PERMITS READY ON WEDNESDAY." By the end of May the system was in full working order. On June 1 there were "LONG LINE-UPS AT ALL LIQUOR DISPENSARIES."

Prohibition had disappeared in Toronto more than half a dozen years before it would disappear in the United States. Some thought had already been given to the regional economic development potential of these circumstances. Late in April 1927 a headline in the *Star* had asked: "WILL SALE OF LIQUOR HELP REAL ESTATE?" On May 18 the *Mail and Empire* reported: "LIQUOR STOCKS AGAIN ACTIVE IN TRADING" and "MANY NEW RECORDS IN ACTIVE MARKET."

Two days later, a dramatic event in the much wider international history of the 1920s was in the papers: "LINDBERGH NOW IN AIR ON N.Y.–PARIS FLIGHT." Now Torontonians could legally celebrate Charles Lindbergh's historic first non-stop solo air journey across the Atlantic Ocean in high style. On Monday, May 23, the *Star* managed to dig up a creative local angle on the great global news story of the moment: "LINDBERGH'S MOTHER VIRILE VIKING TYPE FROM CANADIAN STOCK."

City of Toronto Archives SC 266-10477

Girls' drill, Empire Day Parade, Friday, May 20, 1927 – two days after
liquor permits became available. Empire Day was a schoolchildren's event,
just before the wider celebration of the old Queen Victoria's birthday,
on the 24th of May.

Fergie's new system of government-controlled liquor marketing
was highly draconian. Much of it would last a long time. After
the Second World War, my parents still had to have permits to
buy liquor at the local government store.

Even the more relaxed system of today comes in for much
well-deserved ridicule. Yet I continue to share a little of the
local prejudice that – under the still-primitive conditions of the
New World – the system has also had some virtues. In the U.S.
the sale of alcoholic beverages has tended to be either out-
lawed altogether or altogether wide open. There are a few
things to be said for the more middle-of-the-road approach
involved in government control.

If we ever do decide to face up squarely to our increasingly
serious problems of non-alcoholic drug abuse, we might find
the way that Ontario and other Canadian provinces re-legalized

alcoholic beverages in the 1920s worth a long passing glance. In the later as in the earlier parts of the decade, the deadly drug habit was still an issue that periodically exercised the Toronto press. In fact, the Empire on which the sun never set had played a historic role in promoting the international drug traffic. Selling opium in China was an important element in British imperial expansion during the first half of the nineteenth century. Hong Kong became a British colony as a result of the Opium War of 1839–42. In the late 1920s, some factions of the Toronto press were enthused about a new academic study that claimed to find evidence of a higher morality in this experience. Early in May 1927 the *Mail and Empire* ran an editorial entitled "A NEW AUTHORITY ON THE OPIUM WAR."

ON A SUNDAY AFTERNOON

During the 1926 Ontario election campaign the city's two prohibitionist newspapers, the *Globe* and the *Star*, liked to wonder whether government-controlled liquor marketing would really end the widely acknowledged evils of bootlegging and the illegal speakeasies fostered by the OTA.

Though even today there is still some bootlegging and illegal public drinking in Toronto, the verdict of history is that government control did ultimately bring the rough but romantic age of the speakeasies in the city to an end. On Saturday, May 21, 1927 – just as Fergie's new system was starting to take root – the *Mail and Empire* ran an item that gave some hints about the nature of the vanishing era. It also offered some commentary on the real truth about Toronto the Good's notoriously blue Sundays.

There were a great many things that it was illegal to do in the city of churches on a Sunday, especially during the 1920s. It was illegal to operate almost any kind of business. During the winter months it was even illegal to use the toboggan slides in city parks. It was certainly illegal to go the movies. (Or, more accurately, it was illegal for theatres to open for business.)

Montreal had great contempt for almost everything in Toronto, but especially for its Sunday blue laws. Stephen Leacock, a resident of that city, had once quipped that Toronto on a Sunday would be a good place to die because you wouldn't notice the difference. But in 1927 Sunday movies had become something of an issue in Montreal. Some Montrealers had recently suggested that perhaps it was wrong to go to the movies on a Sunday, even in Montreal.

The suggestion had arisen during a public debate on a Montreal movie theatre disaster. On Sunday, January 9, 1927, seventy-eight children had died tragically in a fire at the Laurier Palace. On May 21, 1927, the *Mail and Empire* reported that Joseph Brunet, president of the Quebec Labour Congress, had given testimony before a provincial commission investigating the event.

Brunet opposed closing down Montreal movie theatres on Sunday. In his opinion it was absurd to assume that Toronto had anything to teach Montreal about morality. As evidence, he told of a recent trip to the city of churches. Inevitably, Sunday had come along and of course he could find nothing to do. A knowledgable local acquaintance had suggested he visit the city's speakeasies. According to Brunet's testimony before the Quebec commission, "I found them all so crowded that I could barely get in. That apparently is what a great many Torontonians do on a Sunday. Here we go to the movies."

The *Mail and Empire* reported Joseph Brunet's story on its front page. Its headline reflected some satisfaction in this one aspect of human endeavour in which, even in the opinion of Montrealers, the second city in the Dominion of Canada came first. It read, in large type: "TORONTO IS SINFUL PLACE ON SUNDAY." Then, in slightly smaller type, it carried on: "Labor Leader Declares There Is More Sin Here Than in Montreal."

On the slopes at Humber Golf Club. (January 1926)

CHAPTER SEVEN

I'VE GOT A FEELING
I'M FALLING

While they waited for the return of the demon rum in early 1927, sinful readers of the Toronto press enjoyed a steady diet of upbeat news: "THE VISION OF CONFEDERATION FULFILLED"; "WILD CLOSING MARKET ON MINE SECURITIES"; "45,000 CANADIANS BACK FROM THE STATES"; "ONTARIO IS POPULOUS, PROSPEROUS, PROGRESSIVE."

Three years later the boom would be over. Three years after that the city was in the middle of the Great Depression.

Sudden turns of fortune, however, are sometimes not as sudden as they seem. On the face of things, in the last half of 1927 and in 1928 and 1929 the good times were rolling, rolling, rolling. Early in 1928 several local financial institutions announced their "best year in history."

But already sceptics could detect subtle signs of fresh trouble ahead. Many of these flowed from events in a larger world. Some were unique to Toronto. In the middle of September 1928 the front page of the *Daily Star* would warn: "BANKERS STATE SPECULATION MANIA NOW BAD." And over the local airwaves one of the smarter new continental tunes was "I've Got a Feeling I'm Falling." The lyrics talked about falling in love, not about the economy or the stock market. Close listeners might have heard something more.

THE CASA LOMA HOTEL

The fate of Henry Pellatt's dream house was a particular case in point. Casa Loma had remained vacant ever since Pellatt moved out, after the failure of the Home Bank in 1923. Its construction had marked the blessings of the great boom in the Canadian economy before the First World War. Sir Henry's departure had shown the sorrows of the postwar bust. Now a failed attempt to revive the place would say something about the dazzling but all-too-transient new prosperity – and about Toronto in the 1920s as well.

When it became clear that Ferguson was determined to abandon the Ontario Temperance Act, W.F. Sparling, a local architect, conceived a scheme for giving Casa Loma a second lease on life as "an apartment hotel." Initial city permits were obtained late in 1926, and renovations and furnishing proceeded during the earlier part of 1927. On Tuesday, April 19, 1927, the new enterprise opened to the public. It advertised "apart-

In this John Boyd photo of the Casa Loma Hotel, February 1928, Henry Pellatt's dream house appears much as it does today. But if you look closely, you can see a discreet sign over the main entrance, somewhat obscured by the tree in the foreground.

City of Toronto Archives SC 266-12724

ments ... for any length of time ... luncheons, afternoon teas, dinners, suppers," and dancing to an "Orchestra."

Certain plutocratic neighbours in the lesser surrounding mansions were alarmed. Some expressed fears about "the cheapest kind of dance hall." Others claimed that Sparling's truest design was "to offer rooms for American visitors to come and drink." A neighbourhood campaign was launched to shut the place down.

At least the first phase of the campaign did not prevail. By the end of May 1927 you could buy liquor in Toronto – and drink it at Casa Loma without breaking the law. In the middle of June Sparling's new enterprise announced that its dining room had "secured the services of Auguste, formerly Chef at the Waldorf-Astoria, New York City." By early July the "Casa Loma Hotel" was advertising "rooms single and en suite – full hotel service – six dollars per day upwards."

Sparling and his associates knew that Casa Loma as Sir Henry had left it was not exactly suited to a hotel operation. It could accommodate large numbers for dancing and dining in high style, but it did not have enough rooms of the right sort to work economically as a haven for upscale, paying guests.

By June 1927 Sparling had completed plans for a $1-million addition on the west end of the building. He claimed that construction would begin "in about a month's time." But raising enough money even to start on this new structure proved to be a problem. Without it the Casa Loma Hotel could not turn a profit.

With plans for the addition hanging in the wind, the Casa Loma Hotel stumbled into its first bout of financial stress as early as December 1927. Just before Christmas Sparling managed to secure some fresh capital from Mrs. Theresa Small, wife (or, some would say, widow) of the Toronto theatre magnate Ambrose Small, who had mysteriously disappeared eight years before.

Alas, it was not enough. By March 1928 Sparling and his associates were in deep trouble. A second group of investors came on board, apparently headed by a Miles H. Knowles. They stressed the "social club" side to the enterprise, which had seemed to be working. But by June 1928 they were in deep trouble as well. This time the doors of Casa Loma were closed to the public.

On June 27, 1928, at a creditors' meeting, the New York businessman W.B. Mosley broached a scheme for a more modest $500,000 addition on the east end of Sir Henry's building. It was well received. Throughout the summer of 1928 many expected that Casa Loma would revive again, under yet another new management. Towards the end of August, Mosley himself assured the local press that the situation was well in hand. He anticipated that the Casa Loma Hotel would reopen in September.

September came and went, however, and the doors of Casa Loma remained closed. Finally, on Friday, November 16, 1928, the newspapers announced a "Sale at Auction" of "the valuable collection of costly furnishings consisting of the contents of the Casa Loma Hotel." The auction was held "under instructions from Humphrey Colquhoun, Trustee." It would last four days, from Tuesday, November 20, to Friday, November 23.

The expansion projects of both Sparling and Mosley had been complicated by some financial encumbrances on Pellatt's existing property. The city by-law that had finally authorized the operation of an apartment hotel had not applied to "further extensions." The plutocratic might of the surrounding neighbours had not stopped Sparling from reopening Casa Loma in the spring of 1927, but it may have killed plans for any sort of addition, from behind the scenes.

SWING, SWING, SWING

Though Sparling and his successors at Sir Henry's house on the hill finally failed, they inadvertently launched a historic legacy in the wider world of entertainment in North America.

July 1, 1927, was the "Sixtieth Jubilee" of the Dominion of Canada. To celebrate, starting at 11 p.m. on June 30, the Casa Loma Hotel had held a "Confederation Masque Ball." Music was provided by "Jean Goldkette's Blue Room Orchestra ... maker of Victor Records ... direct from Book-Cadillac Hotel, Detroit." At this time in the U.S.A., Jean Goldkette was vying for Paul Whiteman's crown as the alleged King of Jazz. A shrewd musical entrepreneur, he operated several Jean Goldkette Orchestras out of Detroit.

Goldkette attended the Confederation Masque Ball in person. And he appeared with his orchestra at a Sunnyside Beach concert during the early evening of June 30, 1927. The musi-

Under New Ownership

CASA LOMA
❋ HOTEL ❋

Dine in the beautiful Palm Room of Toronto's exclusive hostelry.

Dance after the theatre to the elusive strains of the internationally-known Jean Goldkette "Casa Loma" Orchestra, under the direction of Henry Biagini.

Private parties find an atmosphere of elegance and refinement difficult to find elsewhere.

A few delightful suites are still available.

HIllcrest 8383   Ernest G. Borden, Mgr.

The so-called internationally known musical group touted in this March 1928 ad would become the much more famous Casa Loma Orchestra of the 1930s – the first white swing band that unabashedly emulated black musicians and played real jazz.

cians he brought to Toronto, however, were more youthful than those in the Jean Goldkette Orchestra that had just created a sensation at the Roseland Ballroom, in New York City.

When Goldkette left Toronto, his more youthful musicians stayed. They were a kind of farm-team version of the "Goldkette's

Famous Orchestra" that became a popular fixture at the Casa Loma Hotel from mid-1927 to mid-1928. The orchestra gave broadcasts over local radio stations – at first on another short-lived enterprise known as CHIC, and then on CKCL and "the Eveready Battery Station CKNC."

The Toronto Goldkette musicians included a tall, dapper saxophone player then known as Glen Knoblaugh. One night, in Sir Henry's old ballroom, he decided to call himself Glen Gray.

When the Casa Loma Hotel failed for good, Glen Gray and his colleagues broke away from the Goldkette organization. They went to New York City, and from then on called themselves the Casa Loma Orchestra (as they had during the spring of 1928 in Toronto). Though they were all white males, they frankly emulated new black orchestras. They played real jazz, in a new swing style.

In the United States the Casa Loma Orchestra would become what the late twentieth-century jazz historian Gunther Schuller has called "the first white band consistently to feature jazz instrumentals and pursue a deliberate jazz policy, and thus the most influential white big band of the early 1930s until Benny Goodman's breakthrough success of 1935." The "Casa Lomans," in various permutations and combinations, stayed together until 1950. In his old age Glen Gray would claim: "We were the band that made swing commercial."

I first discovered the Casa Loma Orchestra in the early 1960s, when I was learning to play the saxophone. With a view to improving my tone, one night my father brought home a record that revived the band's music for a later generation. The record was called "Casa Loma in Hi-Fi." After listening to it over several weeks, I had some vague sense that it said something about the mystery of Toronto's past. I have been quietly haunted by the thought ever since. I will revive it again, at the end of this book.

THE TROUBLE IN THIS CITY

As the short unhappy saga of the Casa Loma Hotel was unfolding, another critical note about life in the city of churches blew in from south of the Great Lakes.

Like tens of thousands of 1920s Torontonians, Emma Goldman was an east European Jew. She had been born in

1869 in Kovno, a Lithuanian city in the pre-revolutionary Russian empire. At the tender age of seventeen she arrived in the United States, just in time to join anarchist protests against the controversial executions that followed the 1886 Haymarket Square riot in Chicago. Then she embarked on a turbulent career promoting radically progressive causes in Europe and North America.

Her oratorical skills won her two jail sentences, in 1893 and 1917. In 1919 American authorities deported her to Russia. The Soviet experiment with revolutionary communism was not to her taste, and she published a book called *My Disillusionment in Russia* in 1923. Then she toured Weimar Germany, denouncing the emerging totalitarian state in the new Soviet Union.

Chicago had been Emma Goldman's first home in the New World. Following paths from the windy city already travelled by the likes of Ernest Hemingway and Harold Innis, she landed in Toronto in the late fall of 1926. Less than a month after the Casa Loma Hotel opened its doors in the spring of 1927, a headline in the *Daily Star* declared: "2ND DRAMATIC LECTURE BY EMMA GOLDMAN AT THE HELICONIAN CLUB."

Now in her late fifties, Goldman needed a rest. Yet according to the *Daily Star,* during her first Toronto sojourn she kept "busy at correspondence and numerous lectures." She lived in the more southerly Spadina Avenue area – close to the university and to the heartland of the new-community Jews. And she received some unexpected local support from Salem Bland, a United Church clergyman who specialized in preaching the "social gospel."

Her numerous lectures included some particular examples of her gift for oratory. On Thursday, December 1, 1927, she gave a talk on Walt Whitman, at "Hygeia House, 40 Elm Street." At least one branch of the Toronto media sought out her opinions on the local scene. Like Hemingway, she was not impressed. On December 7, 1927, the *Star* reported on its front page: "TORONTO 'DEADLY DULL' EMMA GOLDMAN FINDS."

Her views were moderated by her constructive desire to encourage improvement. She elaborated on some specific themes at a farewell dinner, held to mark her first departure from the city, at the end of January 1928. Despite Salem Bland, one problem was Toronto's "curse of churches." Countervailing cultural currents had trouble taking root because there was "no connection between the university and the city." Even at the university there were problems. Emma Goldman politely alluded to an unnamed professor who thought he was "slumming when he toured the couple of blocks that he called Chinatown." She went on: "He considers it slumming when he studies life itself. That is the great trouble in this city."

Something about Toronto must have redeemed this great trouble, at least a little. Emma Goldman would return a few more times after her first departure in 1928. Eventually she died in Toronto in May 1940. The Reverend Salem Bland delivered a eulogy at her funeral. Then some other friends offered a final critical note on the city of churches. They shipped her body south of the border, to the country that had rejected her. She was buried in Chicago.

RED LIGHTS

Despite what some said, Emma Goldman was not a communist. By the late 1920s, however, Toronto had developed its own representatives of this new global political breed, freshly inspired by the Bolshevik Revolution of 1917. On Thursday, May 26, 1927, the *Daily Star* published a profile of their local life and work. It was headlined "AGAINST EMPIRE SAY TORONTO COMMUNISTS."

In the wake of some broader trouble in the British Empire, the *Star* had sent a reporter to the offices of the Communist Party of Canada, on the third floor of the Tyrell Building, 95 King Street East. Six people worked there, including Maurice Spector, chairman; John Macdonald, secretary; and Tim Buck, organizer.

The *Star* profile also referred to John Macdonald's wife, officially known as "Miss A. Skene," and Tim Buck's wife, "Miss Alice Ayers." The paper stressed that Miss Skene, "like a number of ultra moderns, has retained her maiden name in public life." Wives of communists did not use their husband's name. According to Miss Alice Ayers: "It's just a little offshoot of the communist philosophy ... We are getting away from the old idea of matrimony – the woman belonging to the man and taking his name for some sort of old worn-out protection."

The *Star* was the least anti-communist newspaper in the city. According to the *Globe*, it even suffered from a recurrent inclination "to champion the Soviet cause." The key message of its

A Kensington Market street scene in the Toronto neighbourhood where Emma Goldman lived. (July 1926)

May 26 profile was that the local communists were harmless.

The *Star*'s reporter observed that the atmosphere on the third floor of the Tyrell Building was "interesting. One senses intense activity and sees every evidence of cheerful good humour. Everyone seems to like his work of fomenting discontent with established political and economic conditions."

Even the Liberal *Globe* took a quite different view. On Friday, May 27, 1927, it ran an editorial on "THE COMMUNIST FESTER." It urged that the activities of local communists be repressed, "by regarding them as a menace to political, industrial, and moral life, which they are; by isolating them, discouraging their progress, and declining to regard their views as those of normally healthy people."

JIMMIE SIMPSON

The mainstream Toronto labour movement, headquartered several blocks north of the Tyrell Building, at the Labour Temple, 167 Church Street, had a more practical political influence than the Communist Party of Canada; yet in 1927, 1928, and 1929, local labour activists were not all that influential either.

Toronto in the 1920s was not a strong labour town. Even in the 1919 Ontario election the official political organization run by the Labour Temple had not managed to win a single seat in the provincial legislature. Sergeant-Major MacNamara from Riverdale had supported the Drury regime, but he had been an independent "Soldier-Labour" candidate, with his own personal following.

E.C. Drury, Mackenzie King, and even Howard Ferguson added a few early bits and pieces to what would eventually become the modern Canadian welfare state. But there would be no unemployment insurance in Canada until the early 1940s. There would be no public health insurance until the 1960s. In the 1920s working people had to fend for themselves. For some, hard times in the first half of the decade had meant recurrent bouts of unemployment.

The dazzling boom in the last half of the decade improved short-term conditions for almost everyone. But it also cramped the political style of the local labour movement, even more than before. In the 1926 provincial election the Labour Temple did not bother to run candidates in any Toronto ridings. As the *Globe* explained, this was its "FIRST DEFAULT IN MANY YEARS."

Local labour activists nonetheless carried on with their fight for a better life. James "Jimmie" Simpson was among them. Though he had been born in the north of England in 1873, his Toronto career was well under way by the 1890s.

Jimmie Simpson would serve as an apprentice printer, a journalist with the early *Daily Star*, a printers' union leader, vice-president of the Toronto and District Trades and Labour Council, and eventually manager of the Labour Temple. Throughout the 1920s he took a leading role in the Labour Council's annual meetings with the provincial cabinet.

In the late 1920s Simpson continued to cultivate the voters who would bring his own political career to its culmination in the new hard times of the Great Depression. Soon enough, he would be elected to the Toronto Board of Control five times in a row, from 1930 to 1934. In 1935 he would serve one term as mayor.

Today his work for the working people of the city is commemorated in the name of a Riverdale civic recreation centre, where the old Grand Trunk railway line crosses Queen Street East.

ROGERS BATTERYLESS RADIO

One reason Toronto working people did not pay a lot of attention to the local labour movement in the late 1920s was that they had so much else on their minds.

Almost everyone could at least afford to go to the movies. And in 1927 the movies began to talk. *The Jazz Singer* with Al Jolson opened in New York in October. In December ads for "Phonofilm talking motion pictures" at Massey Hall appeared in the Toronto newspapers. Silent movies would still dominate the local scene for a few more years, but they had reached the beginning of their end.

Television was an even newer communications marvel, pioneered in 1927. In January 1928 television pictures were broadcast at the General Electric radio laboratories in Schenectady, N.Y. On January 14 the *Star* reported: "PERFORMER SEEN BY RADIO AS VOICE IS BROADCAST − REMARKABLE DEMONSTRATION OF TELEVISION IS WITNESSED AT SCHENECTADY LABORATORY." Television would not become a real part of the mechanized mass household until the 1950s. By the late 1920s, however, Toronto newspaper readers knew it was on the horizon.

By 1928 radio was considerably more sophisticated than it had been a mere half-dozen years before. Home-grown Toronto technology had actually played a part in the international progress of the radio age. In 1925 the Torontonian Edward Samuel Rogers perfected the alternating-current tube, which did away with the need for the humming, unwieldy batteries in home radio sets.

In 1927 the Rogers family (most famous today for its cable television empire) started the still-popular local radio station CFRB − the world's first batteryless broadcasting outlet. Down to

Torontonians who saw this October 1929 ad at least knew that television would some day become another part of the mechanized mass household. By the late 1980s, however, General Electric was no longer in the business of manufacturing television receivers.

the present, the "RB" in the station's call letters commemorates the "Rogers Batteryless" radio system.

In November 1928 the Globe included the program listings of five radio stations in Toronto (CFCA, CFRB, CKCL, CKGW, and CKNC), two in Hamilton, one each in Midland and Montreal, and twenty-nine in the United States. In March 1928 CFCA hosted what even the New York press described as "the first North American radio appearance of Maurice Ravel, distinguished French modernist composer." Ravel was visiting the capital city of Ontario, to oversee performances of his work by the Hart House String Quartet.

By 1929 there would be more than 200,000 telephones in Toronto – about twice as many as when the 1920s began. According to a January 1928 article in the *Star:* "CANADA IN FOREFRONT OF THE TELEPHONE DEVELOPMENT." The 1928 edition of *Might's Directory* reported that, of "the total number of families" in Toronto, "practically 67% have telephones in their homes."

There was a parallel modernizing movement in the local press. Just after the Canadian National Exhibition opened, in late August 1928, the *Evening Telegram* finally dropped the archaic habit of covering its front and other early pages with classified ads. From here on, the *Tely* would begin with headlined news stories, just like the *Globe* and the *Star* and the *Mail and Empire.*

CONN SMYTHE'S NEW MAPLE LEAFS

Dramatic developments in Canada's national sport were another distraction for the Toronto masses in the late 1920s. At the start of the 1926–27 hockey season, the St. Patricks were a mere shadow of the team that had won the Stanley Cup in 1922. They soon found themselves in last place. Their owners – J.D. Bickell, Paul Ciceri, N.L. Nathanson, and Charlie Querrie – put them up for sale.

Conn Smythe bought the team for $160,000, using a minimum of cash and much borrowed money. Smythe was a convincing young sand-and-gravel contractor and hockey entrepreneur. He renamed the St. Pats the Maple Leafs, after the local baseball team that had just won the Little World Series. The old green and white uniforms changed to blue and white.

·

These local events took place just after professional hockey had completed the final stages of a great upheaval. In the 1924–25 season the Boston Bruins became the first U.S.-based team in Canada's National Hockey League, and the Montreal Maroons became the second team in Canada's largest city. In the 1925–26 season the Hamilton franchise was transformed into the New York Americans, following an abortive strike by the Hamilton players during the 1925 playoffs. A third U.S.-based team was also set up in Pittsburgh.

Trends of this sort culminated with the creation of a ten-team NHL for the 1926–27 season. It was split into two divisions. The Canadian Division included the Montreal Canadiens, the Montreal Maroons, the New York Americans, the Ottawa Senators, and the Toronto St. Patricks (who quickly became Conn Smythe's new Maple Leafs). The American Division included the Boston Bruins, the Chicago Blackhawks, the Detroit Cougars, the New York Rangers, and the Pittsburgh Pirates.

Much of the personnel for this massive expansion came from the sudden demise of professional hockey in western Canada. As the boom in the last half of the 1920s took hold, Canada's national sport was becoming more of a business than a game. Western cities were not yet large enough for profitable major-league teams. With air travel still in its infancy, Canada was too large for a country-wide circuit.

The Pacific Coast Hockey Association had collapsed after the 1923–24 season. The Vancouver and Victoria franchises survived this first bout of creative destruction and joined the Western Canada Hockey League, but this league collapsed after the 1925–26 season.

In 1926, as NHL historian Brian McFarlane has explained, the WCHL "sold all its talent for a bargain $258,000" to the franchises of the new ten-team NHL that would open the season of 1926–27. Such early western Canadian stars as Jack Adams, Frank Boucher, Dick Irvin, Duke Keats, Eddie Shore, and Jack Walker moved east, to the more profitable geographic region of the Canadian-American Great Lakes. And, starting with the 1926–27 season, the Stanley Cup became the exclusive trophy of the NHL.

Virtually all the players in the NHL of the late 1920s were born in Canada. This would still be true when I was growing up,

*When this ad appeared in the Toronto papers, on November 21, 1927, the
1927–28 NHL season had just begun. Conn Smythe's Maple Leafs had played
two games – one loss and one win – and stood third in the Canadian
Division of the ten-team league.*

after the Second World War. Hockey would remain Canada's
national sport. Yet outside Montreal, Ottawa, and Toronto, only
the bigger cities in the United States could afford major-league
teams. The Great Depression would soon push Ottawa off the list.

It is probably true that a great many hockey fans in such
places as Boston, Chicago, Detroit, and New York were born in
Canada as well. While more than a few of the Canadians who

had gone to the U.S. in the early 1920s (or earlier still) returned later in the decade, the lure of the American colossus remained strong, even during the dazzling boom. As late as December 1927 the *Star* was reporting: "EMIGRATION GREATER THAN IMMIGRATION – INFLUX TO CANADA DOES NOT KEEP PACE WITH QUOTAS GOING TO U.S."

Back in Toronto, the new Maple Leafs would play their first four seasons in what was now being called the "Arena Gardens" on Mutual Street. Since the place was too small for profitable crowds, Conn Smythe began to hatch plans for something bigger. Through the good offices of R.Y. Eaton, he managed to lay his hands on a bargain-priced lot at Carlton and Church streets.

As in the case of the nearby Eaton's College Street, by the time work on the new Maple Leaf Gardens began the Great Depression was showing its first teeth. Conn Smythe was still borrowing much more money than he was making, and it seems that his first name was no accident. McFarlane has told how Smythe talked most of the workers, unions, and contractors on the job into taking "stock in the Gardens as partial payment of wages."

In the long run, it is said, almost everyone who bought into this deal would be pleased. Maple Leaf Gardens was a state-of-the-art hockey arena for its day. According to hockey commentator Foster Hewitt, during its early history the fans who sat in the best box seats dressed for games in top hats and formal wear. The place would be ready in time for the 1930–31 NHL season. The next year the new hockey Leafs would win their first Stanley Cup.

THE TWO LANGUAGES OF CANADA

From the early 1930s to the late 1960s the Toronto Maple Leafs were a hockey legend. But they were never quite like "Les Canadiens" from Montreal. In the late 1920s Toronto newspapers were already describing "the Flying Frenchmen" as "Hockey's Three-Ring Circus."

By this point Italians already outnumbered French Canadians in the city, and French-English bilingualism was far from a practised local art. Like others of my generation, I have assumed that the person who made bilingualism a real issue in Toronto was Pierre Elliott Trudeau, in the late 1960s and 1970s.

But the newspapers of the late 1920s show earlier tender roots.

In May 1927 the *Mail and Empire* ran an editorial called "CANADIANS, ENGLISH AND FRENCH, MUST SPEAK TOGETHER." In March 1928 the *Star* reported: "SAYS BILINGUALISM ASSET THAT TORONTO APPRECIATES." A few weeks later the *Star* published a letter from an anonymous correspondent in its "Voice of the People" section; it bore the caption "THE TWO LANGUAGES OF CANADA." The correspondent began unequivocally: "We have in this great dominion two official languages, English and French, and a great many people don't know it." He went on to express the "wish that Gaelic, which I speak fluently, were also an official language." Then he argued: "No magistrate should be tolerated on the bench who cannot speak this nation's official languages, and every civil service official should be equipped in such respect."

The letter ended on a high and still more utopian note: "A young fellow nowadays can make his mark and his way in the world anywhere, who bears an irreproachable character, and is able to speak French and English fluently – and a knowledge of Gaelic would tend very considerably to BROADEN HIM OUT."

THE PRINCES' GATES

In real life, French Canadians in Toronto during the 1920s were typically treated in the same way as immigrants from non-English-speaking countries. This was partly because no one like Pierre Elliott Trudeau would appear in Canadian federal politics for many years. It was also because mainstream Toronto in the 1920s was still deeply immersed in the British Empire. Anyone who might have forgotten this fact would have been reminded by the city's celebration of Canada's Sixtieth Jubilee, in the summer of 1927.

There was a parade with historical floats on July 1, but the most intense excitement came in August. On Saturday, August 6, the Prince of Wales arrived in Toronto. He was accompanied by his brother, Prince George, and his wife, and the prime minister of the United Kingdom, Stanley Baldwin, and his wife. Even the *Globe* was moved to proclaim: "The Princes and the Baldwins are here. Toronto is ready for them. Three rousing British cheers."

The princes and the Baldwins had just come from Quebec City and Ottawa. They were only in Toronto for the weekend, before leaving for western Canada. Their reception in the city of churches was the "GREATEST WELCOME TO PRINCES AND PREMIER SINCE ARRIVAL IN CANADA." It was reported as well that "PICKPOCK-ETS HAVE FIELD DAY AMONG EXCITED TORONTO CROWDS."

Stanley Baldwin and his wife returned to the United Kingdom a few weeks later, while the royal party rested at the Prince of Wales's ranch in Alberta. At the end of August the princes returned to Toronto to preside over the opening of the new eastern entrance to the Canadian National Exhibition.

The design of this recently erected structure resounded with imperial echoes. It was officially opened by not one, but two princes – the Prince of Wales, who would later briefly become King Edward VIII, and his brother, Prince George, who would later become King George VI. Its proper name is "The Princes' Gates" (not "Prince's" or, as I mistakenly believed myself when I was very young, "Princess").

A year later, in August 1928, the Canadian National Exhibition would celebrate its own 50th Anniversary. For the first time in its history, ticket sales topped two million.

A year before, in August 1926, the Ex had been officially opened by Sir T. Vijayaraghavacharya, the Diwan of Bahadur from the jewel of the Empire in India. In 1928 a delegation of "Empire Parliamentarians" was on hand to help celebrate the 50th Anniversary. George H. Nicols, "member for Zululand in the Parliament of the Union of South Africa," told the local press that he "was glad to observe the Empire-wide scope of the Exhibition." The scope would grow wider still: 1929 was official-ly known as "Empire Year" at the CNE.

EDUCATING BOB ALLEN

The empire on which the sun never set was also a major subject in the Toronto school system of the late 1920s. Canada was growing closer to the United States, in ways that government policy could not touch (the NHL, for example, had to swim in continental currents), but life in the schools was different.

At bottom, the issue went deeper than mere government policy. The nice, sensible plutocracy tended to send its children to private schools, which were even more obsessed by thoughts about England than were the public schools for the mass of the population.

The new Princes' Gates are shown in the background of this August 1927 ad for automobiles manufactured in the Toronto suburb of Leaside.

The most established Toronto private school for boys was Upper Canada College. It had started in 1829 in the old town of York. City newspapers also carried ads for private boys schools in the Ontario hinterland: Albert College, Belleville; Appleby School, Oakville; Pickering College, Newmarket; Ridley College for Boys, St. Catharines; St. Andrew's College, Aurora; and Trinity College School, Port Hope.

Girls were better served by private schools within the city limits. Judging by the ads in the papers, the key names of the late 1920s were Bishop Strachan, Branksome Hall, Glen Mawr, Havergal, and Moulton. For girls who wanted to leave town, there was Alma College in St. Thomas, Bishop Bethune College in Oshawa, and the Ontario Ladies' College in Whitby.

All this was for the lucky few, or for those who aspired to be counted among them. Most late-1920s Torontonians – including even some frugal, sensible plutocrats – sent their children to the tax-supported public school system, run by local boards under the strict eyes of Queen's Park.

According to the 1929 edition of *Might's Directory*, there were more than one hundred public elementary or primary schools in the city of Toronto and its surrounding suburbs. Robert Thomas Allen has left a sketch of the typical boy student of the era. He "chuckled his way through predicate adjectives, the French explorers ... flipping elastics ... and waiting for the whole thing to blow over." Boys and girls alike acquired "vague impressions that England was made up of churchly old buildings that smelled a bit like the Royal Ontario Museum." Canada was "a green carpet miles wide with here and there men with hats on talking to bald Hurons."

High school, or secondary school, was more serious. The most indifferent students did not even start high school. The majority did not graduate. A high school diploma in Toronto during the 1920s was the economic and social equivalent of what a university degree would become in the 1960s and 1970s.

Might's Directory for 1929 listed fifteen secondary schools in the city proper. Nine were academic high schools or "collegiate institutes": Bloor, Harbord, Humberside, Jarvis, Malvern, North Toronto, Oakwood, Parkdale, and Riverdale. Then there were three technical schools (Central, Riverdale, and Western) and three schools of commerce (Central, Eastern, and Western).

Vaughan Road Collegiate, the first secondary school in suburban York Township, was officially opened in May 1927. Since the early 1920s *Might's* had listed Weston High School in the town of Weston among Toronto secondary schools as well. Secondary schools offered both day and evening classes. In the late 1920s there were twice as many evening as day students at Toronto technical schools.

Might's Directory for 1929 listed thirty-five elementary, or primary, "separate" schools in Toronto – from Blessed Sacrament to St. Vincent de Paul. These formed the core of the city's tax-supported Catholic school system, bequeathed by the pre-Confederation era, when Ontario and Quebec were one united province.

Down to as recently as the middle of the 1980s, tax support for Catholic education in Ontario extended only to the lowest secondary school grades. Students who graduated from Toronto Catholic high schools in the 1920s finished their education at private institutions, with fees paid by their parents.

The *Might's* secondary school list for 1929 included two Catholic schools for boys – the Junior De La Salle Collegiate and St. Michael's High School. Both were on Bond Street, adjacent to St. Michael's Cathedral and St. Michael's Hospital (and not far from Holy Blossom Synagogue). Catholic girls could attend St. Joseph's High School on Jarvis Street, just south of Jarvis Collegiate.

Not all Toronto Catholic families supported Catholic separate schools. Morley Callaghan had gone to St. Michael's College, the Catholic branch of the University of Toronto, but because his father "never believed in the parochial school system" at the elementary and secondary level, he was a graduate of Withrow Public School and Riverdale Collegiate.

THE HOUSING MARKET

The clearest technical sign of weaknesses in the fabric of Toronto's late 1920s boom was probably the state of the local housing market. As the city assessment commissioner had noted in 1927, housing prices had fallen somewhat since the early 1920s. The trend would not be reversed in 1928 and 1929.

Flat housing prices in the late 1920s were reflected in other real estate values. In September 1928 the *Evening Telegram*

A world we have lost: lawn bowling in Parkdale, early September 1928. The summer holidays have just ended, and the Exhibition has just closed down for another year.

reported: "NO STRIKING ADVANCES IN DOWNTOWN LAND PRICES IN FIVE YEARS / PREVAILING FRONTAGE RATES OF 1928 ARE EQUIVALENT TO THE SEEMINGLY EXAGGERATED VALUATIONS OF 1923."

The trend was not unique to Toronto. According to John Kenneth Galbraith's classic study of the New York stock market crash of October 1929, throughout the United States of the late 1920s "home-building, a most mercurial industry, had been falling for several years, and it slumped still further in 1929."

New houses were being built in Toronto in 1927, 1928, and 1929. The most talked-about developing area was along the Yonge Street corridor in the old town of North Toronto. In August 1928 the *Tely* real estate section reported: "NORTH TORONTO MADE GREATEST BUILDING GAINS." The accompanying article explained that "the widening of Yonge Street and the extension of the Yonge car line seven years ago gave North Toronto development its greatest impetus."

The pace of new building, however, was not frantic. Prices remained stable. According to the *Tely* want-ads, in the fall of 1926 you could buy a seven-room detached North Toronto house with one bathroom for $6,500. In the fall of 1929 a similar detached house near Yonge and Belsize was advertised for $6,200. If you were more prosperous and wanted to show it, in 1926 you could buy a ten-room house with two bathrooms, on "Hill south of St. Clair," for $14,000. In 1928 a similar "six-bedroom, two-bathroom" house in the Oriole Parkway district was selling for $15,000.

The east end of the city also grew rapidly in the late 1920s. But a five-room "Danforth bungalow" could be had for as little as $4,600 in 1926, and in 1929 you could buy a new six-room house at Danforth and Jones for the same price. A house on Hambly Avenue in the Beach, with "ten rooms and bath," cost $8,000 in 1926. You could buy a similar house with "nine rooms and two sunrooms" on Williamson Road for $8,200 in 1929.

In the west end, a six-room, solid-brick house on Geoffrey near Roncesvalles cost $5,400 in 1926. You could have an eight-room semi-detached house on the more northerly part of Indian Grove for $5,500 in 1929. In 1926 a "beautiful new seven-room home on a large lot," on the more southerly part of Indian Grove, was advertised for $11,250. Three years later, in the Humber-Kingsway district, $14,000 was the advertised price for an eight-room house with two bathrooms and (a sign that the new automobile age had already begun to shape suburban residential design) a two-car garage.

IT'S NEVER OVER

Stable real estate values at least meant affordable housing. The late 1920s marked a kind of apogee for the traditional dreamy Toronto residential neighbourhood that some would try to revive, with varying degrees of success, in the 1960s, 1970s, and 1980s. As the 1928 edition of *Might's Directory* explained: "TORONTO has matchless suburban residential districts in the Beach, Rosedale, the Hill district, North Toronto, Moore Park and High Park, and the Humber district."

On late twentieth-century assumptions, this was an inexact use of the term "suburban." Other still less suburban places had almost equal charms. Morley Callaghan's second novel – *It's Never Over*, published in 1930 – is set in Toronto in the late

1920s. At one point, in the fall of the year, the main character stares out the window of the second-storey room he is renting in a "respectable" house on a street off Broadview Avenue, just south of the Danforth. His "nose pressed against the glass, looking down into the street. Three or four kids were playing on the lawns ... Mrs. Errington ... was raking leaves off the front grass and talking at the same time to the woman next door ... A vegetable man ... called across the street to Mrs. Errington and held up three cobs of fresh corn. The street was all a small, simple, orderly world."

In such a world the assiduous cultivators of the Standard Electric Home went about their work. They took both themselves and their work seriously enough, and they had professional help. Another boast in *Might's* 1928 edition proclaimed that "TORONTO University has the only household science department of any university in the British Empire." The department was housed in a stately structure, on the southeast corner of Bloor Street and Avenue Road, directly across from the Royal Ontario Museum (occupied today by the Ontario Ombudsman's Office). A few years later my mother would be taking household science as part of her prescribed curriculum at Central Technical School.

There could also be danger in the small, simple, orderly world. On Friday, January 20, 1928, the back pages of the *Daily Star* carried the headline "WHERE PROWLERS MOLEST SCHOOL CHILDREN." An accompanying map showed the Chatsworth-Cheritan-Chudleigh area in the matchless suburban residential district of North Toronto.

The best friend of the main character in Morley Callaghan's second novel had risen to the rank of captain during the First World War, but "afterward he had not been successful because he had gone to the war too young." More recently, he had inadvertently killed a policeman, after a night of drinking. When the novel begins, he is about to be hanged in the Don Jail, several blocks south of the street where Mrs. Errington calmly raked leaves off the front grass and talked to the woman next door.

One of the many attractions of the Standard Electric Home. (June 1926)

Auto accident at Manning and Barton. (October 1929)

CHAPTER EIGHT

THE LOCAL CRASH

Today we are bound to see the very late 1920s as an ironic prelude to the Great Crash of October 1929 on the New York stock market and the Great Depression of the 1930s.

At the time no one knew what lay ahead. Despite signs of fresh trouble as read by subtle sceptics, even in the last half of 1929 the public mood was upbeat and optimistic. In 1928 and 1929 downtown Toronto was in the middle of a building boom. Much of the locally compelling corporate and public architecture that Torontonians of my generation would discover after the Second World War had its origins in the late 1920s.

Out in the wider region, there had been a big jump in cars and trucks produced by General Motors of Canada, from 57,000 vehicles in 1926 to 91,000 in 1927. But Sam McLaughlin's branch plant went on to produce 102,000 vehicles in 1928 and 104,000 in 1929.

In late October and early November 1929 there were resounding echoes of the New York crash on both the Standard Mining and Toronto Stock exchanges. Yet in December 1929 there was no sudden sense that a tragic new economic bust was at the door. It took a while for the real shock of the Great Crash to set in. Despite dramatic legends born in British tabloids, even in New York City the number of suicides peaked in 1931 and 1932, not 1929.

THE TALLEST BUILDING IN THE BRITISH EMPIRE

Stable housing prices in Toronto during the late 1920s went hand in hand with the corporate and public building boom downtown. The projects conceived, under way, and in a few cases completed included Greater Simpson's, Eaton's College Street, and Maple Leaf Gardens. But the largest and most impressive was the new head office of the Canadian Bank of Commerce, on King Street West.

Montreal was still the financial capital of Canada, but Toronto was gaining ground. Toronto's banks in the late 1920s included the Dominion, the Imperial, and the Bank of Toronto. The city was also a home away from home for the Bank of Nova Scotia, whose official head office was in Halifax.

The Commerce, however, was Toronto's biggest bank. In November 1928 it bought out the Standard Bank of Canada and became bigger still. This was part of a broader trend. A worried editorial in the *Globe* urged that "the rapidly dwindling number of banks has aroused real fears that the economic destinies of all Canada may be some day controlled by a tiny oligarchy of financiers."

In January 1928 the Bank of Commerce had already announced that it would be erecting a new head office, on the site of its present building at 25 King Street West. Work was being supervised by the local architectural firm of Darling & Pearson. The actual design was by "Messrs. York & Sawyer of New York."

In January 1929 the Commerce purchased the Ogilvie Building at Bay and Wellington streets. As the *Mail and Empire* explained, this served as a "temporary head office of the bank pending construction of the new skyscraper bank building at the site of the present head office." The new skyscraper would reach an unprecedented (on the local office scene at least) twenty-five storeys. Though work was well under way by the end of 1929, it would not be completed until 1931.

The skyscraper genre had been pioneered in Chicago and New York. In this setting the Bank of Commerce building in Toronto hardly broke records. The Chrysler Building, which opened in New York in 1930, had 77 storeys. The Empire State Building, which opened in 1931, had 102.

The great cities of the Old World across the ocean, on the other hand, had arisen on a less colossal vertical scale. London,

At Simpson's, January 1929 – just after completion of the 1928 addition. A
short while later the store ran an essay contest for high school students. First
prize was four years' tuition at the University of Toronto. Contestants were
required to write on "the romance of Greater Simpson's."

England, had some striking architecture, but it did not have tall buildings. When the new Bank of Commerce headquarters in Toronto opened in 1931, it was "the tallest building in the British Empire."

MAYOR MCBRIDE

Just as the Bank of Commerce was making plans for its new corporate headquarters, Toronto municipal politics turned in another direction. This resurrected the crusade against the local dominance of the Orange Lodge, begun by Hiltz's single-term mayoralty of 1924.

The absolute end was still a long way off, and would not actually be in sight until Nathan Phillips first became the mayor of all the people in 1955. But in 1928 and 1929 Sam McBride showed that at least the boldest narrow-mindedness of Tommy Church's era had become a thing of the past.

McBride was born in central Toronto in 1866. He spent eight years as an alderman before the First World War. In 1918 and 1919 he served on the Board of Control, and in 1920 and 1921 he failed to wrest the mayoralty from T.L. Church, candidate of the Orange Lodge. He licked his wounds for two years, then reappeared as an alderman in 1924 and 1925 and as a controller in 1926. In 1927 he was again unsuccessful in a mayoralty bid, this time losing to the venerable Thomas Foster, another candidate of the Orange Lodge.

In 1928 McBride took his second run against Foster, and finally became mayor of Toronto with a majority of more than 15,000 votes. His campaign literature had stressed that he was "not dominated by any set or clique." He aspired to "represent the whole of the city and not one clique alone." He believed that "independence of parties, factions and influences must be the outstanding characteristic of the Chief Magistrate of a city with Toronto's natural advantages." As in 1924 the *Telegram* was bitterly disappointed. Even the *Globe* confessed that it felt the voters "have made a mistake"; yet it also allowed that Sam McBride's victory in 1928 "revealed a revolution in public feeling." The morning after his victory in 1929, McBride announced that he would also be running next year, in 1930. "The *Telegram*," he told a reporter from a rival paper, "can start grooming its candidates right now, because I will be there."

City of Toronto Archives SC 266-12618

Miss Dorothy Lamont in a "jazz" costume at a Bank of Nova Scotia
dance, February 2, 1928 – a month after Sam McBride finally became
mayor of Toronto.

STRANGE FUGITIVE

Though few took notice at the time, 1928 marked yet another kind of new direction in Toronto. In the late winter Morley Callaghan found himself standing outside Scribner's publishing house, on Fifth Avenue in New York. A short while later he had lunch with Max Perkins. At the end of the lunch, "almost as if it had slipped his mind, Perkins said Scribner's would publish my novel."

Scribner's had earlier published successful books by Ernest Hemingway and Scott Fitzgerald. As he promised in 1923, Hemingway had helped Callaghan get started in the transatlantic small magazines run by the likes of Ford Maddox Ford and Ezra Pound. Apparently it was Fitzgerald, however, who had urged Scribner's to publish Callaghan's first novel. In any case, by the late summer of 1928 *Strange Fugitive* was in print.

Its setting was Toronto in the mid- to late 1920s. Callaghan just referred to "the city," never actually mentioning "Toronto," but he used exact local street names. In a casual way he documented the human geography of the place.

The U.S. literary critic Edmund Wilson would later note that the book was "said to be the first of the gangster novels." Its main character is Harry Trotter, described by Wilson as "an almost amoeba-like creature." After losing his job as a foreman at a lumberyard, Harry becomes a successful bootlegger. He murders a rival and is then murdered himself on the book's last page.

According to the Canadian critic F.W. Watt, Harry Trotter is "a kind of automaton, unable to express himself, scarcely conscious of the passions and social forces that mold and impel him." CBC Radio impressario Robert Weaver has claimed there were a lot of Harry Trotters running around Toronto in the 1920s. In real life only a few of them murdered anyone or were murdered themselves. Even Morley Callaghan's city was still Toronto the Good.

Just after the publication of *Strange Fugitive*, in August 1928, the *Star* ran an interview with Callaghan, now in his late twenties. It was headlined "SAYS TORONTO ALOOF FROM LITERARY WORLD." In January 1929 an article on Callaghan appeared in the *Mail and Empire*, headlined "CANADIAN WRITER BECOMES PROPHET IN ANOTHER LAND."

City of Toronto Archives.SC 266-16227

*John Boyd took this photo of an early Dominion store on Wellesley Street
East in April 1929 – just after Morley Callaghan and his new bride left for
Paris. The Toronto-headquartered Dominion grocery chain had started in
1919. At its peak it would operate stores in seven Canadian provinces.*

The *Mail and Empire* article explained that while *Strange
Fugitive* had made a splash of sorts in New York, it was "a flop"
in Toronto: "One book dealer even went to the length of
returning his copies to the publisher with the remark that the
style was not for him. It was not quite the thing, though it dealt
with life in Toronto. It was, in other words, too frank, too
French, too Russian, or too something or other."

In April 1929 Callaghan actually went to Paris for the first
time, with the Toronto girl he had just married. On April 16 a
headline on page 26 of the *Star* reported: "MORLEY CALLAGHAN
LEAVES FOR PARIS TAKING HIS BRIDE." In Paris Callaghan frequent-
ed restaurants with Hemingway and Fitzgerald, and visited
other friends at "the Paris–New York on the rue Vaugirard."

Callaghan finished the manuscript of his second novel, *It's
Never Over*, in Paris during the summer of 1929. He began to

wonder if he could stay in France. Hemingway's view was: "Who would want to stay?" By the fall of 1929 Callaghan had started to think about forging "my own vision in secret spiritual isolation in my native city." Before committing themselves for good, Callaghan and his wife, Loretto, decided to try London, England. As "soon as we got into a London taxi I knew definitely the journey was over and we were on the way home."

Though he would travel again and write about such places as Rome and even Montreal, Morley Callaghan would live in Toronto for the rest of his life. He published more novels and stories, and much journalistic ephemera. With a few exceptions, the local scene would not really start to take his work seriously until the 1960s. And even then, it was prompted by Edmund Wilson's reminder, in a 1960 *New Yorker* article, that "a writer whose work may be mentioned without absurdity in association with Chekhov's and Turgenev's" was "functioning in Toronto." When he died in 1990, Callaghan was at least something of a local grand old man. Toronto began to change in the 1920s. But it would take a long while for the change to become part of the mainstream.

THE ROYAL YORK HOTEL

The city Callaghan and his wife returned to late in 1929 still thought it was booming. In the middle of January 1928 an editorial in the *Globe* noted that "Ottawa says Toronto is to have a brand-new Customs House ... to be built on Front Street, east of the new Union Station." It went on: "Recent announcements of a large number of new office buildings have confirmed the tendency of the city's leading business and financial enterprises to remain downtown."

Ads and headlines in the press over the next few weeks filled the story out: "TEN-STORY BUILDING AT FOOT OF SPADINA PLAN OF FINANCIERS"; "NEW BUILDING FOR NORTHWAYS"; "THE CENTRAL BUILDING — TORONTO'S NEWEST OFFICE BUILDING"; "ANOTHER FINE BUILDING FOR TORONTO." On Friday, March 8, 1929, the *Globe* ran a short item headlined "PULLING DOWN CITY TO BUILD IT ANEW." It told how "to date the City Architect has issued permits to raze 81 buildings ... At this rate there will be around 480 buildings wrecked this year. In most cases the sites are needed for new structures."

Announcing the imminent opening of "the largest hotel in the British Empire." (January 1929)

Reprinted with permission of Canadian Pacific Hotels Corporation.

The building bonanza of the late 1920s demonstrated that the failure of the Casa Loma Hotel did not imply any real dearth of local demand for strategically located and properly designed accommodation of this sort. In October 1928, a little more than a month before the auction of the Casa Loma Hotel furnishings, the *Telegram* reported: "QUEEN'S PLAZA HOTEL PROGRESSING." It would ultimately evolve into today's Park Plaza, at Avenue Road and Bloor, just north of Queen's Park.

The grandest hotel project of the era was the construction of the Royal York by the Canadian Pacific Railway. It had a perfect central location for the day – on Front Street, right across from Union Station. The name "Royal York" reflected the imperial enthusiasms of the city in the late 1920s. Construction began in 1927, and the structural steel started to rise in February 1928. In July 1928 the *Star* reported: "SPEEDING UP WORKS ON ROYAL YORK HOTEL." In October 1928 a headline in the *Telegram* claimed "PROGRESS SHOWN ON ROYAL YORK." The building received its first paying guest on June 11, 1929.

When it opened, it had "over 1,000 rooms with bath." Though it seems to have taken some inspiration from the short-lived Casa Loma Hotel, it lacked the carefully cultivated heritage romance of Henry Pellatt's house on the hill. It would never incubate a musical enterprise like the Casa Loma Orchestra. Yet it would succeed famously as a hotel operation. It boasted a "banquet hall, ball-room, and concert-hall with one of the world's largest organs." It had "convention seating for 4,070." It was "the largest hotel in the British Empire."

CANADA'S FIRST PEOPLES

In April 1928, a few months after the Royal York's structural steel began to rise, Harold Innis heard some welcome news about *The Fur Trade in Canada.*

He had finished his initial manuscript more than a year before and had submitted it to the University of Toronto Studies Committee, which had earlier published one of his shorter projects. The committee decided that it could not afford to publish a book as massive as the one Innis now envisioned.

Innis then approached a British firm, P.S. King & Company, which had earlier published his thesis on the Canadian Pacific Railway. King was willing to publish the fur trade book if the

University of Toronto would at least provide a subsidy. The university decided against this form of support as well.

Finally, Innis sent the thing off to the Yale University Press in Connecticut. According to his biographer, Donald Creighton, Yale "replied that it would like to consider publication provided the French passages were translated and the book as a whole slightly reduced." Innis settled down to the required work of revision. In 1930 Yale University Press would finally publish his book.

It was the ancestors of the Iroquois who had begun Toronto's modern history in the mid-seventeenth century. *The Fur Trade*'s quiet stress on the multiracial aspect of Canada's earliest modern experience was summarized in a key sentence in Innis's conclusion: "We have not yet realized that the Indian and his culture were fundamental to the growth of Canadian institutions." Beyond a handful of early academic enthusiasts, few noted this thought when the book was first published in 1930. Yet as Innis was working on the final revisions to his manuscript in the late 1920s, there were assorted vague intimations of Canada's aboriginal heritage in the Toronto air.

According to census documents, in 1921 there were 183 people with North American Indian "racial origins" living in the city. By 1931 the number would increase to 284. In 1923 the Canadian federal government negotiated one of the last Indian treaties in Ontario, to resolve still-unsettled Mississauga land claims in the wider Toronto region. And in 1924 it introduced a new system of elected local governments on Canadian Indian reserves.

In 1923, the largest group of Six Nations Iroquois in Ontario, who now lived on the Grand River Valley reserve near Brantford, had protested Ottawa's plans for the system at the League of Nations in Geneva. By 1927 controversy over the issue among the Iroquois themselves was making news in the city press. The *Star* covered the story in December 1927: "INDIAN SIX NATIONS RESERVE EQUALLY DIVIDED ON QUESTION OF SELF-GOVERNMENT"; "GOVERNMENT STANDS PAT ON RULE OF SIX NATIONS." There were more articles in 1928: "OTTAWA RIDICULES CLAIM OF INDIAN INDEPENDENCE"; "HEREDITARY CHIEFS OF SIX NATIONS MEET IN SOLEMN COUNCIL ... INDIAN TRIBAL HEADS FORM NEW GOVERNMENT."

In April 1929 the *Star* ran a related item headlined "EAST YORK SCHOOL TEACHER SAYS HISTORY BOOKS WRONG." According to the teacher, Major O.M. Martin, schoolchildren in the Toronto area were being given misleading ideas about Canada's aboriginal peoples. Major Martin was a decorated veteran of the First World War. He was also an Iroquois, from the Mohawk Nation.

Martin particularly objected to a sentence in W.S. Wallace's new textbook on Canadian history, authorized by the minister of education for Ontario. As the *Star* explained, the sentence claimed that the Indians "who inhabited this country when the white man came were 'a very low race of people.'" Martin's objections, seconded by a motley crew of supporters, would lead Wallace to change his description to "savages of a primitive type."

The final version of Wallace's textbook would be published in 1930, the same year as Innis's *The Fur Trade in Canada.* Wallace ended his discussion of "Prehistoric Canada" with the pronouncement that the present Canadian civilization owed "very little to the aboriginal inhabitants of the country."

W.S. Wallace was "Librarian of the University of Toronto," where Harold Innis taught economics. Yet it would be many years before the textbooks read by Toronto schoolchildren even started to present Innis's pioneering view that the "growth of Canadian institutions" in fact owed something deep and even "fundamental" to "the Indian and his culture."

THE APARTMENT BOOM

In 1929 Major O.M. Martin taught at Secord School in suburban East York. But he lived in the city of Toronto, at 117 Wellesley Crescent. Today Wellesley Crescent is more simply known as Wellesley Street East between Jarvis and Sherbourne. As it did in the 1920s, it hosts the Wellesley Hospital. In 1929 it was also host to a few old-Toronto, single-family houses.

The single-family house – preferred setting for the Standard Electric Home, and a kind of urban successor to the rural family farm – was still the typical Toronto residence in 1929. Nevertheless, the era that followed the First World War marked the first significant beginnings of an important secondary trend: the rise of the apartment building.

The trend had reached an initial climax by the end of the

Apartment houses were another part of the late 1920s Toronto building boom. (January 1929)

1920s. In the summer of 1928 the press was full of talk about "THE APARTMENT HOUSE BOOM." In October 1928 the *Tely* ran an article that proclaimed: "CHARM OF A CITY OF HOMES SOON TO PASS FROM TORONTO / NEW YORK REALTOR PREDICTS APARTMENT DWELLINGS WILL SUPERSEDE RESIDENCES."

The new apartment building that Ernest Hemingway and Hadley Richardson moved into in 1923, on Bathurst north of St. Clair, was an early 1920s example of the genre. It was commodious enough for someone who was earning the princely sum of $125 a week, but it was not exactly luxurious. Many more modest variations on the theme were arising in the same neighbourhood.

The late 1920s brought a few real luxury apartment projects to the city, especially in the Hill district around Avenue Road and St. Clair. According to a January 1928 article in the *Star:* "CLARIDGE APARTMENTS WOULD COST $1,250,000." This was a great deal of money in 1928. The Claridge Apartments still qualify as luxury accommodation, even in the Toronto of today.

The late 1920s apartment boom did not last long. According to *Might's Directory*, 117 new apartment buildings were erected in the city in 1928. They did not find as ready a market as their sponsors had hoped: only 29 new buildings went up in 1929. Then there was the Great Depression and the Second World War. More apartments were built when I was growing up in the 1950s and 1960s. But many newcomers to the older areas of Toronto would still favour single-family houses, more than successive generations of real estate experts would recurrently predict.

URBAN DEMOGRAPHY AT THE EDGE OF THE DEPRESSION

Both the apartment boom and the city's unfrantic broader housing market were ultimately shaped by population growth. According to *Might's Directory*, by 1929 the total population of "Toronto City Proper" had grown to 701,454. "Greater Toronto" – the city proper and its surrounding suburbs – included as many as 826,186 people.

These numbers were approximations at best. According to the subsequent decennial census conducted by the federal government, in 1931 the official city of Toronto was home to only 631,207 people. Later expert calculations for the wider metropolitan region, based on federal census data, would suggest a Greater Toronto population of more than 900,000 people in 1931 – some 9 percent higher than *Might's* estimate for 1929.

Already the dynamic edge of growth had shifted from the city proper to the surrounding suburbs. Within the official city limits there was major infilling in both North Toronto and the east end, but city annexation of suburban territory was close to its modern limits. The pressures that would lead to the Municipality of Metropolitan Toronto in the 1950s were already building.

Might's listings for 1929 reported on twenty different "Toronto suburbs." They fell into three broad geographic clusters. From most to least populous, the east end included East York, Scarborough, Birch Cliff, and Leaside; the north end took in Fairbank, Wychwood, Oakwood, Forest Hill, Silverthorn, Earlscourt, and North York; then ten more places covered a broad swath west of the city limits: Mount Dennis, Mimico, Lambton Mills, New Toronto, Runnymede, Weston, Swansea, Humber Bay, Westmount, and Humbermount.

Some of these names merely reflected informal popular designations. From the stricter standpoint of official municipal organization, the surrounding townships of Etobicoke, Scarborough, and York had been created in 1850. The town of Weston had appeared in 1881. The town of Mimico had been established in 1911, and the towns of Leaside and New Toronto in 1913.

Then Queen's Park created the new township of North York in 1922. The village of Forest Hill appeared in 1923, the new township of East York in 1924, and the village of Swansea in 1925. The village of Long Branch – the last component in the original Metro Toronto of the 1950s – would not be established until 1930.

The older Montreal region still had more people than the rising young Toronto metropolis in the late 1920s. Toronto would remain smaller than Montreal for another forty-five years. By 1931, however, Winnipeg's brief reign as the third-largest metropolitan region in Canada had ended, and Vancouver on the Pacific northwest coast had taken its place.

Even in the late 1920s, Toronto still did not cut much of a figure on the wider North American scene. A long-standing symbiosis with Buffalo in western New York was taking on fresh importance. Some continental travellers stressed similarities between Toronto and nearby Cleveland, Ohio. But it was taken for granted that Toronto was the junior partner in all such cases – as in strictly Canadian comparisons with Montreal.

WHITE GIRLS IN CHINESE CAFÉS

According to federal census statistics, in 1931 there were 120,775 Torontonians with non-British racial origins in the city proper – accounting for somewhat more than 19 percent of the total population. And there were 109,622 Torontonians with racial origins that were neither British nor French, nor North American Indian.

In the view of most people of the time, the so-called British groups still made up the decisive majority of the city's population and set the unchallenged pace in public life. From our perspective today, the more interesting point is that by the late 1920s our own more diverse kind of Toronto had already begun to show its face.

The old British Toronto had its own multicultural markings. Only a little more than 55 percent of all British Torontonians had "English" racial origins in 1931; a little less than 23 percent had Irish origins; just over 21 percent were Scottish; and just over one percent were "Other British" (from such places as Wales and the Isle of Man).

British Toronto in the 1920s also had, as it were, its own large immigrant community. The share of people in the city proper born in the United Kingdom declined from 29 percent in 1921 to 25 percent in 1931. Yet even in 1931 close to a third of all so-called British Torontonians had been born outside Canada.

The share of Canadian-born Toronto residents did not change between 1921 and 1931, remaining at approximately 62 percent. By the late 1920s, however, non-British Toronto had its own increasingly substantial Canadian-born population. In 1931 most of the almost 11,000 Torontonians with French racial origins were more-established Canadians than anyone with British roots.

Torontonians with French racial origins had not been the largest non-British group in the city since the late 1860s. As early as 1871 they had been outnumbered by Germans. Migrations from Quebec had reversed this statistic by the early twentieth century. But by this point French Canadians in Toronto had been newly outnumbered by Jews from eastern Europe. By the late 1920s they were outnumbered by Italians as well. There were more than 13,000 Torontonians of Italian origin in the city proper in 1931. There were more than 9,000 Germans, almost 8,500 Poles, more than 5,000 Dutchmen, and almost 4,500 Ukrainians.

The census also listed smaller numbers of another eighteen different Old World cultural and national groups. The overwhelming majority of these other groups also came from Europe. According to the 1931 census, Torontonians with Asian and African origins accounted for only three-quarters of one percent of the city's total population. These non-British Torontonians, even those with origins in Europe, faced harsh pressures to bend to the dominant Anglo-American culture, with its particular British imperial and embryonic Canadian

City of Toronto Archives SC 266-9677

Young Chinese Torontonians at a December 1926 Christmas party, Beverley Street Baptist Church.

twists. In *Strange Fugitive,* even the forward-looking Morley Callaghan could write sentences like "the Chink pushed their plates along the marble counter" and "Harry knew the big wop, Tony, was only half trying" without thinking twice. And black guests were not allowed to stay in some prominent local hotels until after the Second World War.

Some among Toronto's oldest and most secure cultural minorities tried to appreciate how the world looked to the majority. In the late 1920s Holy Blossom Synagogue could no longer claim to speak for the mainstream Jewish community, but it was still concerned to present a sympathetic Jewish image to its non-Jewish neighbours. In November 1928 it was advertising "Sunday Morning Services," with Rabbi Isserman preaching on "Canada's Immigration Problem."

Nevertheless, even the most officially harassed minorities were not altogether cowed into abject submission and silence. After 1923, the federal legislation that effectively prohibited Chinese immigration compounded the difficulty Chinese-restaurant owners had in complying with provincial legislation prohibiting them from hiring white women. Early in 1929 the *Globe* ran an article headlined "HIRING WHITE GIRLS IN CHINESE CAFES UPHELD BY CONSUL / LI TCHUIN PROTESTS TO POLICE COMMISSION AGAINST LEGISLATION."

In the end, there were a few more Asians and Africans in Toronto in 1931 than there had been in 1921. In 1929 Harold Innis was about to publish a book that would quietly demonstrate the precedents for European and non-European multi-racial collaboration in Canada's earliest modern history. The newest multiculturalism of the 1920s would take a long while to reach fruition, but at least it had begun.

IN THE WINGS

In the late 1920s people who migrated to Toronto from outside North America still came by boat. It would be another generation before large numbers of new Torontonians would arrive on airplanes.

Charles Lindbergh's dramatic transatlantic flight in May 1927, however, marked a milestone in the early history of travel by air. On Thursday, January 12, 1928, the *Star* ran an article headlined "TORONTO NEEDS AIRPORT CLEVELAND VISITOR SAYS TWO CITIES ARE ALIKE." In September 1928 the *Star* ran another article on a related theme: "ESTABLISH AIR SERVICE BUFFALO TO TORONTO." In March 1929 the *Globe* reported: "TORONTO–BUFFALO SERVICE BY PLANE APPEARS ASSURED." Two months before, in January 1929, the *Mail and Empire* had noted: "TORONTO AND MONTREAL LINKS IN AERIAL SERVICES."

In August 1929 the *Tely* ran an article headlined "START EXPRESS SERVICE BY AIR, CANADA'S FIRST / CPR EXPRESS PLANE INAUGURATES DAILY SERVICE TO HAMILTON, LONDON AND WINDSOR." A few days later again, the routes for airplane races at the 1929 Canadian National Exhibition were announced. They ran in a kind of oval around Lake Erie – from Toronto to Hamilton to London to Windsor to Toledo to Cleveland to Buffalo to Hamilton, and then back to the CNE grounds on Toronto's Lake Ontario waterfront.

As in the case of television, air travel would be stalled by the Depression and the Second World War. Yet, on the eve of the stock market crash in October 1929, far-sighted readers of Toronto newspapers could glimpse the airplane life we know today, already in the wings.

THE NEW DOWNTOWN PLAN

Something else that briefly seemed to be in the wings for Toronto in 1929 would see the light of day through only the narrowest of cracks. The newly rising apartment houses, department stores, hotels, office buildings, and sports palaces had prompted a more fundamental rethinking about the structure of the city itself.

On Saturday, January 5, 1929, the *Mail and Empire* ran an article headlined "PLANNING BOARD TO COMPLETE TASK." Just over two months later, on Tuesday, March 12, the *Globe* reported: "CITY PLANNERS PROPOSE NEW DOWNTOWN STREETS AND WIDENINGS." The report included a map of the main proposals. The day before, the *Star* had published a more elaborate version of the same map under the heading "CITY PLANNING COMMISSION'S $13,000,000 PLANS FOR IMPROVING DOWNTOWN TORONTO."

The plans were focused on the area within "three quarters of a mile radius" from today's old city hall at Bay and Queen. The apparent objective was to turn downtown Toronto into something that looked less like Cleveland (or even New York) and more like London, England – the "heart of the Empire" across the sea.

The 1929 downtown plan also called for some street widenings, and Bloor Street actually was widened. This was how the intersection at Bloor and Yonge looked on June 20, 1929.

Union Station and the almost-completed Royal York Hotel formed a kind of anchor for the concept. The planners envisioned that a brand-new major thoroughfare – to be known as Cambrai Avenue – would run north from Union Station on Front Street, due east of the Royal York. After dividing to accommodate an elegant boulevard between Adelaide and Richmond, Cambrai Avenue would meet a widened Queen Street at a new public square, to be known as St. Julien Place

North from Front Street, just west of Union Station and the Royal York, a new Queen's Park Avenue would run at an angle towards the intersection of Queen and University. At Richmond it would empty into another new public square, to be known as Vimy Circle.

Another brand-new major thoroughfare, running at an angle from Spadina Avenue just north of Front Street, would

City of Toronto Archives SC 266-15311

Miss Lilian Boyd, boldly perched on the roof of a Toronto automobile,
October 28, 1928 – one year before the Great Crash, when the good times
were still rolling like they would never end.

also empty into Vimy Circle at Richmond. It was to be known as
Passchendaele Road. Heading east from Vimy Circle along
Richmond, a kind of companion to Passchendaele Road, to be
known as Arras Road, would run diagonally from Richmond
and Jarvis to Dundas and Parliament.

There were other more modest elements in the new downtown plan, but these were its most radical features.

The names of the new streets and squares echoed the
European battles of the First World War in which the Canadian
forces of the British Empire had sacrificed so much. The city
planners also hoped to do more than commemorate past glories;
the future Toronto they envisioned would be a new capital of the
British Empire – an imperial metropolis in the New World.

As it happened, the plan met some practical objections as
soon as it was introduced. On Wednesday, March 13, 1929, the

Globe reported: "COUNCIL TO CONSIDER PLANNING REPORT AT SPE-CIAL SESSION / ONE FEATURE OF OBJECTIONS DEVELOPING IS THAT SCHEME MEANS EXTENSIVE USE OF VALUABLE LAND FOR NEW STREETS AND SQUARES."

A day later the press was reporting that Controller Hacker had calculated the scheme could cost as much as $40 million – more than three times as much as its proponents claimed. On Tuesday, March 19, the *Globe* ran an article headlined "CITY PLANNERS' REPORT TO DEPARTMENT HEADS AFTER ROUGH PASSAGE."

The stock market crash and the ensuing extremely grim first half of the 1930s would prove the roughest passage of all. Only a few minor elements of the new plan would ever be implemented. The most notable is probably Queen's Park Avenue. Without the proposed Vimy Circle, it lives today as the southern end of University Avenue, between Queen and Front streets.

The Toronto that began to take shape in the 1920s was not destined to become a new capital of the British Empire in the New World. It would only become a Canadian national metrop-olis in northern North America. Toronto could not really be a part of Europe. It would continue to look and act like a North American city.

FERGIE'S LAST FLING

On Wednesday, October 30, 1929, there was another Ontario provincial election. It would mark G. Howard Ferguson's great-est triumph. His governing Conservatives took a record 57 per-cent of the province-wide popular vote and 92 of the 112 seats in the Legislative Assembly. No party in Ontario history had ever enjoyed a victory of this magnitude before. None has repeated the feat since.

All this happened only six days after the notorious Black Thursday that preceded the Great Crash on the New York Stock Exchange. Fergie's October 30 victory took place a mere twenty-four hours after what John Kenneth Galbraith would subsequently call "the most devastating day in the history of the New York stock market" – and perhaps even "the most devastat-ing day in the history of markets" in the history of the world.

On Friday, October 25, 1929 (the day after Black Thursday), the *Globe* had reported: "CRASH IN NEW YORK ROCKS SHARE PRICES

IN TORONTO MARKETS." The voters in the provincial capital city do seem to have been troubled. On the evening of October 25 the Ontario Conservatives had held what they hoped would be a monster election rally at Massey Hall. On Saturday, October 26, the press reported: "TOTAL OF ATTENDANCE UNEXPECTEDLY SMALL … FERGUSON FOLLOWERS CHEER, BUT FAIL TO FILL MASSEY HALL."

In the fall of 1929 Guy Lombardo began a long history at the Roosevelt Hotel in New York. At the end of the year his Royal Canadians made their first New Year's Eve radio broadcast, starting a national tradition in the U.S.A. Before the band settled into the Roosevelt, it played an engagement at the King Edward Hotel in Toronto. The engagement ended some three weeks before the Great Crash. (October 1929)

Yet few were ready to accept that the boom had really busted again, or that several years of extremely grim times likely lay
ahead. The *Globe* was Toronto's authoritative newspaper of
record, and in the 1920s it had no partisan interest in the
future of the Conservative Party. In an October 26 editorial it
had stressed that "THE MARKET CRASH" did not have fundamental
implications for the broader economic future. On election day,
October 30, its front page announced: "UTTER COLLAPSE IN
STOCK MARKET NARROWLY AVERTED" and "ELECTION BATTLE THRILLS
RADIO PUBLIC."

By this point the provincial Progressives were in utter disar-
ray. Fergie's main opponents were the Liberals, still under
the fanatical prohibitionist William Sinclair. Government-
controlled liquor marketing was working smoothly, and had
brought a surge of public revenue into Queen's Park.

Once again, the Conservatives took every available seat in
the provincial capital city. October 30, 1929, however, marked a
last brilliant blaze of untarnished glory for Tory Toronto.
There would be a final nostalgic sunset in the 1950s. But the
beginning of the end to the rabid Toryism that had appalled
Charles Dickens in the nineteenth century was on the horizon.
In the next provincial contest, in June 1934, the city's fifteen
ridings would be reduced to thirteen as part of a province-wide
economy campaign in the depths of the Depression. Only
seven of the thirteen new Toronto seats would return
Conservatives. The other six would vote for Mitch Hepburn's
resurgent Liberals.

Fergie himself would have the good sense to get out long
before this. In July 1930 R.B. Bennett's federal Conservatives
temporarily replaced Mackenzie's King's Liberals in Ottawa.
Before the end of the year, Bennett appointed Howard
Ferguson Canadian high commissioner to the United Kingdom, in London.

In December 1930 George Henry would become the new
leader of the provincial Conservatives and the premier of
Ontario, without a fresh general election.

ANOTHER SURPRISE

Howard Ferguson did not have to call an Ontario election for
October 30, 1929. Technically, he could have waited much
longer before seeking a renewed mandate from the people.

Perhaps he had guessed that holding an election after the fall of 1929 could mean trouble. Even then, he was almost too late.

Well into the early 1930s, many simply did not accept that the dead hand of economic misfortune was on the land again – with an unusually heavy weight. Yet there had been signs of grief ahead well before October 1929.

In 1924 some 900,000 shares had been traded on the Toronto Stock Exchange; in 1929 more than 10 million shares changed hands. The total value of shares in Canadian mining companies traded in 1921 had been only some $5.6 million; the comparable figure for 1929 was more than $688 million. Between 1927 and 1929 the price of a seat on the Toronto exchange rose from $50,000 to $220,000. As early as September 1928 the front page of the *Star* had warned: "BANKERS STATE SPECULATION MANIA NOW BAD."

On Friday, March 1, 1929, the *Globe* announced: "FAILURE OF HERON AND CO. SHOWN TO INVOLVE ENORMOUS SUMS." Colonel Orlando Heron and his son were local stockbrokers. On March 13, just after the release of the new downtown plan, it was further reported that "COLONEL HERON ARRESTED AFTER CREDITORS MEET" and "LOSSES EXCEED GAINS BY NEARLY 3 TO 1 ON TORONTO MARKET."

Quite quickly things seemed to improve. On Friday, March 15, the *Globe* declared: "STOCK PRICES RALLY WITH STRONG BUYING ON TORONTO MARKET." There were similar ups and downs over the spring and early summer of 1929. Ordinary people with jobs and families were likely not alarmed; life carried on. Early in August the obsolete lake steamer *Jasmine* was "torpedoed and burned" at Sunnyside Beach for the amusement of the citizens of Toronto.

Then on August 6 another headline on the front page of the *Tely* suggested that the Toronto economy was showing signs of stress: "UNSKILLED LABOR FLOODS CITY / TWENTY SEEK EACH JOB OPEN / MAYOR ISSUES WARNING – MEN FROM FARMS, ENGLAND AND UNITED STATES COME HERE IN VAIN HOPE."

On August 27, 1929, insiders predicted that Ferguson would call an election for the end of October. On September 17 the prediction was confirmed. On the morning of Black Thursday, October 24, the *Globe* reported: "PANIC THREATENS NEW YORK." On

October 25 the start of the Great Crash covered the front pages: "STOCK SPECULATORS SHAKEN IN WILD DAY OF PANIC."

The gloom spilled over into early November – in the immediate wake of Fergie's greatest electoral triumph in the history of Ontario politics. Then things seemed to settle down again. For a while it was almost as if nothing had happened.

Late in January 1930 the 1929 *Annual Report of the Assessment Commissioner for the City of Toronto* was made public. In measured official tones it observed that "in the past two years the increases in both assessment and population have been considerably above the average and it is anticipated that our future development will keep pace."

It would be a while before this anticipation vanished from official and unofficial rhetoric in the city. Yet in May 1932 the Dominion Bureau of Statistics index of Canadian stock prices would fall to 38.6, from a high of 235.4 in 1929. On average, in other words, someone who had $1,000 invested on the Toronto Stock Exchange in 1929, and had just left it there, would have only $164 in May 1932.

In 1929 General Motors of Canada in Oshawa, just east of Toronto, produced 104,198 passenger cars and trucks. Production would fall to 55,379 vehicles in 1930, 32,791 in 1931, and 19,565 in 1932. For every 1,000 vehicles that GM Canada made in 1929, it would make only 188 in 1932.

By 1932 no one would be able to deny that a Great Depression had arrived. The stock market crash in October 1929 had signalled something more important than Howard Ferguson's last great Tory fling. By the end of the 1920s, in several different ways, the story of Toronto had set off in new directions. The decade had started with one surprise. It ended with another.

POPULATION OF THE CITY OF TORONTO
BY RACIAL ORIGIN, 1931

ABORIGINALS
(.04%)

North American Indian	284

BRITISH AND FRENCH
(82.59%)

English	282,759
Irish	114,315
Scottish	107,943
Other British	5,415
French	10,869

JEWS
(7.18%)

Hebrew	45,305

WEST/CENTRAL EUROPEANS
(4.42%)

Italian	13,015
German	9,343
Dutch	5,222
Belgian	295

EAST EUROPEANS
(2.97%)

Polish	8,483
Ukrainian	4,434
Finnish	3,453
Russian	1,694
Lithuanian	655

HABSBURG EUROPEANS
(1.20%)

Czech and Slovak	1,535
Austrian	1,403
Bulgarian	1,391
Hungarian	1,354
Jugo-Slavic	1,119
Rumanian	745

ASIANS
(.54%)

Chinese	2,635
Other Asian	787

SCANDINAVIANS
(.34%)

Danish	847
Swedish	778
Norwegian	474
Icelandic	34

GREEKS
(.30%)

Greek	1,922

AFRICANS
(.21%)

Negro	1,344
Other European	494
Other and unspecified	861

TOTAL	**631,207**

Source: Statistics Canada, *Census of Canada,* 1931.

Steel work on the new Bank of Commerce building. (July 1929)

THE FUTURE – THEN AND NOW

Now I've seen the earlier part of the Toronto movie I missed. Or at least I've seen it through the newspapers, the city directories, books and public documents, and John Boyd's photographs. Alas, we cannot really travel back into the past. And, strictly speaking, I've only seen the start of the movie. As of December 1929, a little more than fifteen years will elapse before my own Toronto life begins, and I become an extra in the cast myself.

I want to say a few things by way of conclusion. I want to suggest – more specifically – how Toronto in the 1920s relates to the place I live in now. The kind of history that entertains me the most sheds some more or less direct light on the present and, perhaps, the future as well.

At first I thought I could do this by quickly summarizing what happened in the city during the six decades that followed the Great Crash. But this approach didn't work. It threatened to be too long, and it sounded too serious. I found I had started to write another kind of book altogether. I've finally settled for some bits and pieces that merely hint at the routes Toronto has taken from the end of the 1920s down to the early 1990s – and at what Toronto in the 1920s might have to do with the future of Toronto today.

AN END AND A BEGINNING

The Hungarian-American historian John Lukacs has recently argued that the "twentieth century was a short century." It "lasted seventy-five years – from 1914 to 1989."

In the same spirit, the new era in the story of Toronto that began in the 1920s has recently come to an end. The particular movie that my own personal life stumbled into, early in 1945, is now over. The age that opened with the surprising triumph of E.C. Drury and the Farmer-Labour coalition in the Ontario election of October 1919 closed (it could be said) with the surprising triumph of Bob Rae and the New Democratic Party in the election of September 1990.

As a kind of drawing-room exercise, it is possible to construct a series of similar long eras that stretch back to the middle of the seventeenth century. Toronto's modern history begins with the age of Iroquois and Mississauga villages, from about 1640 to 1710. From 1710 to 1780 the place was a centre for French and Indian fur trade outposts. Then there was the age of the old Upper Canadian capital in British North America, from about 1780 to 1850.

From 1850 to 1920, Toronto was the regional centre for what became the new Canadian province of Ontario in 1867. Then, during the era from 1920 to 1990, it gradually evolved into a kind of cheerfully despised national metropolis for Canada at large (or at least that part of Canada west of the Ottawa River, and east of the Gaspé coast). More exactly, it took over Montreal's ancient role as the economic capital of Canada. The final stages of the transformation were confirmed in the middle of the 1970s, when Toronto at last replaced Montreal as Canada's most populous metropolitan region.

Now we are on the edge of another new era in the life of the city. Historical parallels are always inexact, frequently misleading, and infinitely debatable. Some would say that the closest analogue for the 1920s in the living memory of middle-aged people today is the 1960s. Others would insist that in the 1990s we have returned to the 1930s. But I think it is more provocative to view the times Toronto is living through now, or is about to enter soon, as most similar to the 1920s.

Something was ending in Toronto in the 1920s, and something else was beginning. What was ending would still be

City of Toronto Archives SC 266-6902

In John Boyd's log this January 1926 Toronto photograph is simply called "Indian lecture." Some thirty years later, in 1959, E.C. Drury, who had occupied the premier's office at Queen's Park in the early 1920s, published a book on the earliest French and Indian history of his native Simcoe County, at the northern end of the Toronto Passage. In the story of early seventeenth-century Canada Drury discerned a "vision" of the "production, here in North America, of a new race, stronger for the mingling, as the European races were stronger for the mingling of many and varied strains."

around, long after the decade was over. What was beginning would not reach fruition for a great many years. Yet as Barker Fairley implied in 1921, when he wrote about the "vast gulf between the city's present and its immediate but somehow almost mysterious past," a new era had set in. In this sense at least, I think we are in a similar situation in Toronto today.

THEN AND NOW

As I write these words, almost sixty-four years have passed since the introduction of the new downtown plan in 1929. Though we sometimes imagine that things never change, they do. At the same time, some things that happened only yesterday can remind us of things that happened before many of us were born.

By most statistical measures, the worst years of the Great Depression were 1932 and 1933. The Canada-wide unemployment rate averaged 17.6 percent in 1932 and 19.3 percent in 1933. In the last half of the 1920s the early tensions of Toronto's embryonic multicultural society had drowned in a flood of economic growth. In the early 1930s the tensions resurfaced, with a new sharp edge.

At this point, the new-community Jews from eastern Europe were the most numerous and obvious representatives of the more diverse local society that had begun to show its face in the early twentieth century. And anti-Semitism in the city was mixed in with storms across the ocean. On January 30, 1933, Adolf Hitler became chancellor of Germany. In early August 1933 Toronto proved that it was not altogether immune to the wider neurosis.

The trouble was started by a group known as the Balmy Beach Swastika Club in the east-end Beaches. It climaxed with a riot at Christie Pits in the near west end, close to the home turf of many new-community Jews. At a baseball game between Jewish and non-Jewish teams a swastika sign with the motto "Hail Hitler" appeared among the spectators. After the game, groups of Gentile youths declared that Jews were not allowed at Christie Pits. A few days later a similar incident again took place at the Pits. This time both Gentile and Jewish youths were organized. Baseball bats and lead pipes were on hand. A full-scale riot broke out, lasting six hours and spreading to neighbouring streets. Violence of this sort petered out as the summer of 1933 turned into fall. A Jewish shopkeeper told the *Star* that "people here are too broadminded" to welcome any overtly racist politics. But the riot at Christie Pits left real scars. They would last for many years.

The early August 1933 riot at Christie Pits had some obvious echoes in what may or may not have been a different kind of Toronto race riot, in early May 1992. Yet things do change. Party politics is an example that reflects broader trends in the local society. I was born early in 1945, and the events of the 1930s and most of the 1940s are only second-hand legends to me. The phrase "Tory Toronto," however, was still in the local air when I was growing up. I used to find it puzzling: it didn't seem to describe my city.

I first voted in the Canadian federal election of 1968. In the seven federal elections from 1968 to 1988, more than two-thirds of all seats in today's Metropolitan Toronto were won by Liberals and New Democrats. Conservatives won more seats than Liberals in only two of these seven elections (1979 and 1984). Conservatives won no Toronto seats at all in the 1968 election, only 2 of 20 seats in 1974, and 4 of 23 seats in 1980.

In provincial politics it is true that, from almost two years before the day I was born until shortly after my fortieth birthday, a permutation of the old Tories called the Progressive Conservatives held office at Queen's Park. These new Tories regularly won some seats in Toronto. Yet everyone knew that their real base of support was in rural Ontario, not in the provincial capital city. When I was very young, in the 1950s, there was a kind of Progressive Conservative version of a Tory Toronto last hurrah. But it had limitations, and it did not last.

This is all quite different from the 1920s, when the Tories won every Toronto seat available in the federal and provincial elections of 1921, 1923, 1925, 1926, and 1929. What happened?

The simplest explanation is that the six of thirteen Toronto seats won by Mitch Hepburn's Liberals in the Ontario election of 1934 revived the 1919 project of cutting the local Tory culture down to size. Though Hepburn was a mercurial showboat who spent too much time partying at the King Edward Hotel, he had some authentic progressive streaks. Among other things, he appointed Ontario's first Jewish cabinet minister, David Croll, who swore his oath of office on the Torah.

From here there was the triumph of Mayor Jimmie Simpson in 1935. Then the early Ontario Co-operative Commonwealth Federation, ancestor of today's New Democrats, almost won the provincial election of 1943. By 1943 the capital city was joining the radical cause, and with much more enthusiasm than it had shown in 1919. Four of the thirteen Toronto provincial ridings of the day returned CCF members.

One of them, Mrs. Rae Luckock in Bracondale, was the city's first woman member in the provincial parliament (where she was joined by Agnes Macphail, from suburban York East). An additional two Toronto ridings returned the ostensibly communist duo of Joe Salsberg and Alex MacLeod in 1943, running under a widely recognized "Labour" protective coating (subsequently known as "Labour-Progressive").

The election of Nathan Phillips as mayor of all the people in 1955 prompted the final death throes of Tommy Church's Orange political machine. The two major public squares in Metropolitan Toronto today – Nathan Phillips Square in the old city of Toronto, and Mel Lastman Square in the new city of North York – bear the names of Jewish politicians.

Both the new Canadian maple leaf flag in 1965 and the election of Pierre Trudeau as Canada's third French Canadian prime minister in 1968 prompted the final death throes of the British Empire in the city. There are still a few, sometimes ironic, imperial echoes on the streets of Toronto today. But I can't really say that I have ever actually seen an "Orangeman" myself.

If I try to talk to my children about the Empire, the Orangemen, and the Tories – the way my most progressive aunt once talked to me – their eyes glaze over and they quickly change the subject. Beneath my dated middle-age veneer, I understand why. In the 1990 Ontario provincial election the Progressive Conservatives won only 3 of 28 seats in Metropolitan Toronto. The Liberals took 9, and the New Democrats 16.

Old-fashioned sceptics will rightly urge that it could be a while before the New Democrats do this well again. The Rae regime of the early 1990s may end much as the Drury regime ended in the early 1920s. Yet, whatever else, the 1990s will not exactly repeat the 1920s. Fergie's old Tory Toronto will never reappear.

DEMOGRAPHY, GEOGRAPHY, AND CULTURE

Putting the Toronto of the 1920s under a microscope today shows just how much things can change in as little as an average human lifetime. I think two developments over the more than six decades since 1929 are most striking. The first involves sheer geography and mere numbers of people.

The current official boundaries of the old city of Toronto, or "city proper," are only slightly larger than they were in the 1920s. And according to federal census data, the city of Toronto was home to 635,395 people in 1991 – only a few thousand more than the 631,207 people reported in the census of 1931.

A fund-raising picnic for a new Jewish Old Folks Home – held at Kew Beach on August 7, in the middle of Toronto's troubled summer of 1933.

The old Greater Toronto created by suburban expansion, however, is now much larger than it used to be, in both population and geographic extent. To help bring order to aggressive forces of suburban growth after the Second World War, in 1953 Queen's Park created a new Municipality of Metropolitan Toronto. It joined the old city of Toronto with its surrounding suburbs in a kind of local federal system – the first of its type in North America.

The population of the Municipality of Metropolitan Toronto had already passed the two-million mark by 1971. Its growth was driven by the great, long boom of the 1950s and 1960s. The boom was faltering in a big way by the middle of the 1970s, and there was a bust of sorts in the early 1980s. The mid- to late 1980s brought a strange, short-lived revival, but this deteriorated into an increasingly severe recession in the early 1990s.

The boom periods pushed the geographic growth of Toronto not just beyond the old city proper of the 1920s, but beyond the new metropolitan municipality of the 1950s as well. By the 1970s growth had begun to spill outside the old suburbs and into new "exurbs" – from Oshawa and Whitby on the east to Mississauga and Oakville on the west, and as far north as Aurora, Newmarket, and even the city of Barrie, on the shores of Lake Simcoe.

By the middle of the 1970s Queen's Park had created a reformed municipal political structure for the outer fringes of the burgeoning metropolis. It organized four new regional municipalities, immediately east, north, and west of Metro Toronto. Each of these amounted to a local federal system in its own right. To coordinate its activities in Metro and the surrounding regions, in the late 1980s Queen's Park established an "Office for the Greater Toronto Area," within the bowels of its own bureaucracy.

By this point territory that had been an uncluttered home to the culture of the North American family farm in the 1920s – with provincial electoral ridings that had voted for the United Farmers of Ontario in 1919 – had become part of a sprawling megalopolis with a population of well over four million people. Toronto in this sense is now the largest metropolitan region in Canada, and one of the top-ten big urban markets in North America.

The second most-striking development since 1929 flows from several great waves of migration to the region, also linked with the boom periods of the 1950s, 1960s, 1970s, and 1980s. The most dramatic feature of these migrations is how they have enormously deepened and enriched the early multiculturalism of the 1920s.

For one last time, the Second World War stiffened the city's sense of its British imperial heritage in the narrowest sense. Yet when the war ended, fresh breezes began to blow from other directions. In 1947 the Chinese Immigration Act of 1923 was repealed. In the same year Mackenzie King's government at Ottawa legislated a distinctive "Canadian citizen" status, to supplement and eventually replace the old colonial status of "British subject." In 1952 the Toronto-born Vincent Massey became the first governor general of Canada who, despite splendid uniforms and a patrician accent, was not a real British aristocrat.

Right after the war there was a final surge of immigration from the United Kingdom. But the old British colonial culture began to fade profoundly. In the city of Toronto, 78 percent of all residents had reported "British ethnic origins" in the 1941 census. The proportion would fall to 69 percent in 1951, 52 percent in 1961, and 46 percent in 1971.

Much stronger waves of postwar immigration decisively broadened Toronto's European cultural mix. Italians were at the leading edge, building on the base they had already established by the 1920s. They were followed (in descending numerical order) by Portuguese, Greeks, Poles, Ukrainians, various Yugoslavians, Hungarians, Spanish-speakers, various Czechs and Slovaks, and assorted Baltic peoples.

By the late 1960s a second wave of migrants, with a wide array of African and Asian ancestries, had begun to gather momentum. Pierre Trudeau's official multiculturalism strategy, as well as major changes in Canadian immigration policy and law in 1967 and 1976, pushed the trend. In the 1970s and especially the 1980s non-European immigration gradually eclipsed the earlier postwar wave from Europe beyond the United Kingdom.

By the late 1980s the half-dozen largest sources of migrants to the wider Toronto region were Hong Kong, Guyana, Jamaica, Portugal, India, and the Philippines. The very small local black community of William Peyton Hubbard's era had grown much larger. By the time of the 1991 census, the repressed Toronto Chinese colony of the 1920s was the third-largest "ethnic-origin" group in the Toronto Census Metropolitan Area (an official Statistics Canada region, somewhat smaller than the Ontario government's Greater Toronto Area, but much larger than Metropolitan Toronto).

The 1991 ethnic-origin census shows just how dizzyingly diverse Toronto's multicultural fabric has now become – and how increasingly meaningless the old "racial origin" classifications of the 1920s and 1930s are today.

Almost one-quarter of all 1991 respondents in the Toronto Census Metropolitan Area reported a wide variety of "mixed" origins. Somewhat better than a quarter of these were simply "mixed British" (English-Scottish and so forth). Others were much more mixed, and the pot-pourri defies simple categorization.

Among the three-quarters of respondents reporting "single origins," twenty leading groups accounted for two-thirds of the area's total population. The six largest were British (only some 19 percent of all single origins), Italian, Canadian (still not an officially recognized ethnic origin, but 7 percent of respondents reported it anyway), Chinese, Indian (from India), and black (from various places, but chiefly the West Indies, Africa, and the United States). They were followed (in descending order) by Portuguese, Jewish, Polish, German, Philippino, Greek, French, Ukrainian, Spanish, Dutch, Hungarian, Vietnamese, Korean, and Pakistani.

More than ninety other groups accounted for the balance of single-origin respondents. They included Americans, Australians, Belgians, Brazilians, Cambodians, Colombians, Cubans, Egyptians, Estonians, Iranians, Iraqis, Japanese, Macedonians, Maltese, Mexicans, Punjabis, Sri Lankans, Swedes, Tamils, Turks, and 5,645 "North American Indians."

THE FUTURE TODAY

Toronto in the 1920s may shed a little light on the new long era of Toronto that lies ahead. There is, for instance, much local talk today which suggests that the city may now be entering some kind of "age of the global village."

The January 1993 issue of the *Globe and Mail's Report on Business Magazine* was devoted to "The World in 1993." It

City of Toronto Archives SC 266-8556

The Diwan of Bahadur, Sir T. Vijayaraghavacharya, opening the Canadian National Exhibition in Toronto, August 28, 1926.

included an article entitled "The Nation-State on Trial." The last sentence asked: "With the strains being increasingly put on the nation-state by both the race to a single global economy and by the enduring strength of local attachments, might not a world of city-states become attractive again?"

According to an August 1992 article in the *Toronto Star*, the present "global economy is principally organized through a system of some 30 mega-cities that are the active nodes of the world market." They include "London, New York, Tokyo, Toronto, Chicago, San Francisco, Los Angeles, Houston, Miami, Mexico City, Sao Paulo, Seoul, Taipei, Hong Kong, Singapore, Bangkok, Paris, Zurich, Vienna, Milan, Madrid, and the Randstadt corridor of Holland."

All this echoes Marshall McLuhan's controversial prophecies of the 1960s. McLuhan was born in Alberta and raised in Manitoba. But he was living and working in Toronto when, inspired by Harold Innis's later writings on communications in world history, he began to ponder the fate of the global village.

The 1920s show how this sense of the future has still deeper roots in the local past. The British Empire was its own kind of global village. The Torontonians who celebrated Empire Year at the Canadian National Exhibition in 1929 already had a vision of a world market and a world economy.

It is easy enough to see another kind of global village on the streets of Toronto today. Much of the new multicultural diversity has its own ironic roots in the old British Empire. According to an authorized Ontario school textbook of 1939, the "Empire includes many races ... white men, black men, yellow men, brown men ... Christians, Moslems, Buddhists, Jews" – altogether a "complex assemblage of peoples."

While there was a renewed engagement with the romance of the British Empire in Toronto during the 1920s, there was also a new enthusiasm for the continental commerce of North America. The National Hockey League in Canada had stopped being an exclusively Canadian enterprise as early as 1924. By 1950 almost two-thirds of Canadian exports were destined for the United States.

The central Canadian automobile industry that leaned on the markets of the Empire vanished with the Canada-U.S. Auto

Pact of 1965. Much more recently, an apparently historic free trade agreement between Canada and the United States was signed in the late 1980s. In the 1990s there will apparently be some kind of new North American Free Trade Agreement, which reaches out to Mexico and points to the wider hemisphere beyond.

Some elements in Toronto today have battled against these trends. Like the British Empire, however, the local business elite that sabotaged Laurier's Canada-U.S. Reciprocity Treaty in 1911 vanished sometime after the Second World War. Toronto in the 1990s has at least something of the North American profile that it wanted but lacked in an earlier age.

The North American persona of Toronto today has its own deep local roots. The Ontario Temperance Act of the 1920s was a regional variation on the wider Anglo-American thirst for prohibition. The Blue Jays, who defeated the Atlanta Braves and won the real World Series in 1992, were only the heirs of the old Maple Leafs, who defeated the Louisville Colonels and won the Little World Series in 1926.

Even beyond Mexico, in the wider hemisphere, William Mackenzie had created the Brazilian Traction Light and Power Company as early as 1912. The title page of C.S. Clark's *Of Toronto the Good*, first published in 1898 (in Montreal, of all places), bore the motto: "Not necessarily Toronto alone but every city in America."

Though I am a Canadian and do not want to be anything else, I like to think I can appreciate how, geographically, Canada *is* part of North America. In some broad-brush history of the world, I am a North American. Still, it does seem to me that, even with free trade agreements, the death of the British Empire, the long reach of television, and the real World Series, Toronto today is actually less inclined to be a mere "city in America" than it was in the 1920s.

When Percy Robinson finally published *Toronto during the French Regime* in 1933, he wrote in his preface that the city of his day was "the citadel of British sentiment in America." Few would use this kind of language to describe the Toronto in which I have lived my life since the Second World War. In spite of everything, I think, this can only mark progress in the "making of our nation" – the enterprise that Mackenzie King saw as the crux of the Canadian federal election of 1926, even in the old Tory Toronto.

In terms of Canada's own most authentic traditions, the striking human diversity on the streets of Toronto today reflects an ultimate blossoming of the multiracial wilderness culture of the fur trade in northern North America – the ancient beginnings of modern Canada that the Group of Seven, Harold Innis, Percy Robinson, and many other more obscure people had begun to revive and rediscover in the decade after the First World War.

It seems to be no accident that in the 1990s we have begun to listen to the voice raised by Major O.M. Martin in 1929. At last we are starting to grasp Innis's point about the influence of Canada's aboriginal origins on its modern institutions. In his book of 1930 Innis noted as well that another "interesting survival" of the northern fur trade was the mixed Indian and European groups, now identified in the 1982 Constitution Act as the "Métis peoples of Canada." On one twist of the current kaleidoscope, it could be said, Toronto in the 1990s has started to become a new kind of Canadian Métis city.

Big changes of this sort take time to digest. In the past quarter-century the Toronto region has absorbed a greater variety of new residents than almost any other part of the world. It is not surprising that there is rhetorical controversy over the dynamic mixing and mingling of the various human races in the current metropolis – and over the rights and obligations of citizens of various vintages, from the oldest to the newest. But for practical purposes, "Canadian" today actually does mean what the *Globe* said it ought to mean in 1924: simply a "man or woman who desires to be a Canadian, who takes pride in the name, and who is devoted to the interests of Canada."

TORONTO, CANADA

Canada, according to the novelist Robertson Davies, is a country you worry about. As there were in the 1920s, there are reasons today for worrying about Canada, and about the future of Toronto as a part of Canada.

In the late 1980s Metro bureaucrats liked to say that late twentieth-century Toronto is "Canada's business capital." This could prove even more transient than the earlier status of

Montreal. Calgary, Edmonton, and Vancouver look on Toronto now much as Toronto once looked on Montreal.

It may even be that some vague writing about a softening of Toronto's recently acquired Canadian metropolitan dominance has already appeared on the wall. Early in 1993 local officials argued that half of all jobs lost in Canada during the increasingly dramatic bust of the early 1990s were in the Greater Toronto Area. Eventually Canada will likely enough become, in this as in other respects, a country like the United States, without a single, genuinely dominant metropolitan centre.

At the same time, in the world of tomorrow there may be no more real business capitals in any region of the globe. There will only be strong and weak competitors. In one way or another, I think, strengthening Toronto's Canadian connections is bound to remain a fertile tactic in strengthening its competitive edge.

There is also (as there has been for my entire adult life) the fundamental question of Quebec, and of the impact of its future on Canada at large. Even today Toronto cannot pretend to be any kind of centre for the predominantly French-speaking Canada that lies between the Ottawa River and the Gaspé coast. After a generation of ardent federal and, increasingly, even provincial government promotion, the French language is more alive in the city now than it was in the 1920s. But it is only realistic to acknowledge that this is still not saying much.

The late 1980s and early 1990s have helped to clarify the utopianism of much earlier wishful thinking in Canada after the demise of the British Empire. It now seems clear enough that we will not be able to evade our particular post-colonial language problems by some essentially artificial policy of official bilingualism, from coast to coast to coast. It is clear that we have other kinds of constitutional problems as well. Like so many among us, I am not sure just what our temporary failure to resolve these problems in the early 1990s means for the Canadian future. I do, however, harbour a few residual convictions.

There can be little doubt that the British Empire is now truly dead. I'd guess that the quasi-colonial arrangements of the old Dominion of Canada – with their lack of any formal democratic endorsement in the past or present, and their continuing dependence on assorted obsolete imperial projects, inside and outside the country – really are on their last legs. Somehow, somewhere, sometime, they will have to be changed.

In one way or another, Quebec may have a different position in the new arrangements than the "rest of Canada." Perhaps it will be more distinct within its own borders, but less influential in the wider federal system. Perhaps there is some other kind of future that we have only begun to imagine. Whatever else, in the 1990s the Canada that Harold Innis started to write about in the 1920s seems to me more real, and more aware of itself, than it has ever been before.

During the half-century immediately following the 1867 Confederation, Toronto was obsessed with its role in Ontario. By the 1920s it had begun to discover Canada.

Even now Toronto is still only in the early stages of this discovery. A Toronto that wants to grow beyond V.S. Naipaul's "people far away, living on other people's land and off other people's brains" will press ahead. Whatever may happen to the business capitals of the world, chasing the elusive romance of Canada's unique northern geography has played a large part in the dynamism Toronto has developed in my own lifetime.

Both the global village and the North American continent are bound to figure in Toronto's future, as they have already in its past. But their influence is not infinite. Canada has never really become a nation-state on the traditional European model: the end of the age of the nation-state, if that is in fact what lies before us, does not have all that much to do with the Canadian future.

Even in a wider free-trading universe, the most durable economic development strategy for all big cities in Canada, I think, will be to compete from a strong Canadian base. On the edge of the twenty-first century, there are virtually no decisive practical barriers to building this kind of base. The only strategic asset Canada still does not have enough of is faith in its own destiny, and there is no good reason for believing that this faith cannot continue to grow.

A stronger Canadian future, it seems to me, will prove to be the strongest future for Toronto – culturally, economically, politically, socially, and in every other way imaginable. And I count myself among those who both hope and expect that Toronto's future finally will prove stronger, and better, than either its present or its past.

ENVOI: CASA LOMA STOMP

We can only guess about the future, but history books should end with more than mere guesses. I want to return for one last moment to the city of the 1920s, and to the eventual fate of one of its lesser-known ambiguous and ironic creations.

By the time the Royal York Hotel opened, just over three months before the Great Crash, Glen Gray and his fellow musical refugees from the failed hotel experiment in Sir Henry Pellatt's castle on the hill had already arrived in New York City. By the end of 1929 the Casa Loma Orchestra had made its first phonograph recordings. Late in 1930 it made its first hit record – "Casa Loma Stomp."

The band's guitarist-arranger, Gene Gifford, wrote the piece. It seems that Gifford was not with the group during its formative period in Toronto (though he apparently had worked for the Goldkette organization in Detroit in 1927 and 1928). His "Casa Loma Stomp" nonetheless makes a musical bow to the band's geographic origins, beyond the obvious reference to Pellatt's dream house in the title.

The first white big band that played real jazz had several black models. One of them, the Fletcher Henderson Orchestra, made its own recording of "Casa Loma Stomp" in 1932. Henderson's recording was reissued in 1989. In the accompanying liner notes, the late twentieth-century jazz critic Leonard Feather complains about the lamentably "martial and brisk" style of the piece, even in the hands of Fletcher Henderson.

The martial romantic, Henry Pellatt, knight bachelor and one-time colonel of the Queen's Own Rifles militia regiment, would probably be pleased. "Casa Loma Stomp" sounds a little like something a Toronto militia band might have invented if it had suddenly learned how to swing. Today, I think, it qualifies as an authentic artifact of the city in the 1920s, in all its still-muted but already-kaleidoscopic ambiguity, irony, and variety. If books could have theme songs, "Casa Loma Stomp" would be a good theme song for this book.

Henry Pellatt died in Toronto on March 8, 1939, in much-reduced circumstances from his days at Casa Loma. As a kind of tribute to his contributions to the city, in the late summer of 1939 "Glen Gray and his Casa Loma Orchestra" was the first of several big-name bands hired to play in an Automotive Building dance hall at the CNE. Along with its Canadian origins, at this point the band could actually boast three Canadian musicians – the piano player Howard Hall, from Stratford, Ontario; the drummer Tony Briglia, from London, Ontario (like Guy Lombardo); and the trombonist Murray MacEachern, from Toronto.

Some will object, stressing that neither the Casa Loma Orchestra nor its first hit record was an authentic Toronto creation. This seems to me to miss the point. If there had been no Toronto and no Casa Loma, there would never have been a Casa Loma Orchestra.

The late twentieth-century jazz critic Will Friedwald recently wrote the liner notes to a 1990 reissue of old Casa Loma recordings. They talk about how in 1929, in New York City, "the Casa Loma Band came down swinging from Toronto."

In the late 1980s the jazz historian Gunther Schuller offered a compelling description of the musical Casa Lomans in their prime, during the 1930s. They "played in a flashy, externally exciting manner." They "made a very attractive appearance, dressed impeccably in tails and white tie," and they "gave off an air of optimism, conviction, and youthful exuberance."

The band knew that it had stumbled onto this image during its incubation at the failed Casa Loma Hotel in Toronto, in 1927 and 1928. That's why it called itself the Casa Loma Orchestra. A generation later, the New York literary critic Edmund Wilson "visited for the first time Toronto, a rapidly growing industrial city of which it is customary to say that it is getting to be indistinguishable from our similar cities in the Middle West but which I felt to have its own rhythm and accent." In the era that lies ahead today, Toronto may at last discover its own rhythm and accent itself.

A FINAL NOTE: TOO GOOD TO BE TRUE

Of course, there is another side to the story, and it strikes the right utterly final note. My wife, who was not born in Toronto, tells me that too many natives of the place are too sentimental about its past. From the standpoint of the 1990s, there are some brutal and unpleasant historical facts that we ought to face squarely. In several different senses, Toronto the Good in the 1920s was too good to be true.

After the 1920s, as well, the city's goodness has too often been superficial. It has been said that you can do anything you want in late twentieth-century Toronto, so long as you don't spit on the sidewalk. Like others I know, I hope that in the years ahead we Torontonians will develop less passion for this kind of goodness and more passion for truth.

Yet the world is a complicated place. Historically, the north-western shore of Lake Ontario has welcomed successive waves of ambiguity and irony. Even now that I've seen the earlier part of the old Toronto movie, I still feel that when you strip away all its false goodness and untruthfulness, and even its stridently unjust and evil sides, Toronto in the 1920s at least had the beginnings of a spirit that actually was good.

For all its faults, in the grim times of the early 1930s the city was too broad-minded to embrace any overtly racist politics. Some white girls took jobs in Chinese cafés in the late 1920s, even though this was against the law. On various fringes of the political mainstream after the First World War, a few Toronto residents had begun to think about Canada's future beyond the British Empire. The Group of Seven was exploring the native wilderness of the second-largest country in the world.

Banting, Best, Collip, and MacLeod discovered insulin. The Rogers Batteryless Radio helped advance the early phases of the twentieth-century communications revolution. Agnes Macphail struck early blows for women's liberation, and Morley Callaghan wrote the first modern Toronto novel. The Standard Electric Home was a symbol of mass civility. Without taking themselves too seriously, many among the mass of the people believed in the significance of their ordinary lives, and tried to live them well. Already the city's population had some ancient ancestries in all of Africa, Asia, Europe, and the New World.

The beginnings of the spirit that actually was good in the 1920s had their own origins in a more distant past. The best sides of Toronto in the 1990s owe something to the growth and development of this spirit in the decades that followed the Great Crash. The spirit is still evolving. It deserves a little more respect than it gets in the city today, perhaps especially from people like myself. Along with everything else, it has earned the right to survive. And, in one way or another, I think it will.

BIBLIOGRAPHY

As noted in the text, the major primary sources for this book are the Toronto newspapers of the 1920s. They are available on microfilm in the newspapers department at the Metropolitan Toronto Reference Library. Other important sources consulted include the *Might's Directory* and Toronto map collections at the Reference Library; the city council minutes and annual reports of the city assessment commissioner at the Archives of the City of Toronto; the admirably accessible collection of Statistics Canada (or old Dominion Bureau of Statistics) publications, in the Robarts Library at the University of Toronto; and the reports of the chief election officers for Canada and Ontario.

The publications listed below indicate the major secondary sources for material directly quoted or otherwise referred to or employed in the text. Where appropriate, the date of first publication for an item is inserted before the date of the edition cited.

Allen, Robert Thomas. *When Toronto Was for Kids*. Toronto: McClelland and Stewart, 1961, 1967.

Armstrong, Frederick H. *Toronto: The Place of Meeting*. Burlington, Ontario: Windsor Publications, 1983.

_____. *A City in the Making: Progress, People and Perils in Victorian Toronto*. Toronto: Dundurn Press, 1988.

Arthur, Eric. *Toronto: No Mean City*. Toronto: University of Toronto Press, 1964, 1974, 1986. Third edition revised by Stephen A. Otto.

Baker, Carlos, ed. *Ernest Hemingway: Selected Letters, 1917-1961*. New York: Charles Scribner's Sons, 1981.

Bissell, Claude. *The Young Vincent Massey*. Toronto: University of Toronto Press, 1981.

Bliss, Michael. *The Discovery of Insulin*. Toronto: McClelland and Stewart, 1982.

Bromley, John F. *TTC '28: The Electric Railway Services of the Toronto Transportation Commission in 1928*. Toronto: Upper Canada Railway Society, June 1968.

Brown, Ian. "The Empire That Timothy Built." *Financial Post Magazine*, May 1978.

Callaghan, Morley. *Strange Fugitive*. Toronto: Macmillan of Canada, 1928, 1973.

_____. *It's Never Over*. Toronto: Macmillan of Canada, 1930, 1972.

_____. "The Big League," in B.T. Richardson, ed. *Toronto '59*. Toronto: The City of Toronto, 1959.

_____. *That Summer in Paris*. Toronto: Macmillan of Canada, 1963, 1976.

Careless, J.M.S. *Toronto to 1918: An Illustrated History*. Toronto: James Lorimer & Company, 1984.

Clark, C.S. *Of Toronto the Good: A Social Study*. Toronto: Coles Canadiana Collection, 1898, 1970.

Clark, Gregory. *Greg's Choice*. Toronto: Ryerson Press, 1961.

Creighton, Donald. *Harold Adams Innis: Portrait of a Scholar*. Toronto: University of Toronto Press, 1957, 1978.

_____. *The Forked Road: Canada 1939-1957*. Toronto: McClelland and Stewart, 1976, 1986.

Dendy, William. *Lost Toronto*. Toronto: Oxford University Press, 1978.

_____. and William Kilbourn. *Toronto Observed: Its Architecture, Patrons, and History*. Toronto: Oxford University Press Canada, 1986.

Denison, John. *Casa Loma and the Man Who Built It*. Erin, Ontario: Boston Mills Press, 1982.

Donegan, Rosemary. *Spadina Avenue*. Vancouver and Toronto: Douglas & McIntyre, 1985.

Drury, E.C. *All for a Beaver Hat: A History of Early Simcoe County*. Toronto: Ryerson Press, 1959.

_____. *Farmer Premier. Memoirs of the Honourable E.C. Drury*. Toronto: McClelland and Stewart, 1966.

Dykes, James G. "Background on the Automotive Products Trade Agreement." Toronto: Motor Vehicle Manufacturers' Association, June 1983.

Filey, Mike. *A Toronto Album: Glimpses of the City That Was*. Toronto: University of Toronto Press, 1970.

_____. *Look at Us Now*. Toronto: Mike Filey and the *Toronto Telegram*, 1971.

_____. *Toronto: Reflections of the Past*. Toronto: Nelson, Foster & Scott, 1972.

_____. *Toronto Sketches: "The Way We Were."* Toronto: Dundurn Press, 1992.

Firth, Edith G. *Toronto in Art: 150 Years through Artists' Eyes*. Toronto: Fitzhenry & Whiteside, 1983.

Fleming, R.B. *The Railway King of Canada: Sir William Mackenzie, 1849-1923*. Vancouver: University of British Columbia Press, 1991.

Forster, John. *The Life of Charles Dickens*. London: J.M. Dent & Sons, 1872, 1966. Volume 1.

Galbraith, John Kenneth. *The Great Crash 1929*. Harmondsworth, Middlesex: Penguin Books, 1954, 1975.

Glazebrook, G.P. de T. *The Story of Toronto*. Toronto: University of Toronto Press, 1971.

GM in Canada: The Early Years. Oshawa, Ontario: General Motors of Canada Limited, n.d.

Granatstein, J.L. *Mackenzie King: His Life and World*. Toronto: McGraw-Hill Ryerson, 1977.

_____. and Peter Stevens, eds. *Forum: Canadian Life and Letters 1920-1970, Selections from the Canadian Forum*. Toronto: University of Toronto Press, 1972.

Harney, Robert F., ed. *Gathering Place: Peoples and Neighbourhoods of Toronto, 1834-1945*. Toronto: Multicultural History Society of Ontario, 1985.

Hemingway, Ernest. *In Our Time*. New York: Macmillan Publishing Company, 1925, 1986.

Hubbard, Stephen L. *Against All Odds: The Story of William Peyton Hubbard, Black Leader and Municipal Reformer*. Toronto: Dundurn Press, 1987.

Humber, William. *Cheering for the Home Team: The Story of Baseball in Canada*. Erin, Ontario: Boston Mills Press, 1983.

Hunkin, Harry. *There is no finality ... A Story of the Group of Seven*. Toronto: Burns & MacEachern, 1971.

Hutchison, Bruce. *The Incredible Canadian*. Don Mills, Ontario: Longmans Canada, 1952, 1970.

Innis, Harold. *The Fur Trade in Canada: An Introduction to Canadian Economic History*. Toronto: University of Toronto Press, 1930, 1956, 1970.

Johnston, Charles M. *E.C. Drury: Agrarian Idealist*. Toronto: University of Toronto Press, 1986.

Kaplan, Harold. *Urban Political Systems: A Functional Analysis of Metro Toronto*. New York: Columbia University Press, 1967.

Kilbourn, William, ed. *The Toronto Book: An Anthology of Writings Past and Present*. Toronto: Macmillan of Canada, 1976.

Knowles, Valerie. *First Person: A Biography of Cairine Wilson, Canada's First Woman Senator*. Toronto: Dundurn Press, 1988.

_____. *Strangers at Our Gates: Canadian Immigration and Immigration Policy, 1540-1990*. Toronto: Dundurn Press, 1992.

Lees, Gene. *Meet Me at Jim and Andy's: Jazz Musicians and Their World*. New York: Oxford University Press, 1988.

Lemon, James. *Toronto Since 1918: An Illustrated History*. Toronto: James Lorimer & Company, 1985.

Lukacs, John. "The End of the Twentieth Century: Historical Reflections on a Misunderstood Epoch." *Harper's*, January 1993.

Lustiger-Thaler, Henri, ed. *Political Arrangements: Power and the City*. Montreal: Black Rose Books, 1992.

MacDougall, Heather. *Activists and Advocates: Toronto's Health Department 1883-1983*. Toronto: Dundurn Press, 1990.

MacIntosh, Robert. *Different Drummers: Banking and Politics in Canada*. Toronto: Macmillan of Canada, 1991.

MacLachlan, Colin M., and Jaime E. Rodriguez O. *The Forging of the Cosmic Race: A Reinterpretation of Colonial Mexico*. Berkeley: University of California Press, 1980.

Marchand, Philip. *Marshall McLuhan: The Medium and the Messenger*. Toronto: Random House, 1989.

Marshall, Herbert, Frank Southard Jr., and Kenneth W. Taylor. *Canadian-American Industry*. Toronto: McClelland and Stewart, 1936, 1976.

Marshall, John. *The Structure of Urban Systems*. Toronto: University of Toronto Press, 1989.

McCarthy, Albert. *The Dance Band Era. The Dancing Decades from Ragtime to Swing: 1910-1950*. London: Studio Vista Publishers, 1971.

McClement, Fred. *The Strange Case of Ambrose Small*. Toronto: McClelland and Stewart, 1974.

McFarlane, Brian. *The Story of the National Hockey League*. New York: Charles Scribner's Sons, 1973.

McGowan, Mark George, and Brian P. Clarke, eds. *Catholics at the "Gathering Place": Historical Essays on the Archdiocese of Toronto, 1841-1991*. Toronto: Canadian Catholic Historical Association (English Section), 1993.

McLuhan, Marshall. *The Mechanical Bride: Folklore of Industrial Man*. New York: Vanguard Press, 1951.

Mellen, Peter. *The Group of Seven*. Toronto: McClelland and Stewart, 1970.

Meyers, Jeffrey. *Hemingway: A Biography*. New York: Harper & Row, 1985.

Miller, Mark. *Jazz in Canada, Fourteen Lives*. Toronto: University of Toronto Press, 1982.

Minister of Education for Ontario. *Ontario*

Readers: Third Book. Toronto: T. Eaton Co. Ltd., 1925.

Morley, Patricia. *Morley Callaghan.* Toronto: McClelland and Stewart, 1978.

Naipaul, V.S. *A Bend in the River.* Harmondsworth, Middlesex: Penguin Books, 1979, 1980.

Neufeld, E.P., ed. *Money and Banking in Canada.* Toronto: McClelland and Stewart, 1964.

Obojski, Robert. *Bush League: A History of Minor League Baseball.* New York: Macmillan Publishing Company, 1975.

Oliver, Peter. *Public and Private Persons: The Ontario Political Culture 1914-1934.* Toronto: Clarke, Irwin & Company, 1975.

_____. *G. Howard Ferguson: Ontario Tory.* Toronto: University of Toronto Press, 1977.

_____. *Unlikely Tory: The Life and Politics of Allan Grossman.* Toronto: Lester & Orpen Dennys, 1985.

Once upon a Century: 100 Year History of The 'Ex.' Toronto: J.H. Robinson Publishing, 1978.

Ondaatje, Michael. *In the Skin of a Lion.* Toronto: McClelland and Stewart, 1987.

Ontario Ministry of Transportation and Communications. *Footpaths to Freeways: The Story of Ontario's Roads.* Toronto: The Ministry, n.d.

Oreskovich, Carlie. *Sir Henry Pellatt: The King of Casa Loma.* Toronto: McGraw-Hill Ryerson, 1982.

Pennington, Doris. *Agnes Macphail, Reformer.* Toronto: Dundurn Press, 1989.

Reid, Dennis. *The Group of Seven.* Ottawa: National Gallery of Canada, 1970.

Rivers, F.S., C.C. Goldring, and Gilbert Paterson. *The Empire Story.* Toronto: Ryerson Press, 1939.

Robinson, Percy. *Toronto during the French Regime.* Toronto: University of Toronto Press, 1933, 1965.

Schmalz, Peter S. *The Ojibwa of Southern Ontario.* Toronto: University of Toronto Press, 1991.

Schuller, Gunther. *The Swing Era: The Development of Jazz 1930-1945.* New York: Oxford University Press, 1989.

Seidensticker, Edward. *Low City, High City. Tokyo from Edo to the Earthquake: how the shogun's ancient capital became a great modern city, 1867-1923.* New York: Alfred A. Knopf, 1983.

Simon, George T. *Simon Says: The Sights and Sounds of the Swing Era, 1935-1955.* New Rochelle, N.Y.: Arlington House, 1971.

Simpson-Housley, Paul, and Glen Norcliffe, eds. *A Few Acres of Snow: Literary and*

Artistic Images of Canada. Toronto: Dundurn Press, 1992.

Speisman, Stephen A. *The Jews of Toronto: A History to 1937.* Toronto: McClelland and Stewart, 1979, 1987.

Spelt, Jacob. *Urban Development in South-Central Ontario.* Toronto: McClelland and Stewart, 1955, 1972.

_____. and Donald P. Kerr. *Toronto.* Don Mills, Ontario: Collier Macmillan Canada, 1973.

Toronto Harbour Commissioners. *Toronto Harbour: The Passing Years.* Toronto: The Commissioners, n.d.

Toronto Stock Exchange. *The Toronto Stock Exchange: Toward an Ideal Market.* Toronto: The Exchange, 1983.

Town, Harold, and David P. Silcox. *Tom Thomson: The Silence and the Storm.* Toronto: McClelland and Stewart, 1977, 1989.

Underhill, Frank. *In Search of Canadian Liberalism.* Toronto: Macmillan Canada, 1960.

Wallace, William Stewart. *A History of the Canadian People.* Toronto: Copp Clark, 1930.

West, Bruce. *Toronto.* Toronto: Doubleday Canada, 1967, 1979.

Wexler, Alice. *Emma Goldman in Exile: From the Russian Revolution to the Spanish Civil War.* Boston: Beacon Press, 1989.

White, William, ed. *Ernest Hemingway. Dateline: Toronto. The Complete Toronto Star Dispatches, 1920-1924.* New York: Charles Scribner's Sons, 1985.

Wilson, Edmund. *O Canada: An American's Notes on Canadian Culture.* New York: Noonday Press, 1964, 1965, 1966.

Woodcock, George. "Callaghan's Toronto: the persona of a city." *Journal of Canadian Studies,* August 1972.

INDEX